Reincarnation
AN EAST-WEST ANTHOLOGY

Reincarnation is frequently regarded as an Oriental concept incompatible with Western thinking and traditional belief. This encyclopedic compilation of quotations from eminent philosophers, theologians, poets, scientists, and other thinkers of every period of Western culture, and the thoroughly documented survey of reincarnation in the world religions, will serve to dispel this idea. In no sense dogmatic, the ideas presented are stimulating, challenging and inspiring. Both adherents and dissenters to the rebirth theory are represented.

This book was highly acclaimed when it was first published in a hard cover edition in 1961. It was listed in the annual report of the famous Bodleian Library, Oxford University, England, as among their sixty-nine "Chief Donations" received 1961-1962.

Some Readers' Comments

"Reincarnation: An East-West Anthology *goes far beyond the area suggested in its title. What is gathered here covers an exploration of the meaning of life and death. The impressive quality of the volume is not whether it will prove or disprove reincarnation but rather the continuing concern with the problem right down to the rational and scientific present."* — Los Angeles Times *(Robert R. Kirsch).*

"*A highly impressive collection of the reflections of many wise men in many places."* — *Karl Menninger, M.D., Psychiatrist, Menninger Institute.*

"*I am glad to know of this book. I feel confident that I shall be referring students to it in the years to come."* — *Huston Smith, author of* The Religions of Man, *Professor of Philosophy at Massachusetts Institute of Technology.*

"*Will open the eyes of many people who dismissed the rebirth theory as something oriental."* — *Dr. S. Radhakrishnan, former President of India and eminent Hindu philosopher.*

"*In its field, this anthology is the most complete and exciting that has ever come to my desk."* — *Rev. Dr. Daniel A. Poling, Editor of* The Christian Herald, *President of the World's Christian Endeavor Union.*

QUEST BOOKS
are published by
The Theosophical Society in America,
a branch of a world organization
dedicated to the promotion of brotherhood and
the encouragement of the study of religion,
philosophy, and science, to the end that man may
better understand himself and his place in
the universe. The Society stands for complete
freedom of individual search and belief.
In the Theosophical Classics Series
well-known occult works are made
available in popular editions.

Reincarnation

AN EAST-WEST ANTHOLOGY

*Including quotations from the world's religions &
from over 400 western thinkers*

Compiled and edited by

JOSEPH HEAD and S. L. CRANSTON

A QUEST BOOK
Published under a grant from The Kern Foundation

THE THEOSOPHICAL PUBLISHING HOUSE
Wheaton, Ill., U.S.A.
Madras, India / London, England

CONTENTS

PREFACE

Although a surprising number of distinguished thinkers of every period of history have either championed or on occasion favorably considered the idea of repeated existences upon earth, as this Anthology attests, such testimony hardly establishes reincarnation as a fact. It does suggest, however, that an idea that has occupied so many exceptional minds cannot be lightly dismissed, but is worthy of questioning, study, and investigation.

Henry T. Buckle spoke movingly of this interest when he wrote: "If immortality be untrue, it matters little whether anything else be true or not." A similar feeling is joined with clarifying logic by W. Macneile Dixon in The Human Situation (Gifford Lectures 1936-37):

To live is by universal consent to travel a rough road. And how can a rough road which leads nowhere be worth the travelling? Mere living, what a profitless performance; mere painful living, what an absurd! . . . There is, then, nothing to be hoped for, nothing to be expected and nothing to be done save to await our turn to mount the scaffold and bid farewell to that colossal blunder, the much-ado-about-nothing world . . . Think, if only for a moment, think. Proclaim to men that 'Death is the only immortal' and . . . [they] will not be easily consoled for so much courage, so much endurance, so much faith, so much affection, so much sweetness cast into the void, when they recall the faithful hearts, friendly faces, strong intelligences forever gone. . . .

Beyond all peradventure it is the thought that death appears to proclaim, the thought of frustration and final unreason at the heart of things, that is itself the root of the pessimist's despair. . . . Give assurance that it is not so, and the scene is changed. The sky brightens, the door is left open for unimagined possibilities, things begin to fall into an intelligible pattern. . . .

If you have not here among men who reflect, however unwilling they are to acknowledge it . . . the pivot of the human situation, the question upon the answer to which all turns, I know not where to look for it. . . . Immortality is a word which stands for the stability or permanence of that unique and precious quality we discern in the soul, which, if lost, leaves nothing worth preservation in the world.

"What kind of immortality is at all conceivable?" Dixon answers: "Of all doctrines of a future life palingenesis or rebirth, which carries with it the idea of pre-existence, is by far the most ancient and most widely held, 'the only system to which,' as said Hume, 'philosophy can hearken.'"

But we must let the writers presented in the Anthology speak for themselves. Dissenting opinions have also been included, and readers inclined to dismiss all theories of immortality as wishful thinking will find this view considered at pages 249-50 and 279-84.

Other terms for reincarnation variously used by the authors quoted include rebirth, metempsychosis, transmigration, palingenesis, and re-embodiment. While each word may have a distinctive meaning of its own, many writers appear to employ them interchangeably.

Some of the authors cited are chiefly concerned with one phase of reincarnation, the pre-existence of the soul, plainly disregarding the theological notion that each soul is a new creation at birth. Of this view, Rev. William R. Alger, a noted scholar on the subject of immortality, has written: "The pre-existence of the soul, whether taught by Pythagoras, sung by Empedocles, dreamed by Fludd, or contended for by Beecher, is the principal foundation of the belief of metempsychosis." Occasionally the reader will come upon a suggestive quotation on the soul or on immortality, with no direct reference to rebirth. This has been included because of its implications or philosophical bearing on the question.

The first sizable treatise on reincarnation, with numerous quotations, was published in 1888 by Houghton Mifflin Company under the title Reincarnation, A Study of Forgotten Truth. This book, by E. D. Walker, went through numerous editions, but is now out of print and of course somewhat dated. A reference work on the subject, The Ring of Return, compiled by Eva Martin, was published in London in 1927, but has also long been out of print.

The present volume is the most extensive collection of reincarnation quotations from modern and ancient literature thus far published, although further research will no doubt uncover additional material. To avoid unduly extending the book, however, extracts have been confined chiefly to the writings of the more widely known authors, and were selected to include various facets of the reincarnation idea.

Brief summaries of background considerations introduce several sections of the Anthology. Some of these, for example, trace the line of Platonic influence from Greece to the Alexandrian philosophers, to Arabia, then (after expulsion of the Platonists from Christian Europe for almost a thousand years) to Italy, Germany, England, and America. A historical view of the emergence of reincarnation in Western thought is thus provided, since wherever Plato and the Neoplatonists have exerted an influence, there the idea of metempsychosis inevitably gains fresh currency.

The fact that people often recognize, as familiar, scenes and landscapes which they see for the first time, is adduced by some as proof of rebirth. A number of these déjà vu experiences have been included, not because they are especially "evidential," but because the individual recording the experience

himself looked to the idea of reincarnation for an explanation. Other explanations are possible, for instance, the exercise of extrasensory powers during sleep. Dr. Ian Stevenson, University of Virginia psychiatrist, has made a
study of hundreds of other types of cases where children and adults claimed
to have remembered their former lives, and he is hopeful that this kind of
investigation may lead to decisive evidence concerning the survival question
(see page 302).

The real case for or against reincarnation, however, will probably rest not
so much on evidence of a phenomenal character but on its capacity to provide a rational explanation of life and its mysteries, based on the ascertainable
laws of nature. One of America's foremost physicists, Dr. W. F. G. Swann,
considering the possible relationship to the law of the universe of an immortal
entity within man, has said:

In contemplating the harmonization of life with what we call the laws of
inanimate matter, I expect to find a new set of laws, laws which do not deny
anything we had before except in the denial of the claim of those laws to
finality. I do not expect it to be necessary to find a new *particle* which will
cement the old materialistic realm with the realm of life and all that goes
with it, but I may expect to find the formal recognition of some kind of a
new entity differing from those which we have encountered in physics. I do
not necessarily expect that this entity will be something which can be described in terms of space and time, although I shall expect it to be accompanied by well-defined laws of operation which provide, not only for the
activities peculiar to its own purposes, but for the possibility of cementing
it logically with the knowledge of the past.   *Saturday Review, June 4, 1960*

It has been pointed out by the Viennese psychiatrist Viktor Frankl * that
Freudian psychoanalysis introduced into psychological research what it calls
the pleasure principle, or what may be termed the will-to-pleasure, while
Adlerian psychology made men conversant with the role of the will-to-power
as a main factor in the formation of neuroses. Dr. Frankl is of the opinion
that man is neither dominated by the will-to-pleasure nor the will-to-power,
but by what he should like to call the will-to-meaning—man's deep-seated
striving for a higher meaning to existence. The majority of a psychoanalyst's
clientele these days, says Dr. Erich Fromm, are "sick" because they know
that life runs out of their hands like sand, and that they will die without having lived.

Many of the individuals quoted in these pages seemed to have been able
to conceive of meaning and purpose only in a universe of unbroken continuity, where birth is not a beginning nor is death an end. Not as "authori-

* From *Death Camp to Existentialism*, Beacon Press, 1959.

ties" are their views presented, rather as coadventurers on the sea of discovery. The question of "authority"—whether religious or scientific—has been a benumbing weight upon the inquiring mind for many centuries, but now there appears to be a growing awareness that each individual must become his own authority, and that whatever of fundamental truth there is to be known must be discovered anew each for himself. The open-minded inquirer examines on its merits alone every idea that may point the way to self-knowledge.

The following advice, proffered by Schelling in his Philosophie der Mythologie, seems particularly applicable to a consideration of the phenomena of life, death, and consciousness, now to be discussed in this volume:

First and above all, an explanation must do justice to the thing that is to be explained, must not devaluate it, interpret it away, belittle it, or garble it, in order to make it easier to understand. The question is not "At what view of the phenomenon must we arrive in order to explain it in accordance with one or another philosophy?" but precisely the reverse: "What philosophy is requisite if we are to live up to the subject, be on a level with it?" The question is not how the phenomenon must be turned, twisted, narrowed, crippled so as to be explicable, at all costs, upon principles that we have once and for all resolved not to go beyond. The question is: "To what point must we enlarge *our* thought so that it shall be in proportion to the phenomenon. . . ."

PART ONE

Reincarnation in the World's Religions

In the East the life of man is held to be a pilgrimage, not only from the cradle to the grave, but also through that vast period of time, embracing millions upon millions of years, stretching from the beginning to the end of a Manvantara, or period of evolution, and as he is held to be a spiritual being, the continuity of his existence is unbroken. Nations and civilizations rise, grow old, decline and disappear; but the being lives on, spectator of all the innumerable changes of environment. Starting from the great ALL, radiating like a spark from the central fire, he gathers experience in all ages, under all rulers, civilizations and customs, ever engaged in a pilgrimage to the shrine from which he came. To symbolize this, the whole of India is dotted with sacred shrines, to which pilgrimages are made.

Echoes from the Orient

The Bhagavad-Gita and the Upanishads contain such Godlike fulness of wisdom on all things that I feel the authors must have looked with calm re- membrance back through a thousand passionate lives full of feverish strife for and with shadows, ere they could have written with such certainty of things which the soul feels to be sure.

George W. Russell (Æ)

The calmness and gentleness with which the Hindoo philosophers ap- proach and discourse on forbidden themes is admirable. What extracts from the Vedas I have read fall on me like the light of a higher and purer lumi- nary, which describes a loftier course through a purer stratum,—free from particulars, simple, universal.

Thoreau

THE ORIENT

·HINDUISM·

KRISHNA: I myself never was not, nor thou, nor all the princes of the earth; nor shall we ever hereafter cease to be. As the Lord of this mortal frame experienceth therein infancy, youth, and old age, so in future incarnations will it meet the same. One who is confirmed in this belief is not disturbed by anything that may come to pass. . . . As a man throweth away old garments and putteth on new, even so the dweller in the body, having quitted its old mortal frames, entereth into others which are new. . . .

The deluded do not see the spirit when it quitteth or remains in the body, nor when, moved by the qualities, it has experience in the world. But those who have the eye of wisdom perceive it, and devotees who industriously strive to do so see it dwelling in their own hearts. . . .

This exhaustless doctrine of Yoga* I formerly taught unto Vivaswat; Vivaswat communicated it to Manu and Manu made it known unto Ikshwaku; and being thus transmitted from one unto another it was studied by the Rajarshees (Royal Sages), until at length in the course of time the mighty art was lost. . . . It is even the same exhaustless, secret, eternal doctrine I have this day communicated unto thee because thou art my devotee and my friend.

---

* [Raja Yoga, the "Great" Yoga, which purports to reveal how man's lower self may be united with his Divine Immortal SELF. Hatha or body Yoga, a far lower practice, recommends physical disciplines—postures, breathing exercises, etc.—to gain desired ends. Eds.]

ARJUNA: Seeing that thy birth is posterior to the life of Ikshwaku, how am I to understand that thou wert in the beginning the teacher of this doctrine?
KRISHNA: Both I and thou have passed through many births! Mine are known unto me, but thou knowest not of thine. . . . I produce myself among creatures, O son of Bharata, whenever there is a decline of virtue and an insurrection of vice and injustice in the world; and thus I incarnate from age to age for the preservation of the just, the destruction of the wicked, and the establishment of righteousness. . . .
ARJUNA: What end, O Krishna, doth that man attain who, although having faith, hath not attained to perfection in his devotion because his unsubdued mind wandered from the discipline? Doth he . . . become destroyed, O strong-armed one, being deluded in the path of the Supreme Spirit? . . .
KRISHNA: Such a man, O son of Pritha, doth not perish here or hereafter. For never to an evil place goeth one who doeth good. The man whose devotion has been broken off by death goeth to the regions of the righteous, where he dwells for an immensity of years and is then born again on earth in a pure and fortunate family; or even in a family of those who are spiritually illuminated. But such a rebirth into this life as this last is more difficult to obtain. Being thus born again he comes in contact with the knowledge which belonged to him in his former body, and from that time he struggles more diligently towards perfection, O son of Kuru. For even unwittingly, by reason of that past practice, he is led and works on. Even if only a mere enquirer, he reaches beyond the word of the Vedas. But the devotee who, striving with all his might, obtaineth perfection because of efforts continued through many births, goeth to the supreme goal.

The Bhagavad-Gita
Trans. Wm. Q. Judge

All the worlds, and even the heavenly realm of Brahma, are subject to the laws of rebirth. . . .

> There is day . . . and night in the universe . . .
> Day dawns, and all those lives that lay hidden asleep
> Come forth and show themselves, mortally manifest:
> Night falls, and all are dissolved
> Into the sleeping germ of life.
> Thus they are seen, O Prince, and appear unceasingly,
> Dissolving with the dark, and with day returning
> Back to the new birth, new death. . . .*

* The translators explain: "When, at the end of a time-cycle, or kalpa, the universe is dissolved, it passes into a phase of potentiality, a seed-state, and thus awaits its next creation."

But behind the manifest and the unmanifest, there is another Existence, which is eternal and changeless. This is not dissolved in the general cosmic dissolution. It has been called the unmanifest, the imperishable. To reach it is said to be the greatest of all achievements.

> The Bhagavad-Gita
> *Trans. Prabhavananda and Isherwood*

That which giveth sustenance to the Universe and to ourselves, from which all doth proceed and unto which all must return—That Thou Art. In the golden vase of thine earthly body may the pure Light of the Spiritual Sun shine forth, that thou may'st know the Truth, and do thy whole duty, on the journey back to the Sacred Seat!

> The Gayâtri, a Hymn from the Rig-Veda†

Let him reflect on the transmigrations of men. . . .
On the departure of the individual soul from this body and its new birth in another womb, and on its wanderings through ten thousand millions of existences;
On the infliction of pain on embodied spirits, which is caused by demerit, and the gain of eternal bliss, which is caused by the attainment of their highest aim through spiritual merit.

> Laws of Manu, Book V.

[*A young man, by name Nachiketas, goes to the House of Death, and the god of death, Yama, grants him three wishes.*]

NACHIKETAS SPEAKS: This doubt that there is of a man that has gone forth [died]: "He exists," say some; and "He exists not," others say: "a knowledge of this, taught by thee, this of my wishes is the third wish."
DEATH SPEAKS: Even by the gods of old it was doubted about this; not easily knowable, and subtle is this law. Choose, Nachiketas, another wish; hold me not to it, but spare me this. . . . Choose sons and grandsons of a hundred years, and much cattle, and elephants and gold and horses. . . . Choose wealth and length of days. . . . Ask me not of death, Nachiketas.
NACHIKETAS SPEAKS: To-morrow these fleeting things wear out the vigour of a mortal's powers. Even the whole of life is short. . . . Not by wealth can a man be satisfied. Shall we choose wealth if we have seen thee? Shall we desire life while thou art master? . . . This that they doubt about, O Death, what is in the great Beyond, tell me of that. This wish that draws near to the mystery, Nachiketas chooses no other wish than that. . . .

---

† A sacred verse that Brahmins repeat mentally every morning and evening during their devotions.

DEATH SPEAKS: Thou indeed, pondering on dear and dearly-loved desires, O Nachiketas, hast passed them by. Not this way of wealth hast thou chosen, in which many men sink. . . . Thou art steadfast in the truth; may a questioner like thee, Nachiketas, come to us. . . .

That resting-place which all the Vedas proclaim, and all austerities declare; seeking for which they enter the service of the Eternal, that resting-place I briefly tell to thee. It is the unchanging Eternal, it is the unchanging supreme; having understood that unchanging one, whatsoever a man wishes, that he gains. It is the excellent foundation, the supreme foundation; knowing that foundation, a man is mighty in the eternal world.

The knower is never born nor dies, nor is it from anywhere, nor did it become anything. Unborn, eternal, immemorial, this ancient is not slain when the body is slain. . . . Smaller than small, greater than great, this Self is hidden in the heart of man. . . . Understanding this great lord the Self, bodiless in bodies, stable among unstable, the wise man cannot grieve.

Know that the Self is the lord of the chariot, the body verily is the chariot; know that the soul is the charioteer, and emotion the reins. They say that the bodily powers are the horses, and that the external world is their field. When the Self, the bodily powers and emotion are joined together, this is the right enjoyer; thus say the wise. But for the unwise, with emotion ever unrestrained, his bodily powers run away with him, like the unruly horses of the charioteer. . . . He whose charioteer is wisdom, who grasps the reins—emotion—firmly, he indeed gains the end of the path, the supreme resting-place of the emanating Power. . . . This is the hidden Self; in all beings it shines not forth; but is perceived by the piercing subtle soul of the subtle-sighted. . . .

He is released from the mouth of Death, having gained the lasting thing which is above the great, which has neither sound nor touch nor form nor change nor taste nor smell, but is eternal, beginningless, endless.

This is the immemorial teaching of Nachiketas, declared by Death. Speaking it and hearing it the sage is mighty in the eternal world. Whosoever, being pure, shall cause this supreme secret to be heard, in the assembly of those who seek the Eternal . . . he indeed builds for endlessness, he builds for endlessness.

Katha Upanishad*
Trans. Chas. Johnston

As a wagon heavy-laden might go halting and creaking, so the embodied soul goes halting, overburdened by the Soul of Inspiration when it has gone so far that a man is giving up the ghost. . . . Then as a caterpillar when

---

* *Selections from the* Upanishads *and* The Tao Te King, Cunningham Press, Los Angeles 32, Calif.

it comes to the end of a leaf, reaching forth to another foothold, draws itself over to it, so the soul, leaving the body, and putting off unwisdom, reaching another foothold there, draws itself over to it. As a worker in gold, taking an ornament, moulds it to another form newer and fairer; so in truth the soul, leaving the body here, and putting off unwisdom, makes for itself another form newer and fairer: a form like the forms of departed souls, or of the seraphs, or of the gods. . . .

Through his past works he shall return once more to birth, entering whatever form his heart is set on. When he has received full measure of reward in paradise for the works he did, from that world he returns again to this, the world of works. . . . This mighty Soul unborn grows not old, nor dies, for the Soul is immortal and fearless. The Soul is the fearless Eternal. He grows one with the Eternal, the fearless Eternal, who knows this.

Brihad Aranyaka Upanishad*
Trans. Chas. Johnston

There was a great god-sage called Narâda. . . . He travelled everywhere, and one day he was passing through a forest, and he saw a man who had been meditating until the white ants had built a huge mound round his body, so long had he been sitting in that position. He said to Narâda, "Where are you going?" Narâda replied, "I am going to heaven." "Then ask the God of Heaven when he will be merciful to me, when I shall attain freedom." Further on Narâda saw another man. He was singing and dancing, and he said, "O Narâda, where are you going?" Narâda said, "I am going to heaven." "Then ask when I shall attain freedom."

So Narâda went on. In the course of time he came again by the same road, and there was the man who had been meditating till the ant-hills had grown round him. He said, "O Narâda, did you ask about me?" "O yes." "What did he say?" "He told me that you would attain freedom in four more births." Then the man began to weep and wail, and said, "I have meditated until an ant-hill has been raised around me, and I have to endure four more births yet!"

Narâda went on to the other man. "Did you ask about me?" "O yes. Do you see this tamarind tree? I have to tell you that as many leaves as there are on that tree, so many times you will be born, and then you will attain freedom." Then the man began to dance for joy, and said, "After so short a time I shall be free!" A voice came, "My child, you shall have freedom this instant."

Kurma Purâna

* *Ibid.*

Patanjali

FOUNDER OF THE HINDU SCHOOL OF YOGA PHILOSOPHY

The soul is the Perceiver; is assuredly vision itself pure and simple; unmodified; and looks directly upon ideas. For the sake of the soul alone, the Universe exists. . . .

A knowledge of the occurrences experienced in former incarnations arises in the ascetic from holding before his mind the trains of self-reproductive thought and concentrating himself upon them. . . . By concentrating his mind upon the true nature of the soul as being entirely distinct from any experiences, and disconnected from all material things, and dissociated from the understanding, a knowledge of the true nature of the soul itself arises in the ascetic. . . .

The modifications of the mind are always known to the presiding spirit, because it is not subject to modification. The mind is not self-illuminative, because it is an instrument of the soul, is colored and modified by experiences and objects, and is cognized by the soul. . . . When the understanding and the soul are united, then self-knowledge results. . . .

The knowledge that springs from this perfection of discriminative power is called "knowledge that saves from re-birth." It has all things and the nature of all things for its objects, and perceives all that hath been and that is, without limitations of time, place, or circumstance, as if all were in the present and the presence of the contemplator. When the mind no longer conceives itself to be the knower, or experiencer, and has become one with the soul—the real knower and experiencer— . . . the soul is emancipated.

The Yoga Aphorisms of Patanjali
Trans. Wm. Q. Judge

Sankharâchârya (510-478? B.C.)

CELEBRATED VEDANTIC PHILOSOPHER

For beings a human birth is hard to win, then manhood and holiness, then excellence in the path of wise law; hardest of all to win is wisdom. Discernment between Self and not-Self, true judgment, nearness to the Self of the Eternal and Freedom are not gained without a myriad of right acts in a hundred births. . . .

The food-formed vesture is this body, which comes into being through food, which lives by food, which perishes without food. It is formed of cuticle, skin, flesh, blood, bone, water; this is not worthy to be the Self, eternally pure. The Self was before birth or death, and now is; how can it be born for the moment, fleeting, unstable of nature, not unified, inert, beheld like a jar? For the Self is the witness of all changes of form. The body has hands and feet, not the Self; though bodiless, yet because it is the Life, because its power is indestructible, it is controller, not controlled.

Since the Self is witness of the body, its character, its acts, its states, therefore the Self must be of other nature than the body. A mass of wretchedness, clad in flesh, full of impurity and evil, how can this body be the knower? The Self is of other nature. Of this compound of skin, flesh, fat, bone and water, the man of deluded mind thinks, "This is I"; but he who is possessed of judgment knows that his true Self is of other character, is nature transcendental. . . . Therefore, O thou of mind deluded, put away the thought that this body is the Self . . . discern the universal Self, the Eternal, changeless, and enjoy supreme peace. . . .

Putting off the body is not Freedom, any more than putting away one's staff and waterpot; but getting free from the knots of unwisdom in the heart—that is Freedom, in very deed. . . . Like the loss of a leaf, or a flower, or a fruit, is the loss of the body, or powers, or vital breath, or mind; but the Self itself, ever one's own, formed of bliss, is like the tree and stands. . . . Indestructible, verily, is the Self . . . it is not destroyed when all its changing vestures are destroyed. . . .

The great and peaceful ones live regenerating the world like the coming of spring, and after having themselves crossed the ocean of embodied existence, help those who try to do the same thing, without personal motives.

Vivekachûdâmani, or The Crest-Jewel of Wisdom

❁

In the Hindu view, spirit no more depends on the body it inhabits than body depends on the clothes it wears or the house it lives in. When we outgrow a suit or find our house too cramped we exchanged these for roomier ones that offer our bodies freer play. Souls do the same. . . .

This process by which an individual *jiva* passes through a sequence of bodies is known as reincarnation or transmigration of the soul—in Sanskrit *samsara* . . . On the subhuman level the passage is through a series of increasingly complex bodies until at last a human one is attained. Up to this point the soul's growth is virtually automatic. It is as if the soul were growing as steadily and normally as a plant and receiving at each successive embodiment a body which, being more complex, provides the needed largess for its new attainments.

With the soul's graduation into a human body this automatic, escalator mode of ascent comes to an end. Its assignment to this exalted habitation is evidence that the soul has reached self-consciousness, and with this estate come freedom, responsibility, and effort.

The mechanism that ties these new acquisitions together is the law of *Karma.* . . . *Karma* means, roughly, the moral law of cause and effect. . . . Every physical event, we are inclined to believe, has its cause, and every cause will have its determinate effects. India extends this concept of universal causation to include man's moral and spiritual life as well. . . . The present condition of each individual's interior life—how happy he is, how confused or serene, how much he can see—is an exact product of what he has wanted and got in the past; and equally, his present thoughts and decisions are determining his future states. Each act he directs upon the world has its equal and opposite reaction on himself. Each thought and deed delivers an unseen chisel blow toward the sculpturing of his destiny.

This idea of *Karma* and the completely moral universe it implies . . . commits the Hindu who understands it to complete personal responsibility. . . . Most persons are unwilling to admit this. They prefer, as the psychologists would say, to project—to locate the source of their difficulties outside themselves. . . . This, say the Hindus, is simply immature.

*The Religions of Man**
Prof. Huston Smith

Mohandas K. Gandhi (1869-1948)

[From Gandhi's Letters to a Disciple (Harpers, 1950) the following is taken, the disciple being Madeleine Slade, daughter of a distinguished British Admiral, who renounced position and comfort to follow Gandhi:]

The more I observe and study things, the more convinced I become that sorrow over separation and death is perhaps the greatest delusion. To realize that it is a delusion is to become free. There is no death, no separation of the substance. And yet the tragedy of it is that though we love friends for the substance we recognize in them, we deplore the destruction of the insubstantial that covers the substance for the time being. Whereas real friendship should be used to reach the whole through the fragment. You seem to have got the truth for the moment. Let it abide for ever. . . .

What you say about rebirth is sound. It is nature's kindness that we do not remember past births. Where is the good either of knowing in detail the numberless births we have gone through? Life would be a burden if we carried such a tremendous load of memories. A wise man deliberately forgets many things, even as a lawyer forgets the cases and their details as soon as they are disposed of. Yes, "death is but a sleep and a forgetting." . . .

* *Harpers,* 1958; *Mentor,* 1959.

Mother is slowly going. It will be well if the end comes soon. It is better to leave a body one has outgrown. To wish to see the dearest ones as long as possible in the flesh is a selfish desire and it comes out of weakness or want of faith in the survival of the soul after the dissolution of the body. The form ever changes, ever perishes, the informing spirit neither changes nor perishes. True love consists in transferring itself from the body to the dweller within and then necessarily realizing the oneness of all life inhabiting numberless bodies. . . . Both birth and death are great mysteries. If death is not a prelude to another life, the intermediate period is a cruel mockery.

· THE SIKHS ·

In Arnold Toynbee's foreword to *The Sacred Writings of the Sikhs* (Macmillan, N.Y., 1960) he states that the principal meeting-ground between the Indian and Judaic religions—which are notoriously different in spirit and have sometimes behaved like oil and vinegar—has been in India, where Islam has come in violent contact within Hinduism. The Sikh religion, he thinks, has achieved the spiritual triumph of discovering the fundamental harmony underlying the discord. Toynbee believes that the living higher religions of mankind are going to influence each other more than ever, and that in the coming debate the doctrines of the Sikhs will have a special contribution to make.

Dr. S. Radhakrishnan, the eminent Hindu scholar and Vice President of India, wrote the introduction to the above work, and therein states that the Sikhs and their founder, Nānak (1469-1539), teach both reincarnation and karma, holding that men are born with varying temperaments, some kind and unselfish, others greedy, fretful or passionate, all the result of past karma. While circumstances may stimulate these qualities, evil dispositions may be weakened, and good tendencies strengthened through effort. True happiness is not to be found in perishable things but only in union with the Supreme. Men are caught in the whirling wheel of samsara —of births and deaths—because of self-identification with the body and its environment.

"The aim of liberation is not to escape from the world of space and time but to be enlightened, wherever we may be. It is to live in this world knowing that it is divinely informed. . . . For those who are no longer bound to the wheel of samsara, life on earth is centred in the bliss of eternity. Their life is joy and where joy is, there is creation. They have no other country here below except the world itself. They owe their loyalty and love to the whole of humanity." Dr. Radhakrishnan thus throws a revealing light on the puzzling and oft-repeated instruction found in oriental scriptures that human beings should seek escape from the wheel of rebirth. It is from the *compulsory* necessity to reincarnate, springing from ceaseless involvement in material existence, that a being must free himself. The emancipated soul who has discharged all personal karmic obligations may choose to incarnate *voluntarily* as a helper of the human race.

· B U D D H I S M ·

I, Buddh, who wept with all my brothers' tears,
     Whose heart was broken by a whole world's woe,
Laugh and am glad, for there is Liberty!
     Ho! ye who suffer! know
Ye suffer from yourselves . . .

The Books say well, my Brothers! each man's life
     The outcome of his former living is;
The bygone wrongs bring forth sorrows and woes
     The bygone right breeds bliss.

That which ye sow ye reap. See yonder fields!
     The sesamum was sesamum, the corn
Was corn. The Silence and the Darkness knew!
     So is a man's fate born.

He cometh, reaper of the things he sowed,
     Sesamum, corn, so much cast in past birth;
And so much weed and poison-stuff, which mar
     Him and the aching earth.

If he shall labour rightly, rooting these,
     And planting wholesome seedlings where they grew,
Fruitful and fair and clean the ground shall be,
     And rich the harvest due . . .

Such is the Law which moves to righteousness,
     Which none at last can turn aside or stay;

The heart of it is Love, the end of it
　　Is Peace and Consummation sweet.　Obey!

> *The Light of Asia*
> *Sir Edwin Arnold*

Gautama Buddha speaks: With his heart thus serene, made pure, trans-
lucent, cultured, devoid of evil, supple, ready to act, firm and imperturbable,
he [the saint] directs and bends down his mind to the knowledge of the
memory of his previous temporary states. He recalls to his mind . . . one
birth, or two or three . . . or a thousand or a hundred thousand births,
through many an aeon of dissolution, many an aeon of both dissolution
and evolution.

> Samannaphala Sutta
> *Trans. T. W. Rhys Davids*

[Buddha discourses on old age:] Why this laughter, why this jubilation,
when this world is burning, burning? Shrouded in darkness why do you not
seek for light? Behold this painted image, this body full of sores, stuck
together, sickly, and full of many thoughts devoid of permanence and
stability. This body is wearing out; it is a nest of diseases; it is frail. This
heap of corruption is breaking to pieces. Life ends in death. . . . The
splendid chariots of kings wear away; the body also comes to old age; but
the virtue of the good never ages. Thus the saintly teach each other. A man
who has learnt but little grows old like an ox; his flesh increases, but his
knowledge does not grow.

> Many a House of life
> Hath held me—seeking ever him who wrought
> These prisons of the senses, sorrow-fraught;
> 　　Sore was my ceaseless strife!
>
> But now,
> Thou Builder of this Tabernacle—Thou!
> I know Thee! Never shalt Thou build again
> 　　These walls of pain,
> Nor raise the roof-tree of deceits, nor lay
> 　　Fresh rafters on the clay;
> Broken Thy House is, and the ridge-pole split!
> 　　Delusion fashioned it!
> Safe pass I thence—deliverance to obtain.

Him I called a Brahamana who knows the mystery of death and rebirth
of all beings, who is free from attachment, who is happy within himself

and enlightened. . . . Him I call a Brahamana who knows his former lives, who knows heaven and hell, who has reached the end of births, who is a sage of perfect knowledge and who has accomplished all that has to be accomplished.

The Dhammapada*

Although the Master [Buddha] was preaching, yet, of five laymen who sat there in His presence, one, being drowsy, fell asleep; another sat grubbing in the ground with his finger; the third idly shook a tree to and fro; the fourth sat gazing at the sky and paid no heed to what was said; while the fifth was the only one of them who gave heed to the teaching.

So the Elder Ananda, who stood there fanning the Master, observing the behaviour of these men, said to Him: "Lord, Thou art teaching the Truth to these men even as the voice of the thunder when the heavy rains are falling. Yet, behold! they sit doing this and that, while Thou dost preach. . . . Thy teaching cleaveth even through the skin and reacheth unto bones and marrow. How can it be that when Thou preachest the Law these men pay no heed thereto?"

"Ananda, such things as The Buddha, or The Law, or The Order of Brethren, through countless hundred thousand cycles of time have never been heard of by these beings. Therefore they cannot listen to this Law. In this round of births and deaths, whose beginning is incalculable, these beings have come to birth hearing only the talk of divers animals. They spend their time in song and dance, in places where men drink and gamble and the like. Thus they cannot listen to the Law."

"But what, Lord, is the actual reason, the immediate cause why they cannot?"

The Master replied: "Ananda, owing to hatred, owing to delusion, owing to lust, they cannot do so. There is no such fire as the fire of lust. It burns up creatures, nor even leaves an ash behind. . . . But this one, who, sitting, hears the Law attentively, for many, many times successively was a master of the Vedas three, a brâhmana who could repeat the Sacred Texts. So now also he pays good heed unto my words. . . ."

Dhammapala Commentary
Trans. F. L. Woodward

❁

The distinctive genius of Buddhism as a civilized religion can be approached by a brief explanation of the fundamental concepts in which this mystical philosophy . . . is formulated.

* Cunningham Press, Los Angeles 32, Calif.

First and quite central is the concept of Brahman, the metaphysical absolute. Out of Brahman come all things; to Brahman all things return. . . . Second, there is the concept of *atman*, the soul or self. And the very meaning of this concept is determined by the central Hindu conviction that the true self of each human being is identical with Brahman, and that when that identity is realized the quest for salvation is fulfilled. . . .

What makes possible the realization of identity with Brahman is the freeing of the self from control by longings which bind it to the needs of the body and to other transitory concerns. Now only in rare cases will an individual be sufficiently purged of these cravings in his present existence so that he can hope for *moksha* [liberation] before the death of the body which his soul now tenants. But this soul will survive this event and continue to exist, taking new forms one after another until the purgation is complete; in fact, it has existed in innumerable forms in the past.

Teachings of the Compassionate Buddha*
Prof. Edwin A. Burtt

Did Buddha Really Teach Immortality?

The foregoing quotations clearly suggest that Buddha taught the existence in man of an immortal reincarnating individuality. However, as so many Westerners have gained the opposite impression, we quote the following from a valuable essay on Buddha's thought contained in a translation of The Dhammapada *published by the Cunningham Press:*

It is a mistake to attempt a final estimate of the views of either Buddha, Plato, Jesus, or any other teacher of religious philosophy, by means of a literal analysis of the printed record of what they taught. In the case of Buddha, there is reason to think that, like Jesus, he taught an inner, higher doctrine to his immediate disciples. What may be called "popular" Buddhism is generally conceded to have been preserved by the Southern or Ceylonese School, and it is from the scriptures of Southern Buddhism that Western scholars have gained the impression that Buddha denied the possibility of immortality. Rhys Davids, the Orientalist whose interpretations are best known to the West, has written: "There is no passage of a soul or I in any sense from the one life to the other." . . . Davids also concludes that "death, utter death," is the sequel to Nirvana.

Edmond Holmes is convinced that this is a mutilation, a complete misreading, of Buddhist philosophy, and his chapter in *The Creed of*

* Mentor Religious Classic.

Buddha to correct the mistake seems a well-reasoned discussion of the central implication of Buddhist teachings. The Southern version, briefly, is that at death a man's tendencies and traits of character are resolved into psychic residues termed by the Buddhists *Skandhas*, and that these are all that remain of the man that has died. The Skandhas (carriers of Karma) are then reborn in some other person or individual, but without any connecting link of continuing egoity.

Northern Buddhism [the Buddhism of Tibet, China, and Japan], on the other hand, while exuberantly metaphysical in form, is said to have preserved the teaching given by Buddha to his *arhats*, or initiated disciples, and here one finds unmistakably taught the doctrine of a permanent identity which unites all the incarnations of a single individual. This latter is the view adopted by Holmes: "The question which we have to ask ourselves with regard to the Buddhist conception is a simple one: Is the identity between me and the inheritor of my Karma . . . as real as the identity between the me of today and the me of 20 years hence . . . ? If it is not as real, the doctrine of reincarnation is pure nonsense."

Holmes continues, showing that the doctrine of Karma, the key teaching of Buddhism, becomes almost senseless when divorced from the idea of a reincarnating ego.

Significantly enough, Buddha's reputed dying words were: "All compounds are perishable. Spirit is the sole, elementary, and primordial unity, and each of its rays is immortal, infinite, and indestructible. Beware of the illusions of matter."

Japanese Buddhism

> Blind, blind are sentient creatures all,
> Yet know they not their blindness.
> Again, again they are reborn
> To darkness and to sadness:
> Again, again they pass and die
> Blinded by sense eternally!
>
> *Japanese Buddhist Hymn*
> *Eighth century* A.D.

At that moment when faith in the Enlightened One is perfected, pure and lasting as the diamond, then shall the Spiritual Light shine upon us and guard us, the light which forever guideth us from rebirth and death. . . .

Throughout the long, long Kalpa [cycle] of my lives that are overpast could I never find the way of Deliverance, and if Hōnen Shōnin [1133-1212], the Great Teacher, had not arisen in this world, vainly had I spent the precious hours of my life. . . . Having taken birth in that small and remote island, Hōnen Shōnin spread abroad the doctrine of the Holy Name for the sake of all men's salvation. And thus had he done not only then, but many times in ages gone by.

Japanese Buddhist Psalms

Daisetz T. Suzuki (1870-   )

ZEN BUDDHIST WRITER AND UNIVERSITY TEACHER

When the Master Daito saw the Emperor Godaigo (reigned 1318-1338) who was another student of Zen, the Master said, "We were parted many thousands of Kalpas ago, yet we have not been separated even for a moment. We are facing each other all day long, yet we have never met."

Here we have the same idea as expressed by Shakyamuni [Buddha] himself in the *Saddharma-Pundarika*. . . . In spite of the historical fact that he attained Enlightenment near Buddhagaya at a definite moment of time, he says that he was fully enlightened even before the world was created. The historical fact of his Enlightenment is a record which we time-minded make with the intellect, because the intellect likes to divide, and cuts time into years and days and hours, and constructs history, whereas time itself underlying history knows no such human artificial cuttings. We are living partly in this time-space-conscious history but essentially in history-transcending time-space. Most of us would recognise the first, but not the second phase of our life. Daito the Master here wishes to remind the Emperor of this most fundamental experience. . . .

We are now in a position to say something about Karma. Human suffering is due to our being bound in Karma, for all of us, as soon as we are born, carry a heavy burden of past Karma. . . . In this sense, human beings are the only beings which have their Karma. All others move in accordance with the laws of their being, but it is human beings alone that can design and calculate and are conscious of themselves and of their doings. . . . From thinking, from thinking consciously, we develop the faculty of seeing, designing, and planning beforehand, which demonstrates that we are free, and not always bound by the "inevitable laws" of Nature. . . .

Not only are we wrapped up in our Karma but we know the fact that we are so wrapped up. . . . This very fact of our being aware of the Karma-bondage is the spiritual privilege of humanity. For this privilege, implying freedom, means our being able to transcend Karma. . . . We must make full use of it, and, accepting the Karma-bondage as far as it extends, resolutely face all forms of suffering and thereby qualify ourselves for transcending them.

The Essence of Buddhism

Tibetan Buddhism

A distinctive feature of Tibetan religion is belief in the successive rebirths of the highest Lamas, the Dalai, the Teshu, and some others. Westerners are accustomed to think of all Tibetan monks as lamas. This title, however, is formally allowed only to such high ranking "Incarnations" and to monks who have lived unusually saintly lives. Heinrich Harrer, once tutor to the present (fourteenth) Dalai Lama, observes in Seven Years in Tibet:

Birthdays are unimportant dates in Tibet. They are generally not known and never celebrated. For the people the date of their King's birth [the Dalai Lama] is quite without interest. He represents in his person the return to earth of Chenrezi, the God of Grace, one of the thousand Living Buddhas who have renounced Nirvana in order to help mankind. . . .
With us it is generally, but mistakenly, believed that each rebirth takes place at the moment of the predecessor's death. This does not accord with Buddhist doctrine, which declares that years may pass before the god once more leaves the fields of Heaven and resumes the form of man.

Chapter 16 of Harrer's book provides an eye-witness account of the long search for and final identification of the now living Dalai Lama.

The first authentic Western story of the supposed reincarnation of the same Living Buddhas in the succession of Grand Lamas is to be found in one of the early volumes of the Royal Asiatic Society, which contains the official recital by an English agent of the East India Company of two visits to Lhassa to interview the Dalai Lama. The Lama was, on the first occasion, an aged priest. At the second visit the Englishman was introduced to a mere babe who received him with every mark of intelligent understanding and the greatest dignity.

Nearly a century later Abbé Huc recounted a similar story in his famous Travels in Tartary, Thibet and China, coupled with details of many marvels witnessed by himself and his companion Catholic priest. The Abbé stated that the baby-oracle makes good his claim to being an old mind in a young body by giving to those who ask him "and who knew him in his past life, the most exact details of his anterior earthly existence." Chevalier des Mousseaux expatiates at length on the phenomenon, attributing it as a matter of course to the Devil.

· C H I N A ·

Lao Tzu (born c. 604 B.C.)

[From the books of Chwang Tzu, the celebrated disciple of Lao Tzu, the following extracts are taken concerning the Great Sage and his teaching:]

To have attained to the human form must be always a source of joy. And then, to undergo countless transitions, with only the infinite to look forward to—what incomparable bliss is that! Therefore it is that the truly wise rejoice in that which can never be lost, but endures always. . . .

The Master [Lao Tzu] came, because it was his time to be born; he went, because it was his time to die. For those who accept the phenomena of birth and death in this sense, lamentation and sorrow have no place. . . . The ancients described death as the loosening of the cord on which the Tao is suspended. What we can point to are the faggots that have been consumed; but the fire is transmitted, and we know not that it comes to an end. . . .

Birth is not a beginning; death is not an end. There is existence without limitation; there is continuity without a starting-point. . . . There is birth, there is death, there is issuing forth, there is entering in. That through which one passes in and out without seeing its form, that is the Portal of the Heavenly Tao.

[NOTE: *In explaining the nature of Tao, Lao Tzu wrote in The Tao Te King: "There is something which existed before Heaven and Earth. Oh how still it is, and formless, standing alone without changing, reaching everywhere without suffering harm. It must be regarded as the Mother of the Universe. It appears to be everlasting. Its name I know not. To designate it, I call it Tao."*]

Po Chü-I (A.D. 772-846)

TAOIST POET

If I depart, I cast no look behind
Still wed to life, I still am free from care.
Since life and death in cycles come and go,
Of little moment are the days to spare.

Thus strong in faith I wait, and long to be
One with the pulsings of Eternity.

"Peaceful Old Age"
Trans. Lionel Giles

· Z O R O A S T R I A N I S M ·

[The teachings of Zoroaster of ancient Persia are preserved to this day by the Parsis of India.]

Mezdam separated man from the other animals by the distinction of a soul, which is a free and independent substance, without a body or anything material, indivisible and without position, by which he attaineth to the glory of the angels.

And everyone who wisheth to return to the lower world [the earth] and is a doer of good shall, according to his knowledge and conversation and actions, receive something, either as a King or a Prime Minister, or some high office or wealth, until he meeteth with a reward suited to his deeds. ... Those who, in the season of prosperity, experience pain and grief, suffer them on account of their words or deeds in a former body, for which the Most Just now punisheth them.

The Desatir

According to Faredun's opinion, a man's soul, on departing from this world, ascends until it reaches the mountain of fire which lies under the Moon. If it is entirely pure and stainless it would easily cross the fire, without any disturbance in its course. Then it would be an angel. On the contrary, if it is rather impure or stained during earth life it would not be able to get over the fire. Then it returns to earth. ... If the soul, during earthly life does not purify itself, remains ignorant, and cherishes any worldly desires, afterwards it must return, and take physical bodies one after another until it is quite pure.

Zoré Pastan

After leaving this body a virtuous man acquires a still better place and body and his wisdom constantly increaseth.

Jam-i-Kaikhoshra

"Creator of the material world, Pure one! If a (female) dog that has ceased to bear, or a (male) dog whose seed is dried up, happens to die, where does its consciousness (*baodhangh*) go?"

[Ahura-Mazda replies:] "O holy Zarathushtra! it goes into a stream of water, where, from a thousand male, and a thousand female dogs, a pair, —one male and one female—of the *Udra*,* that reside in the waters, comes into being."

Vendidad, fargard, XIII, para. 50, 51

---

* Among the ancient Iranians the *Udra* or water-dog (probably the seal, or walrus) was considered of far greater value than even the dog, of which they took the greatest care.

EGYPT

Osiris

[*In his Treatise on Providence, Synesius, one of the Fathers of the Christian Church, thus records the instructions received by Osiris, the great teacher of Egypt, concerning the periodical rebirth amongst men of wise bene-factors:*]

Yet you must not think that the gods are without employment, or that their descent to this earth is perpetual. For they descend according to orderly periods of time, for the purpose of imparting a beneficent impulse in the republics of mankind. . . . But this happens when they harmonize a Kingdom and send to this earth for that purpose souls who are allied to themselves. For this providence is divine and most ample, which frequently through one man pays attention to and affects countless multitudes of men. . . .

For there is indeed in the terrestrial abode the sacred tribe of heroes who pay attention to mankind, and who are able to give them assistance even in the smallest concerns. . . . This heroic tribe is, as it were, a colony from the gods established here in order that this terrene abode may not be left destitute of a better nature.

Hermes

From one Soul of the Universe are all Souls derived. . . . Of these Souls there are many changes, some into a more fortunate estate, and some quite contrary. . . . Not all human souls but only the pious ones are divine. Once separated from the body, and after the struggle to acquire piety, which consist in knowing God and injuring none, such a soul becomes all intelligence. The impious soul, however, punishes itself by seeking a human body to enter into, for no other body can receive a human soul; it cannot enter the body of an animal devoid of reason. Divine law preserves the human soul from such infamy. . . .

The Soul passeth from form to form; and the mansions of her pilgrimage are manifold. Thou puttest off thy bodies as raiment; and as vesture dost thou fold them up. Thou art from old, O Soul of Man; yea, thou art from everlasting.

Books of Hermes

Homage to thee, O Governor of those who are Amenti [Heaven], who makest mortals to be born again, who renewest thy youth. . . .

I am Yesterday, Today, and Tomorrow; and I have the power to be born a second time. I am the hidden Soul who createth the gods. I am the Lord of those who are raised up from the dead. . . .

I am the Great One, Son of the Great One; I am Fire, the Son of Fire. I have knit together my bones; I have made myself whole and sound; I have become young once more; I am Osiris, the Lord of Eternity.

The Book of the Dead

Popular Stories of Ancient Egypt

In the book of the above name, Sir G. Maspero, the French Egyptologist, translates a tale concerning Horus, a magician, son of Panishi, who knowing that Egypt was menaced by an Ethiopian invader, caused himself to be reborn as Senosiris, the son of Princess Mahîtuaskhît, in order to save his country. According to the story Horus lived in Egypt fifteen hundred years prior, and so also had the Ethiopian invader. In this new incarnation Horus underwent all the stages of human existence but retained the acquirements and consciousness of his former life, and only returned to the heavenly region after victoriously accomplishing his self-imposed task.

Egyptian Belief and Modern Thought

[*James Bonwick's book of the above title originally published in 1878, but reissued in 1956 by Falcon's Wing Press, devotes a chapter to "Re-Incarnation; or Transmigration of Souls." He writes:*]

The Ritual [Book of the Dead] is full of allusions to the doctrine. Chapters 26 to 30 relate to the preservation of the heart or life for this purpose. . . . [Deveria, the] French writer shows how this esoteric doctrine was revealed in that portion of Egyptian sacred Scripture, known as the "Book of that which is in the Lower Hemisphere." He admits that "the funeral books show us clearly that resurrection was, in reality, but a renovation, leading to a new existence, a new infancy, and a new youth." He says further, "The *sahou* was not truly the mortal body. It was *a new being* formed by the re-union of corporeal elements elaborated by nature, and in which the soul was reborn in order to accomplish a new terrestrial existence under many forms. . . ."

Absurd as this notion [of reincarnation] may appear to a modern European, there can be no doubt that it ranks among the very oldest entertained by man. It would seem, by the approximate universality of this opinion throughout the world, that it was not so out of joint with reason as some have supposed. . . . An infant may take one breath of outer air, and die; a child may live only through the few years of supposed non-responsibility; a man may have diseased brain, or defective brain, and be idiotic or weak-headed for life. . . . Something seems wanting to vindicate Divine Providence, to vindicate the goodness and justice of Deity to *all* the race. It was, then, natural that some proposed a return to earth, under other conditions, to carry on the work of spiritual progression and soul discipline. The pampered sensualist returned a beggar; the proud oppressor, a slave; the selfish woman of fashion, a seamstress. A turn of the wheel gave a chance for the development of neglected or abused intelligence and feeling.

JUDAISM

•THE OLD TESTAMENT•

[Moses addressing the Lord concerning the death of human beings:] Thou turnest man to destruction; and sayest, Return, ye children of men. For a thousand years in thy sight are but as yesterday when it is past, and as a watch in the night.

Psalms 90:3-4

[King Solomon:] The Lord possessed me in the beginning of his way, before his works of old. I was set up from everlasting, from the beginning, or ever the earth was. When there were no depths, I was brought forth; when there were no fountains abounding with water.

Before the mountains were settled, before the hills was I brought forth: While as yet he had not made the earth, nor the fields, nor the highest part of the dust of the world. When he prepared the heavens, I was there. . . . When he established the clouds above . . . when he appointed the foundations of the earth: Then I was by him, as one brought up with him: and I was daily his delight, rejoicing always before him; rejoicing in the habitable part of his earth; and my delights were with the sons of men.

Book of Proverbs 8:22-31

Then the word of the Lord came unto me saying, before I formed thee in the belly I knew thee; and before thou camest forth out of the womb I sanctified thee, and I ordained thee a prophet unto the nations.

Jeremiah 1:5

The thing that hath been, it is that which shall be . . . and there is no new thing under the sun. Is there any thing whereof it may be said, See, this is new? it hath been already of old time, which was before us. There is no remembrance of former things.

Ecclesiastes 1:9-11

· THE ESSENES AND THE PHARISEES ·

[*In his Antiquity of the Jews (Book 18, Chap. 1, No. 2), the Jewish historian Josephus states that there were three sects of philosophy amongst the Jews: the Essenes, the Pharisees, and the Sadducees. The doctrine of the Sadducees was that souls die with the bodies, but both the Essenes and the Pharisees, he affirms, believed in rebirth. As to the Essenes, who have now become famous owing to the discovery of the Dead Sea Scrolls, he states elsewhere:*]

They contemn the miseries of life, and are above pain, by the generosity of their mind. And as for death . . . our war with the Romans gave abundant evidence what great souls they had in their trials. . . . They smiled in their very pains and laughed to scorn those who inflicted torments upon them, and resigned up their souls with great alacrity, as expecting to receive them again.

For their doctrine is this, that bodies are corruptible, and that the matter they are made of is not permanent; but that the souls are immortal, and continue for ever: and that they come out of the most subtile air, and are united to their bodies as to prisons, into which they are drawn by a certain natural enticement; but that when they are set free from the bonds of flesh, they then, as released from a long bondage, rejoice and mount upward. . . . These are the divine doctrines of the Essenes about the soul, which lay an unavoidable bait for such as have once had a taste of their philosophy.

Jewish War, Book 2, Chap. 8, Nos. 10-11

[The Pharisees] believe that souls have an immortal vigour in them [and that the virtuous] shall have power to revive and live again: on account of which doctrines they are able greatly to persuade the body of the people.

Antiquity of the Jews, Book 18, Chap. 1, No. 3

Philo Judæus (20 B.C.-A.D. 54)

ALEXANDRIAN PHILOSOPHER

The air is full of souls; those who are nearest to earth descending to be tied to mortal bodies return to other bodies, desiring to live in them.

De Somniis

The company of disembodied souls is distributed in various orders. The law of some of them is to enter mortal bodies and after certain prescribed periods be again set free. But those possessed of a diviner structure are absolved from all local bonds of earth. Some of these souls choose confinement in mortal bodies because they are earthly and corporeally inclined. . . .

All such as are wise, like Moses, are living abroad from home. For the souls of such formerly chose this expatriation from heaven, and through curiosity and the desire of acquiring knowledge they came to dwell abroad in earthly nature, and while they dwell in the body they look down on things visible and mortal around them, and urge their way thitherward again whence they came originally: and call that heavenly region . . . their citizenship, fatherland, but this earthly region in which they live, foreign.*

Flavius Josephus (A.D. 37-100)

HISTORIAN

[*From an address of Josephus to some Jewish soldiers who desired to kill themselves rather than be captured by the Romans:*]

The bodies of all men are, indeed mortal, and are created out of corruptible matter; but the soul is ever immortal, and is a portion of the divinity that inhabits our bodies. . . . Do ye not remember that all pure Spirits when they depart out of this life obtain a most holy place in heaven, from whence, in the revolutions of ages, they are again sent into pure bodies; while the souls of those who have committed self-destruction are doomed to a region in the darkness of Hades?

Jewish War, Book 3, Chap. 8, No. 5

* *Versuch eines systematischen Entwurfs des Lehrbegriffs Philo's von Alexandrien.* E. H. Stahl. Eichhorn's Allgem. Bibl. 1792. (IV, 767-890).

The Kabala

The Kabala is said to represent the hidden wisdom behind the Hebrew scriptures, derived by the Rabbis of the middle ages from still older secret doctrines. The first Jews to call themselves Kabalists were the Tanaiim who lived in Jerusalem about the beginning of the third century B.C. Two centuries later three important Jewish Kabalists appeared: Jehoshuah ben Pandira; Hillel, the great Chaldean teacher; and Philo Judæus, the Alexandrian Neo-Platonist. During medieval times there were many celebrated Kabalists, Spain being one of the important seats of their activity. Rabbi Isaac Luria founded a school of the Kabala around 1560, and the great exponent of his teachings, Rabbi Chajim Vital, wrote a famed work called Otz Chiim, or the Tree of Life, from which Baron Knorr von Rosenroth, a Christian Kabalist, took the Book on the Rashith ha Gilgalim, revolutions of souls, or scheme of reincarnations.

A Talmudic Miscellany by Paul Isaac Hershon provides the following quotations from the Kabala:

If a man be niggardly either in a financial or a spiritual regard, giving nothing of his money to the poor, or not imparting of his knowledge to the ignorant, he shall be punished by transmigration into a woman. . . . Know thou that Sarah, Hannah, the Shunamite (2 Kings, iv. 8), and the widow of Zarepta, were each in turn possessed by the soul of Eve. . . . The soul of Rahab transmigrated into Heber the Kenite, and afterwards into Hannah; and this is the mystery of her words: "I am a woman of a sorrowful spirit" (I Sam. i. 15)—for there still lingered in her soul a sorrowful sense of inherited defilement. . . . Sometimes the souls of pious Jews pass by metempsychosis into Gentiles, in order that they may plead on behalf of Israel and treat them kindly.

Yalkut Reubeni, Nos. 1, 8, 61, 63

We have it by tradition that when Moses . . . said in the law, "O God, the God of the spirits of all the flesh," (*Numbers* xvi, 22), he meant mystically to intimate that metempsychosis takes place in all flesh, in beasts, reptiles, fowls [i.e., animals also reincarnate].

Avodath Hakodesh, fol. 49, col. 3

The Zohar

[Tradition assigns the authorship of this Kabalistic classic to Rabbi Simeon ben Jochai, A.D. 80, although additions were made by medieval Hebrew scholars. Rabbi Moses de Leon, of Guadalaxara in Spain, edited and first published the work as a whole in 1280.]

All souls are subject to the trials of transmigration; and men do not know the designs of the Most High with regard to them: they know not how they are being at all times judged, both before coming into this world and when they leave it. They do not know how many transformations and mysterious trials they must undergo; how many souls and spirits come to this world without returning to the palace of the divine king.

The souls must reenter the absolute substance whence they have emerged. But to accomplish this end they must develop all the perfections, the germ of which is planted in them; and if they have not fulfilled this condition during one life, they must commence another, a third, and so forth, until they have acquired the condition which fits them for reunion with God.

Vol. II, fol. 99, et seq.

Rabbi Manasseh ben Israel (1604-1657)
THEOLOGIAN AND STATESMAN

[History informs us that owing to the efforts of this revered son of Israel, Oliver Cromwell removed the legal prohibition of Jews from England that had existed for three hundred fifty years since the reign of Edward I. In his book Nishmath Hayem, Rabbi Manasseh wrote:]

The belief or the doctrine of the transmigration of souls is a firm and infallible dogma accepted by the whole assemblage of our church with one accord, so that there is none to be found who would dare to deny it. . . . Indeed, there are a great number of sages in Israel who hold firm to this doctrine so that they made it a dogma, a fundamental point of our religion. We are therefore in duty bound to obey and to accept this dogma with acclamation . . . as the truth of it has been incontestably demonstrated by the Zohar, and all books of the Kabalists.

Hasidism and Karaism

The following quotation is taken from The Universal Jewish Encyclopedia, section "Souls, Transmigration of (gilgul hanefesh)":

The doctrine of transmigration of souls, which was especially accepted by the Karaites . . . is generally attacked by Jewish philosophers, but is defended by Isaac Abravanel and Manasseh ben Israel. It appears often in Cabala; it is found in organized form in the Zohar, it is further developed in the teachings of Isaac Luria [1534-1572], and in Hasidism it becomes a universal belief.

According to these teachings, all human souls have a common origin in the spiritual unity of the primordial man (Adam Kadmon), sparks (nitzotzoth) of which form the individual souls. . . . The sin of [the later] Adam brought higher and lower souls into confusion; as a result, every soul has to pass through a series of incarnations. . . . The soul itself has no sex, which is determined by the body and may vary from incarnation to incarnation.

The Karaites were a Jewish sect which rejected Rabbinism and Talmudism, basing its tenets on interpretation of the scriptures. It was founded in Bagdad about A.D. 765 by Anan ben David, was formerly widespread, but now has only some 12,000 adherents, chiefly in southern Russia.

Hasidism was an influential movement among Polish Jews of the eighteenth century that spread to the Ukraine, Galicia, and Lithuania, and still persists. The Jewish philosopher Martin Buber has devoted his life to spreading its teachings and way of life.

S. Ansky (1863-1920)
SOLOMON JUDAH LÖB RAPOPORT

["He was a unique figure in Yiddish literature. . . . His masterpiece is the dramatic legend Tzvishen Tzvei Velten, better known as the Dybbuk; it is mystical and symbolical, yet taken from actual Hasidic life."—The Universal Jewish Encyclopedia]

It's not only the poor it pays to be careful with. You can't say for a certainty, who any man might have been in his last existence, nor what he is doing on earth. . . . Through many transmigrations, the human soul is drawn by pain and grief, as the child to its mother's breast, to the source of its being, the Exalted Throne above. But it sometimes happens that a soul which has attained to the final state of purification suddenly becomes the prey of evil forces which cause it to slip and fall. And the higher it has soared, the deeper it falls.

The Dybbuk

Sholem Asch (1880-1957)

Not the power to remember, but its very opposite, the power to forget, is a necessary condition of our existence. If the lore of the transmigration of souls is a true one, then these, between their exchange of bodies, must pass through the sea of forgetfulness. According to the Jewish view we make the transition under the overlordship of the Angel of Forgetfulness. But it sometimes happens that the Angel of Forgetfulness himself forgets to remove from our memories the records of the former world; and then our senses are haunted by fragmentary recollections of another life. They drift like torn clouds above the hills and valleys of the mind, and weave themselves into the incidents of our current existence. . . . Then the effect is exactly the same as when, listening to a concert broadcast through the air, we suddenly hear a strange voice break in, carried from afar on another ether-wave and charged with another melody.

The Nazarene

CHRISTIANITY

[For statements on pre-existence and rebirth from the Old Testament, see prior section under Judaism.]

• THE NEW TESTAMENT •

The ancient Jews were continually expecting the reincarnation of their great prophets. Moses was in their opinion Abel, the son of Adam; and their Messiah was to be the reincarnation of Adam himself, who had already come a second time as David. It seems especially significant then that the closing words of the Old Testament (Malachi 4:5) make this prophecy:

Behold, I will send you Elijah the prophet before the great and terrible day of Jehovah come.

Elijah had already lived amongst the Jews. Now the first book of the New Testament refers to this prophecy on three occasions, thus linking the Old and New Testament on the idea of rebirth (In the King James version of the New Testament, the Greek form of "Elijah," namely "Elias," is used).

When Jesus came into the coasts of Caesarea Philippi, he asked his disciples, saying, Whom do men say that I, the Son of man, am? And they said, Some say that thou art John the Baptist; some, Elias; and others, Jeremias, or one of the prophets.

Matthew 16:13-4

And as they came down from the mountain, Jesus charged them, saying, Tell the vision to no man, until the Son of man be risen again from the dead.

And his disciples asked him, saying, Why then say the scribes that Elias must first come? And Jesus answered and said unto them, Elias truly shall first come, and restore all things. But I say unto you, That Elias is come already, and they knew him not, but have done unto him whatsoever they listed. Likewise shall also the Son of man suffer of them.

Then the disciples understood that he spake unto them of John the Baptist [who had already been beheaded by Herod].

Matthew 17:9-13

Among them that are born of women there hath not risen a greater than John the Baptist. . . . For all the prophets and the law prophesied until John. And if ye will receive it, this is Elias, which was for to come. *He that hath ears to hear, let him hear.* (Italics ours.)

Matthew 11:11-15

The foregoing statement from Matthew 17 is repeated in Mark 9:13, omitting the name of John.

❀

When there was brought into the presence of Jesus a man who was born blind, the disciples naturally wondered why he had been thus punished, and asked Jesus: "Which did sin, this man or his parents" (John 9:34). The disciples must have had the idea of reincarnation in mind, for obviously if the man had been born blind, his sin could not have been committed in this life. If the doctrine was wrong and pernicious, then, it would seem, was the time for Jesus to deny the whole theory. Yet he did not do so, although in this case he said the blindness was for other reasons.

❀

Returning again to the case of John the Baptist, one finds this statement in John 1:6: "There was a man sent from God, whose name was John." The obvious sense of this verse to the church fathers who lived closest to the time of Jesus appears in the comments on it by Origen, who says that it implies the existence of John the Baptist's soul previous to his terrestrial body. He states:

And if the Catholic opinion hold good concerning the soul, as not propagated with the body, but existing previously and for various reasons clothed in flesh and blood this expression, "Sent from God," will no longer seem extraordinary as applied to John.

❁

St. Paul also appears to point to the theory of pre-existence in Romans 9:10-13, where he refers to the case of Jacob and Esau, saying that the Lord loved the one and hated the other before they were born. Chevalier Ramsay comments on this at page 45.

❁

St. John in Revelations 3:12 states:

Him that overcometh will I make a pillar in the temple of my God, and *he shall go no more out.*

Evidently he had gone out into incarnation before the words "no more" could have no place or meaning. It was probably the old idea of the exile of the soul and the need for it to be purified by long wandering before it could be admitted as a "pillar in the temple of God."

· THE APOCRYPHA ·

The fourteen books of The Apocrypha, of which The Wisdom of Solomon is one, are appended to the Vulgate (Roman Catholic) and to the Septuagint (Greek Catholic) versions of the Old Testament, although the Jews themselves do not include them in their Bible. The following is from the King James translation:

Now I was a child good by nature, and a good soul fell to my lot. Nay, rather, being good, I came into a body undefiled.

The Wisdom of Solomon 8:19-20

Early Church Fathers on Reincarnation

Justin Martyr (A.D. 100-165)

[E. D. Walker writes:] "Justin Martyr expressly speaks of the soul inhabiting more than once the human body, and denies that on taking a
second time the embodied form it can remember previous experiences.
Afterwards, he says, souls who have become unworthy to see God in human
guise, are joined to the bodies of wild beasts. Thus he openly defends the
grosser concept of metempsychosis."

St. Clement of Alexandria (A.D. 150-220)

[In Stromata, Vol. 3, p. 433 (Edition des Benedictins), St. Clement
says that although man was created after other beings, "the human species is
more ancient than all these things." In his Exhortations to the Pagans he
wrote:]

We were in being long before the foundation of the world; we existed in
the eye of God, for it is our destiny to live in Him. We are the reasonable
creatures of the Divine Word; therefore, we have existed from the beginning, for in the beginning was the Word. . . . Not for the first time does
He show pity on us in our wanderings, He pitied us from the very beginning. . . . Philolaus, the Pythagorean, taught that the soul was flung into
the body as a punishment for the misdeeds it had committed, and his opinion was confirmed by the most ancient of the prophets.

Origen (A.D. 185-254)

[The Encyclopædia Britannica states that Origen was "the most prominent
of all the Church Fathers with the possible exception of Augustine," while
St. Jerome at one time considered him as "the greatest teacher of the Church
after the apostles." St. Gregory of Nyssa called him "the prince of Christian
learning in the third century."]

Is it not more in conformity with reason that every soul for certain mysterious reasons (I speak now according to the opinion of Pythagoras and

Plato and Empedocles, whom Celsus frequently names) is introduced into a body, and introduced according to its deserts and former actions? . . .

Is it not rational that souls should be introduced into bodies, in accordance with their merits and previous deeds, and that those who have used their bodies in doing the utmost possible good should have a right to bodies endowed with qualities superior to the bodies of others? . . .

The soul, which is immaterial and invisible in its nature, exists in no material place without having a body suited to the nature of that place; accordingly, it at one time puts off one body, which was necessary before, but which is no longer adequate in its changed state, and it exchanges it for a second.

Contra Celsum

The soul has neither beginning nor end. . . .

Every soul . . . comes into this world strengthened by the victories or weakened by the defeats of its previous life. Its place in this world as a vessel appointed to honor or dishonor is determined by its previous merits or demerits. Its work in this world determines its place in the world which is to follow this. . . .

I am indeed of the opinion that as the end and consummation of the saints will be in those [ages] which are not seen, and are eternal, we must conclude that rational creatures had also a similar beginning. . . . And if this is so, then there has been a descent from a higher to a lower condition, on the part not only of those souls who have deserved the change by the variety of their movements, but also on that of those who, in order to serve the whole world, were brought down from those higher and invisible spheres to these lower and visible ones, although against their will. . . . The hope of freedom is entertained by the whole of creation—of being liberated from the corruption of slavery—when the sons of God, who either fell away or were scattered abroad, shall be gathered into one, and when they shall have fulfilled their duties in this world.

De Principiis

St. Gregory (A.D. 257-332)
BISHOP OF NYSSA

It is absolutely necessary that the soul should be healed and purified, and if this does not take place during its life on earth it must be accomplished in future lives.

Arnobius (fl. 290)

Arnobius wrote in his Adversus Gentes: "We die many times, and often do we rise from the dead." He also informs us that Clement of Alexandria had written wonderful stories of metempsychosis, and many worlds before Adam.

Lactantius (early fourth century)

CHRISTIAN WRITER; TUTOR OF SON OF CONSTANTINE THE GREAT

In Divinarum Institutionum 3, 18, Lactantius, whom St. Jerome called the Christian Cicero, states that the soul was capable of immortality and of bodily survival only on the hypothesis that it existed before the body.

St. Jerome (340-420)

[In the early centuries of the Christian era the leading churchmen held varying opinions as to the origin of the soul. From St. Jerome's summary of these views it is evident that all but one involves some form of pre-existence:]

As to the origin of the soul, I remember the question of the whole church: whether it be fallen from heaven, as Pythagoras and the Platonists and Origen believe; or be of the proper substance of God, as the Stoics, Manicheans and Priscillian heretics of Spain believe; or whether they are kept in a repository formerly built by God, as some ecclesiastics foolishly believe; or whether they are daily made by God and sent into bodies. . . or whether by traduction, as Tertullian, Apollinarius, and the greater part of the Westerns believe, i.e., that as body from body so the soul is derived from the soul. . . .

[In his 94th Epistle to Avitus, Jerome agrees with Origen as to the interpretation of the passage mentioned by Origen in De Principiis, "Who hath chosen us before the foundation of the world" (St. Paul's Ephesians 1:4), and states:]

A divine habitation, and a true rest above, I think, is to be understood, where rational creatures dwelt, and where, before their descent to a lower position, and removal from invisible to visible [worlds], and fall to earth, and need of gross bodies, they enjoyed a former blessedness. Whence God the Creator made for them bodies suitable to their humble position, and created this visible world and sent into the world ministers for their salvation.

❁

The doctrine of transmigration has been secretly taught from ancient times to small numbers of people, as a traditional truth which was not to be divulged.

Hyeronym., Epistola ad Demetriadem

❁

The order of things is regulated by the providential government of the whole world; some powers falling down from a loftier position, others gradually sinking to earth: some falling voluntarily, others being cast down against their will: some undertaking of their own accord the service of stretching out the hand to those who fall, others being compelled to persevere for a long time in the duty which they have undertaken.

St. Augustine (354-430)

The message of Plato, the purest and most luminous in all philosophy, has at last scattered the darkness of error, and now shines forth mainly in Plotinus, a Platonist so like his master that one would think they lived together, or rather—since so long a period of time separates them—that Plato is born again in Plotinus.

Contra Academicos

Say, Lord to me . . . say, did my infancy succeed another age of mine that died before it? Was it that which I spent within my mother's womb? . . . and what before that life again, O God my joy, was I anywhere or in any body? For this I have none to tell me, neither father nor mother, nor experience of others, nor mine own memory.

The Confessions of St. Augustine

Synesius (370-430)
BISHOP OF PTOLEMAIS

The Church Fathers Nemesius, Synesius, and Hilarius, it appears, openly defended pre-existence, though not always agreeing to Origen's form of it.

Nemesius who was Bishop of Emissa in Syria and a Christian philosopher declared that every Greek who believed in immortality believed also in the pre-existence of the soul. Of Synesius, most familiar to English readers as the convent patriarch in Charles Kingsley's Hypatia, it is known that when the citizens of Ptolemais invited him to their bishopric, he declined that dignity at first for the reason that he cherished certain opinions which they might not approve, as after mature reflection they had struck deep roots in his mind. Foremost among these he mentioned the doctrine of pre-existence. In his Treatise on Dreams he wrote:

Philosophy speaks of souls being prepared by a course of transmigrations. . . . When first it comes down to earth, it [the soul] embarks on this animal spirit as on a boat, and through it is brought into contact with matter. The soul's object is to take this spirit back with her; for if she were to abandon it and leave it behind on earth . . . the manner of her return would bring disgrace on her. . . . The soul which did not quickly return to the heavenly region from which it was sent down to earth had to go through many lives of wandering.

The Anathemas Against Pre-existence

It has been generally believed that in the year A.D. 553 an important church council anathematized (cursed) the doctrine of the pre-existence of the soul, and, by implication, reincarnation as related to man's past. Recent evidence advanced by Catholic scholars throws a new light on the whole matter, as we shall shortly see.

In the early centuries of Christian history, many battles were waged over issues of doctrine, church councils being convened to settle disputes. In the sixth century the Byzantine Emperor Justinian declared war against the Origenists, the followers of the learned church father Origen (A.D. 185-254). Origen's high standing in the early church is clearly attested by St. Jerome and St. Gregory (see page 35, where also are printed Origen's statements on reincarnation). At Justinian's instigation a local synod, convened in Constantinople in the year 543, condemned the teachings of Origen, and ten years later, in 553, Justinian issued his anathemas against Origen, possibly submitting them for final ratification at an extra-conciliary session of the Fifth Ecumenical Council (also called the Second Council of Constantinople). The anathemas cursed among other teachings the doctrine of the pre-existence of the soul.

The Catholic Encyclopedia (Vol. 11, p. 311 under "Origen," and Vol. 4, p. 308-309 under "Councils of Constantinople") gives some rather astonishing information concerning this Fifth Ecumenical Council, permitting the conclusion, on at least technical grounds, that there is no barrier to belief in reincarnation for Catholic Christians. With the exception of six western bishops from Africa, the council was attended entirely by oriental bishops, no representative from Rome being present. Although Pope Vigilius was in Constantinople at the time, he refused to attend. The president of the Council was Eutychius, Patriarch of Constantinople. The Columbia Encyclopedia (under "Orthodox Eastern Church") remarks: "From the time of Justinian the emperor controlled the patriarch absolutely."

There had apparently been intense conflict between Justinian and Pope Vigilius for several years. Violating previous agreements, Justinian in 551 issued an edict against what was known as "The Three Chapters," the teachings of three supposed heretics. "For his dignified protest Vigilius thereupon suffered various personal indignities at the hands of the civil authority and nearly lost his life." (Vol. 4:309) Later, to bring peace between the eastern and western branches of the church, this Fifth Ecumenical Council was called. Justinian, however, refused Pope Vigilius' request for equal representation of bishops from east and west, and summarily convened the council on his own terms; hence the pope's refusal to attend. When we learn that as many as 165 bishops were present at the final meeting on June 2, only six of whom could possibly be from the western church, it can safely be concluded that the voting during all the sessions was very much in Justinian's hands.

Quoting directly from The Catholic Encyclopedia (Vol. 11, p. 311,* italics ours):

Were Origen and Origenism anathematized? Many learned writers believe so; an equal number deny that they were condemned; most modern authorities are either undecided or reply with reservations. Relying on the most recent studies on the question it may be held that:

1. It is certain that the fifth general council was convoked exclusively to deal with the affair of the Three Chapters, *and that neither Origen nor Origenism were the cause of it.*

2. It is certain that the council opened on 5 May, 553, in spite of the protestations of Pope Vigilius, who though at Constantinople refused to attend it, and that in the eight conciliary sessions (from 5 May to 2 June), the Acts of which we possess, *only the question of the Three Chapters is treated.*

3. Finally it is certain that *only the Acts concerning the affair of the*

---

* The section on Origen was written by Father Ferdinand Prat, S.J., member of the Biblical Commission, College St. Michel, Brussels.

Three Chapters were submitted to the pope for his approval, which was given on 8 December, 553, and 23 February, 554.

4. It is a fact that Popes Vigilius, Pelagius I (556-61), Pelagius II (579-90), Gregory the Great (590-604), in treating of the fifth council deal only with the Three Chapters, *make no mention of Origenism, and speak as if they did not know of its condemnation.*

5. It must be admitted that *before the opening of the council,* which had been delayed by the resistance of the pope, the bishops already assembled at Constantinople had to consider, by order of the emperor, *a form of Origenism that had practically nothing in common with Origen,* but which was held, we know, by one of the Origenist parties in Palestine. . . .

6. The bishops [at this extra-conciliary session referred to in No. 5 above] certainly subscribed to the fifteen anathemas proposed by the emperor [against Origen]; an admitted Origenist, Theodore of Scythopolin, was forced to retract; *but there is no proof that the approbation of the pope, who was at that time protesting against the convocation of the council, was asked.*

7. It is easy to understand how this extra-conciliary sentence *was mistaken at a later period* for a decree of the actual oecumenical council.

It seems clear from the above that Catholic scholars are beginning to disclaim that the Roman Church took any part in the anathemas against Origen, suggesting that during the many centuries when the Church believed it had condemned Origen, it was mistaken. However, one disastrous result of the mistake still persists, namely, the exclusion from the Christian creed of the teaching of the pre-existence of the soul and, by implication, reincarnation.

What do Protestant scholars and theologians say about the supposed condemnation of Origen? Henry R. Percival writes in A Select Library of Nicene and Post-Nicene Fathers, published in 1900 (Vol. 14, Series 2, p. 316):

Did the Fifth synod examine the case of Origen and finally adopt the XV. Anathemas against him which are usually found assigned to it? It would seem that with the evidence now in our possession it would be the height of rashness to give a dogmatic answer to this question. Scholars of the highest repute have taken, and do take to-day, the opposite sides of the case. . . . To my mind the chief difficulty in supposing these anathematisms to have been adopted by the Fifth Ecumenical is that nothing whatever is said about Origen in the call of the council, nor in any of the letters written in connexion with it; all of which would seem unnatural had there been a long discussion upon the matter, and had such an important dogmatic definition been adopted as the XV. anathemas. . . .

Whatever the truth of this obscure phase of early church history, the anathemas themselves are most revealing and well worth consideration. They are reprinted in their entirety in the Appendix. Special attention is drawn to the maledictions at the conclusions of both series, the anathemas of Justinian being directed not only against Origen and one other "who set forth these opinions together with their nefarious and execrable and wicked doctrine," but also against "whomsoever there is who thinks thus, or defends these opinions, or in any way hereafter at any time presumes to protect them."

In the light of the references to reincarnation in the Bible, and of statements by the early church fathers, and now of the position of Catholic scholars in disclaiming the crusade against Origen, it is not remarkable that a growing number of the Christian clergy and religious writers are speaking favorably of the new interest in reincarnation, and are even hoping that this "lost chord of Christianity" may once more vibrate in harmony with Christ's teaching of hope and responsibility.

Early Christian Sects

During the Dark Ages the doctrine of metempsychosis did not disappear entirely, but was perpetuated by so-called heretical Christian groups, the most prominent of which was the widespread Cathari movement. The latter included the Albigenses and the Waldensians of France, who were later mercilessly wiped out; the Bogomiles of Bulgaria, and the Paulicians of Armenia. In The Troubadours and Courts of Love, J. F. Rowbotham states:

The Cathari believed that the soul was forced to migrate from body to body, until it became reincarnated in a member of the sect. . . . Many believed that they had passed through hundreds of bodies. Paul was said to have passed through thirteen bodies, according to some, and through thirty-two according to others before he attained the grace of God.

Still earlier groups such as the Priscillians in Spain, the Simonists (followers of Simon Magus), and Christian Gnostics such as the Manicheans, Marcionists, Basilidians, and Valentinians, also taught reincarnation, the Manicheans alone comprising more than seventy sects. The Encyclopædia

Britannica states that the doctrine was held by a group of early Christian heretics spoken of by Jeremy Collier as the "Metempsychi."

According to the Pistis Sophia, a sacred book of the early Gnostics or primitive Christians, "The discarnate soul which has not solved the mystery of the breaking of the bonds of the seals is brought before the virgin of light, who, after judging it, hands it over to her agents, who carry it into a new body."

Returning to the sects of the Middle Ages, some mention should be made of the legendary Knights of the Round Table and similar orders. In reviewing the book King Arthur's Avalon (The Story of Glastonbury) by Geoffrey Ashe (Dutton, 1958) DeLancey Ferguson writes in the New York Herald Tribune for June 8, 1958:

The Grail stories mostly grew up outside the Church. . . . Mr. Ashe suggests possible reasons why the Church fought shy of this cult. A wonder-working vessel is a recurrent theme in ancient religions; so is the idea of special knowledge to be achieved by an initiate who performs secret rituals. "The Grail cult may well have been only the most complex codification of a bold strain of mysticism, persisting through the centuries but never openly unfolded." To the Church, of course, the hint of spiritual knowledge hidden even from the clergy was flat heresy.

One of the King Arthur legends made this prophecy: "He shall come again full twice as fair to rule over his people." Glastonbury, by the way, was an old Druidical holy place.

Clergymen and Religious Writers on Reincarnation

Jacob Boehme (1575-1624)
CHRISTIAN PHILOSOPHER AND MYSTIC

Those who are often and much hindered by the contrarious life, and thus are involved in the mixed life, and travail in desire for the birth of the holy life: for them are these writings written. . . . Let them imagine a life which is the outcome and growth of all lives, and is mixed. But let them also imagine another life to grow in it from all the lives, which, though it had grown from all the lives, was free from all the other lives, and yet possessed of all the essential properties of those lives. This other new life (let them imagine) is illuminated with the light, and only in itself; so that it could behold all the other lives, and they (the other lives) could not see nor apprehend the new life. Thus is every one, who, out of the mixed life, evil and good, is born again.

Six Theosophic Points

Death is a breaking up of the three kingdoms in man. It is the only means by which the spirit is enabled to enter into another state and to become manifest in another form. When the spirit dies relatively to its selfhood and its self-will becomes broken in death, then out of that death grows another will, not according to that temporal will, but according to the eternal will.

The Signature of All Things

Joseph Glanvill (1636-1680)

ENGLISH DIVINE; CHAPLAIN OF KING CHARLES II

[*The following is taken from Glanvill's* Lux Orientalis, *which bears this subtitle:* "An Inquiry into the opinions of the Eastern sages concerning the Præexistence of Souls. Being a Key to unlock the Grand Mysteries of Providence in Relation to man's sin and misery."]

Christ and His Apostles spoke and writ as the condition of the persons, with whom they dealt, administered occasion. . . . Therefore doubtless there were many noble theories which they could have made the world acquainted with. . . . Few speculative truths are delivered in Scripture but such as were called forth by the controversies of those times; and Pre-existence was none of them, it being the constant opinion of the Jews, as appears by that question, "Master, was it for this man's sin or his father's that he was born blind?" . . . And the author of the Book of Wisdom, who certainly was a Jew, probably Philo, plainly supposeth the same doctrine in that speech, "For I was a witty child and had a good spirit, wherefore . . . being good, I came into a body undefiled."

. . . Every soul brings a kind of sense with it into the world, whereby it tastes and relisheth what is suitable to its peculiar temper. . . . What can we conclude but that the soul itself is the immediate subject of all this variety and that it came prejudiced and prepossessed into this body with some implicit notions that it had learnt in another?

To say that all this variety proceeds primarily from the mere temper of our bodies is methinks a very poor and unsatisfying account. For those that are the most like in the temper, air, and complexion of their bodies, are yet of a vastly differing genius. . . . What then can we conjecture is the cause of all this diversity, but that we had taken a great delight and pleasure in some things like and analogous unto these in a former condition?

William Law (1686-1761)

CELEBRATED ENGLISH DIVINE

It has been an Opinion commonly received, though without any Foundation in the Light of Nature, or Scripture, that God created this whole visible World and all Things in it *out of Nothing*; nay, that the souls of Men and the highest Orders of Beings were created in the same Manner. The Scripture is very decisive against this Origin of the Souls of Men. . . . God *breathed into Man (Spiraculum Vitarum) the Breath of Lives, and Man became a Living Soul.* Here the Notion of a Soul created *out of Nothing* is in the plainest, strongest Manner rejected by the first Written Word of God. . . . Therefore there is in all Men . . . a *divine, immortal, never-ending* Spirit, that can have nothing of Death in it, but *must* live forever, because it is the Breath of the *everliving* God. . . .

Thinking and *Willing* are Eternal, they never began to be. Nothing can think, or will *now*, in which there was not Will and Thought from *all Eternity.* . . . Herein also appears the high Dignity, and never-ceasing Perpetuity of our Nature. The *Essences* of our Souls can never cease to be, because they never began to be; and nothing can live eternally, but that which hath lived from all Eternity. . . . Properly and strictly speaking, nothing *can begin* to be: The Beginning of every Thing is nothing more than its beginning to be in a *new State.*

*An Appeal To All that Doubt or
Disbelieve in the Truths of the Gospel*

Chevalier Ramsay (1686-1743)

The holy oracles always represent Paradise as our native country, and our present life as an exile. How can we be said to have been banished from a place in which we never were? This argument alone would suffice to convince us of pre-existence, if the prejudice of infancy inspired by the schoolmen had not accustomed us to look upon these expressions as metaphorical, and to believe, contrary to Scripture and to reason, that we were exiled from a happy state, only for the fault of our first parents. . . .

St. Paul seems to confirm this when he says: For the children being not yet born, having neither done good nor evil, it was said unto Rebecca, "Jacob have I loved, but Esau have I hated." [Romans 9: 13] God's love and hatred depend upon the moral dispositions of the creature. Since God says that he loved Jacob and hated Esau ere they were born, and before they had done good or evil in this mortal life, it follows clearly that they must have pre-existed in another state.

If it be said that these texts are obscure; that pre-existence is only drawn from them by induction, and that this opinion is not revealed in Scripture by express words, I answer, that the doctrines of the immortality of the soul are nowhere revealed expressly in the sacred oracles of the Old or New Testament, but because all their morals and doctrines are founded upon these great truths. We may say the same of pre-existence. The doctrine is nowhere expressly revealed, but it is evidently supposed, as without it original sin becomes not only inexplicable, but absurd, repugnant, and impossible.

*The Philosophical Principles of Revealed Religion**

William R. Alger (1822-1905)

[To appreciate the bearing of the Reverend Mr. Alger's remarks on reincarnation, the following background information from E. D. Walker's Reincarnation is of particular interest:]

The noblest work of modern times, and probably of all time, upon immortality, is a large volume by the Rev. William R. Alger, entitled "A Critical History of the Doctrine of a Future Life."† It was published in 1860 and still remains [1888] the standard authority upon that topic throughout Christendom. . . . The author is a Unitarian minister, who devoted half his lifetime to the work, undermining his health thereby. In the first edition (1860) the writer characterizes reincarnation as a plausible delusion, unworthy of credence. For fifteen years more he continued studying the subject, and the latest edition (1878) gives the final result of his ripest investigations in heartily endorsing and advocating reincarnation. No more striking argument for the doctrine could be advanced than this fact. That a Christian clergyman, making the problem of the soul's destiny his life's study, should become so overpowered by the force of this pagan idea as to adopt it for the climax of his scholarship is extremely significant.

[Now to quote from the Reverend Mr. Alger:]

The argument [for reincarnation] from analogy is especially strong. It is natural to argue from the universal spectacle of incarnated life that this is the eternal scheme everywhere, the variety of souls finding in the variety of worlds an everlasting series of adventures in appropriate organisms . . .

---

* Chevalier Ramsay's book appears to have had an important influence on Coleridge. See index under "Coleridge."

† [Alger's work also contains a complete bibliography, comprising 4,977 books relating to the nature, origin, and destiny of the soul, compiled by Ezra Abbot, Librarian of Harvard University. Eds.]

It must be confessed that of all the thoughtful and refined forms of the belief in a future life none has had so extensive and prolonged prevalence as this. It has the vote of the majority, having for ages on ages been held by half the human race with an intensity of conviction almost without a parallel. Indeed, the most striking fact at first sight about the doctrine of the repeated incarnations of the soul . . . is the constant reappearance of the faith in all parts of the world, and its permanent hold on certain great nations. . . .

It is not propounded with the slightest dogmatic animus. It is advanced solely as an illustration of what may possibly be true, as suggested by the general evidence of the phenomena of history and the facts of experience. The thoughts embodied in it are so wonderful, the method of it so rational, the region of contemplation into which it lifts the mind is so grand, the prospects it opens are of such universal reach and import, that the study of it brings us into full sympathy with the sublime scope of the idea of immortality, and of a cosmopolitan vindication of providence uncovered to every eye. It takes us out of the littleness of petty themes and selfish affairs, and makes it easier for us to believe in the vastest hopes mankind has ever known.

Other Nineteenth-Century Clergymen

In Boston in 1853, Dr. Edward Beecher (1803-1895), a leading Congregational minister and theological writer, published The Conflict of Ages, his theme being that the teaching of pre-existence is necessary to a reasonable explanation of the world, and that the facts of sin and depravity compel the acceptance of this doctrine to exonerate God from the charge of maliciousness. The book caused lively controversy and was soon followed by The Concord of Ages in which Dr. Beecher answered objections and endeavored to strengthen his position.

Pre-existence was also preached by the celebrated Congregational minister, lecturer, and reformer, Henry Ward Beecher (1813-1887), brother of Edward, and later by Phillips Brooks (1835-1893), bishop of the Episcopal Church and noted pulpit orator. In Ireland, the Irish-Anglican clergyman William Archer Butler upheld the idea (see index), while on the continent Dr. Julius Muller, a German theologian of prodigious influence, spread the doctrine there through his profound work The Christian Doctrine of Sin.

For reincarnation quotations from the writings of American Unitarian ministers, see index under: Frederic Hedge, James Freeman Clarke, Cyrus Bartol, and William J. Potter; and for European theologians, see under: Friedrich Schleiermacher and Johann Peter Hebel.

George Foot Moore (1851-1931)

CLERGYMAN, BIBLE SCHOLAR, AND ORIENTALIST
FROTHINGHAM PROFESSOR OF HISTORY OF RELIGION, HARVARD UNIVERSITY

A theory [metempsychosis] which has been embraced by so large a part of mankind, of many races and religions, and has commended itself to some of the most profound thinkers of all time, cannot be lightly dismissed. . . . If man's earthly existence be conceived as a probation, it must be admitted that in any one life men are put upon this probation under very unequal conditions of every kind, and that the theory of a series of embodiments in which the soul is tested under various conditions accords better with our · opinions of justice in the order of things. Finally, if an end of perfection is set for the soul, metempsychosis affords the opportunity for a progressive approach to that infinite attainment. . . .

Metempsychosis
Ingersoll Lecture on Immortality

William R. Inge (1860-1954)

DEAN OF ST. PAUL'S CATHEDRAL, LONDON

The doctrine of transmigration offers us "chains of personalities linked together by impersonal transitions" [quoting Bosanquet]. Nothing survives except the bare being of the Soul, and, we may add, its liabilities. But Plato does not hold the doctrine in an uncompromising form: Souls do not all drink enough of the waters of Lethe to forget everything; the importance of "recollection" in his writings is well known. Leibnitz thought that "immortality without recollection is ethically quite useless"; and many others profess that such an immortality would have no attraction for them. But others would be satisfied to know that they will live on in the great spiritual interests with which they identified themselves; they could say with Browning, "Other tasks in other lives, God willing." It is not continuity of consciousness which they prize, but perpetuity of life amid the eternal ideas.

The Philosophy of Plotinus
Gifford Lectures 1917-18

Has an ex-dignitary of the Anglican Church any business to dabble in these heathen beliefs? Well, they are not so alien as we think. Rebirth is plainly asserted in the Wisdom of Solomon (viii, 19, 20,) which the Roman Church rightly accepts as canonical.*

---

* For quotation see index under "Apocrypha."

It is implied in St. John's Gospel, where the disciples ask whether the blind man is punished for his sins in a former life. Herod thought that Jesus might be one of the old prophets, or even John the Baptist, whom he had beheaded himself. The belief was widely held among the Jews. . . .

I believe there is an element of truth in this belief about our personality, which is common to India and all the mystics. Practically it amounts to disinterestedness, which is the core of all higher religion.

London Evening Standard, Mar. 23, 1944

Harry Emerson Fosdick (1878-   )

[In his book, The Assurance of Immortality, Dr. Fosdick considers briefly the subject of birth in relation to the soul and lists as the first possibility that the soul already pre-exists, the second being that God creates the soul complete and injects it into the body. On the logic of immortality he states:]

The necessity of personal permanence to the reasonableness of human life may be, perhaps, most clearly seen when we consider the essentially limitless possibilities which inhere in knowledge and character. If death ends all, these possibilities are involved in man's very nature only that without excuse they may be brusquely and abruptly snatched away. . . . Death is a thief who breaks into the character and steals from it its essential nature of endless aspiration. . . . One generation of incomplete, aspiring persons is wiped off the earth, as a child erases unfinished problems from his slate, that another generation of incomplete, aspiring persons may be created —created and then annihilated.

Paul Tillich (1886-   )

THEOLOGIAN AND PHILOSOPHER

[Dr. Tillich, considered by many to be the foremost Protestant theologian of our time, is professor of theology at Harvard University Divinity School. The following extracts are taken from his lecture "Symbols of Eternal Life," delivered at the University of California:]

The Nirvana symbol for eternal life points to the life of absolute fullness, not to the death of absolute nothingness, as sometimes is assumed. The life of Nirvana is beyond distinction of subject and object. It is everything because it is nothing definite. . . . But in order to reach this, many reincarnations are necessary. They are continuations of temporal existence, and therefore they are considered as punishment and suffering. Only the end of temporal existence brings the full participation in eternal life. In it individualization is conquered by participation. The full recession to the ground has taken place. . . . The individual is preserved, but only in its reunion with the realm of essences. . . .

We would like to go into the history of these ideas, but important for us in this moment is the use of this idea [of eternal life] in present American Protestantism, especially in the more secularized forms of Protestantism. It is used as a description of a desirable continuation of life after death indefinitely. This popular belief has actually pushed aside most of the tenets of Christian symbolism. Eternal life has been replaced by endless *temporal* life after death. The life hereafter, as it is called, is imagined as a bodiless continuation of the experiences and activities of this life. . . . One continues to live after one has died in almost the same way as before, only without a body. Blessed spirits walking on beautiful meadows. . . . This has nothing to do with Christianity. . . . One is not aware of the fact that endless living in finitude would be Hell. Whatever the content of such life would be, to continue the finite beyond the limits of its finitude is endless punishment. Eternal fulfillment it is not.

Leslie D. Weatherhead

PRESIDENT OF THE CITY TEMPLE LITERARY SOCIETY OF LONDON

[Extracts from Rev. Weatherhead's lecture "The Case for Reincarnation," * delivered at the opening session of the Society's 1957-58 season:]

The intelligent Christian asks not only that life should be just, but that it shall make sense. Does the idea of reincarnation help here? I think it does. Let us suppose that a very depraved or entirely materialistic person dies. Let us suppose that from a religious point of view he has entirely misused his earth-life. Will his translation to a spiritual plane do all that needs doing? Will it not be like putting a person who has never given himself any chance to understand music, into an everlasting concert . . . ? Can a man who has entirely neglected spiritual things be happy in a spiritual environment? If you say, "Oh well, he can learn in the next phase"—can he? Doesn't such a speculation make the earth-life meaningless? I don't think we shall be able to skip the examinations of life like that. It would be as incongruous and unsound as telling a medical student, who failed his qualifying examination,

* Published by M. C. Peto, 16 Kingswood Rd., Tadworth, Surrey, England.

not to bother, but to go on treating people as if he had qualified. If I fail to pass those examinations in life which can only be taken while I dwell in a physical body, shall I not have to come back and take them again? . . .

If every birth in the world is the birth of a new soul, I don't see how progress can ever be consummated. Each has to begin at scratch. . . . How then can there be progress in the innermost things of the heart? We can pass on *some* wisdom and, in outward circumstance, those who follow us can in some ways go on where we left off. They will not have to re-discover electricity or atomic energy. But they *will* have to discover, for example, each for himself, the vital supremacy of love. Each child is born a selfish little animal . . . not able in character to begin where the most saintly parent left off. . . . How can a world progress in inner things—which are the most important— if the birth of every new generation fills the world with unregenerate souls full of original sin? There can never be a perfect world unless gradually those born into it can take advantage of lessons learned in earlier lives instead of starting at scratch.

Roman Catholic Clerics and Writers on Reincarnation

Cardinal Mercier (1851-1926)
BELGIAN CARDINAL AND SCHOLASTIC PHILOSOPHER

Under the term *Wiedermenschwerdung,* metempsychosis, or the transmigration of souls, a great variety of ideas may be understood: either a series of repetitions of existence under the twofold condition that the soul maintains consciousness of its personality and that there is a final unit in the series of transmigrations; or a series of repetitions of existence without any final unit, and yet with the presupposition that the soul maintains consciousness of its personality; or, finally, an endless series of repetitions of existence with the loss of consciousness of personal identity. . . . So far as concerns the first assumption, we do not see that reason, if left to itself, would declare this to be impossible or certainly false.

Psychologie

Archbishop Passavalli (1820-1897)

[Prof. Wincenty Lutoslawski, a noted Platonic scholar, and Professor of Philosophy at the University of Wilno, Poland, wrote in his book Pre-existence and Reincarnation (Allen & Unwin, London, 1928):]

For those who are interested in the relation of the Church to the dogmas of palingenesis, an Italian book, published in 1911, is of the greatest important: Attilio Begey e Allessandro Favero, Monsignor Arcivescovo L. Puecher Passavalli (Milano: Fratelli Bocca, 1911).

Here we find the life and letters of a pious and learned Roman Catholic archbishop who at the age of sixty-four accepted the truth of pre-existence and reincarnation from two disciples of the Polish seer Towianski, namely Stanislaw Falkowski and Tancredi Canonico. Archbishop Passavalli admitted that reincarnation is not condemned by the Church, and that it is not at all in conflict with any Catholic dogma. He lived up to the age of seventy-seven, unshaken in his conviction that he had already lived many times on earth and that he was likely to return.* [He remained archbishop until his death.]

Another Catholic priest, who also after long discussion gave up the prejudice against reincarnation . . . was Edward Dunski, whose Letters, edited by Attilio Begey and Jozef Komenda, were published by Bona in Torino in 1915. Many other priests in Poland and Italy believe in reincarnation, being influenced by the great mystic Andrzej Towianski (1799-1878) whose works were printed privately in three large volumes at Torino in 1882. . . .

The Catholic Encyclopedia

[The Catholic Encyclopedia (Vol. 10, p. 236) states in its article on Metempsychosis:]

It was a tenet common to many systems of philosophic thought and religious belief widely separated from each other both geographically and historically. . . . There is evidence that at one period or another it has flourished in almost every part of the world. . . . This universality seems to mark it as one of those spontaneous or instinctive beliefs by which man's nature responds to the deep and urgent problems of existence. . . .

* [Eds.: The Catholic theologian Baron Friedrich von Hügel also speaks of the Archbishop's "acceptance of a doctrine of successive lives for human souls;" see Essays and Addresses on the Philosophy of Religion, Dutton, 1921.]

St. Jerome tells us that metempsychosis was a secret doctrine of certain sectaries in his day, but it was too evidently opposed to the Catholic doctrine of Redemption ever to obtain a settled footing. It was held, however, in a Platonic form by the Gnostics, and was so taught by Origen in his great work, Περὶ ἀρχῶν [*de* Principiis *].

In the face of a belief at first sight so far fetched and yet at the same time so widely diffused, we are led to anticipate some great general causes which have worked together to produce it. A few such causes may be mentioned: (1) The practically universal conviction that the soul is a real entity distinct from the body and that it survives death; (2) connected with this, there is the imperative moral demand for an equitable future retribution of rewards and punishments in accordance with good or ill conduct here. The doctrine of transmigration satifies in some degree both these virtually instinctive faiths; (3) As mentioned above, it offers a plausible explanation of the phenomena of heredity. . . .

The world thus seems to become, through and through, moral and human. Indeed, where the belief in a personal Providence is unfamiliar or but feebly grasped, some form of metempsychosis understood as a kind of ethical evolutionary process, is almost a necessary makeshift.

Maude Gonne (1866-1953)

IRISH PATRIOT AND REVOLUTIONARY

In her autobiography, A Servant of the Queen, Maude Gonne writes that when a priest asked her why she was not a Catholic, and she answered, "Because I believe in reincarnation," she received the rejoinder: "The Soul comes from God and returns to God when purified, when all things will become clear; and who can tell the stages of its purification? It may be possible that some souls work out their purification on this earth."†

Other Twentieth Century Clergymen

Rev. Columbus Bradford, Methodist Episcopal clergyman of Illinois: Birth— a New Chance.

Rev. Ernest C. Wilson, Christ Church, Los Angeles: Have You Lived Other Lives?

---

* Quoted at p. 36.

† [There has never been a papal encyclical against reincarnation, it would appear. See Mentor Religious Classic The Papal Encyclicals in Their Historic Context by the Catholic religious scholar Prof. Anne Fremantle of Fordham University. Eds.]

Rev. Dr. Emmet Fox, Church of the Healing Christ, New York City: Power Through Constructive Thinking (Harper & Bros.), Chapter "Reincarnation."

Rev. Dr. Robert G. Katsunoff, United Church of Canada (Presbytarian), Montreal: Pamphlet "Does the Bible Teach Reincarnation and Karma?"

Rev. A. Henderson, Vicar of St. John of the Sepulchre, Norwich, England: The Wheel of Life.

MOHAMMEDANISM

The early days of Islam in the sixth century A.D. have a history related to our subject. The persecution of scholars by the Christian Church for over four hundred years had gradually driven most students of science and philosophy out of Europe. These people found refuge in Arabia, the land of liberty in those days. The Christian Gnostics gave the Arabs a knowledge of Greek philosophy; the Nestorians made them acquainted with the Neoplatonic philosophers, and the exiled Jews instructed them in the Kabala. These several influences combined to make Islamic thinkers natural heirs to the philosophy of rebirth.

The Nestorians were by this time powerful. Nestorius, the founder of the Order, was the excommunicated Christian Bishop who in the fifth century refused to accept the Virgin Mary as the Mother of God. After his death his followers emigrated to Asia Minor, China, Tartary, and India, where they soon outnumbered all the Christians of the Greek and Roman churches put together.

Mohammed as a boy came in contact with a Nestorian monastery in Busra, and grew deeply interested in the religious and philosophical views of the monks. Upon reaching manhood, he fell more and more under Nestorian influence. In fact, for many centuries after Mohammed's death, Muslim followers regarded his teachings as an offshoot of Nestorian doctrines.

Neoplatonic thought, which had been carried on from the fifth century by the Nestorians, gained new life in the eighth century from the great Arabian philosopher Al-Kindi, and in the ninth century from Al-Ferabi, who in turn taught the Persian-born physician and philosopher, Avicenna. Spain had been conquered by the Muslims in the eighth century and under Islamic influence the Iberian Peninsula became a great center of civilization and enlightenment. An important link in the Neoplatonic succession was Ibn Gebirol, a Spanish Jew, known to medieval scholastics as Avicebron (died c. 1070), for it was through him that the long-exiled teachings of Plato returned to Europe.

Dr. W. Y. Evans-Wentz, a scholar known for his books on Celtic mythology and on Tibetan religion, has stated in his lecture, "The Christian Doctrine of Re-Birth":

During the Dark Ages of Europe, when the Moors of Spain almost alone in the Western World kept alight the sacred Torch of Learning . . . the Doctrine of Re-birth was being taught by the great Saracenic philosophers— Al Ghazali and Al Batagni—in the Schools of Bagdad in the East and of Cordova [Spain] in the West. And in Europe, the disciples of these great teachers were Paracelsus and the martyred Bruno. It was due chiefly to Moslem scholars of those days that to Europe was restored the classical culture of Greece, and that the Light from the Orient was re-lit in the Occident. . . .

It was, however, among the Mohammedan mystical sect of Persia, called the Sufis (from Sophia, wisdom), that the teaching of reincarnation was more especially preserved, for just as had happened in Christianity and Judaism, in Islamic countries the doctrine became obscured. The Sufis claimed to possess the esoteric philosophy of Islam. Saadi, Rumi, Hafiz, and other celebrated Persian poets were Sufis, and like Dante and some of the troubadours, appeared to hide their ideas behind the symbolism of the "Beloved" (see p. 95).

The Koran

God generates beings, and sends them back over and over again, till they return to Him.

The Koran

And when his body falleth off altogether, as an old fish-shell, his soul doeth well by the releasing, and formeth a new one instead. . . . Ye who now lament to go out of this body wept also when ye were born into it. . . . The person of man is only a mask which the soul putteth on for a season; it weareth its proper time and then is cast off, and another is worn in its stead. . . .

I tell you, of a truth, that the spirits which now have affinity shall be kindred together, although they all meet in new persons and names.

The New Koran

Ibn 'Arabī (1164-1240)

SPANISH-BORN SUFI PHILOSOPHER AND POET

[*Ibn 'Arabī is said to have exercised a considerable influence upon Dante and upon Raymond Lully, the Spanish mystic (see p. 95). However, owing to his profound metaphysical views, especially concerning an absolute impersonal Deity, his teachings have only recently become known in the West.*]

There is some difference of opinion among the Muslim learned men as regards the method of Resurrection. Some of them say that Resurrection will be by reincarnation and quote passages from the Quran and authenticated sayings of the Prophet in support of their contention.

Al Futūhat Al-Makkiyyah

Jalālu 'D-Din Rumi (1207-1273)

SUFI POET

I died as mineral and became a plant,
I died as plant and rose to animal,
I died as animal and I was Man.
Why should I fear? When was I less by dying?
Yet once more I shall die as Man, to soar
With angels blest; but even from angelhood
I must pass on. . . .

Rumi, Poet and Mystic
Trans. R. A. Nicholson

Sharf-U'D-Din-Maneri

SUFI TEACHER

O Brother, know for certain that this work has been before thee and me in bygone ages, and that each man has already reached a certain stage. No one has begun this work for the first time.

THE DRUSES

The Druses of Mount Lebanon, Syria, first came to prominence in the eleventh century. Many theories of their origin have been suggested, and their religion is described as a blending of Judaism, Christianity, and Mohammedanism, strongly tinged with Gnosticism, Tibetan Lamaism, and the Magian system of Persia. The Druses are thought to be the descendants of the persecuted mystics of all nations who found refuge in the mountains of Syria during the early years of the Christian era. Some of them trace their order back to Hemsa, the uncle of Mohammed who in 625 went to Tibet in search of secret wisdom. He is said to have incarnated again in the eleventh century as H'amsa, the founder of the Druses. From that time he is supposed to have reincarnated successively in the body of the chief Druse hierophant (or Okhal) in the same way that some of the Buddhas are said to reincarnate in the Tibetan Lamas.

Lawrie in his History of Freemasonry claims that the Knights Templar, founded in 1118, inherited their knowledge from the Druses of Mount Lebanon.

Blackwood's Magazine for January, 1881, reviewing Laurence Oliphant's book The Land of Gilead, with Excursions in the Lebanon, states: "Mr. Oliphant gives an anecdote, which is worthy of quotation, as illustrating the character of the Druse ideas of metempsychosis." In the book itself, Oliphant observes that the Druses accept the doctrine of reincarnation as one of their fundamental teachings, and that remembering of past lives is not uncommon amongst them. The anecdote now follows:

A child, five years old, in Djebel el A'ala, complained of the life of poverty which his parents led, and alleged that he had been a rich man in Damascus; that on his death he was born in another place, but lived only six months; that he was born again among his present friends, and desired to be carried to that city [Damascus].

He was taken there by his relatives, and on the way astonished them by his correct knowledge of the names of the different places which they passed. On reaching the city, he led the way through the various streets to a house which he said had been his own. He knocked, and called the woman of the house by her name; and on being admitted, told her that he had been her husband, and asked after the welfare of the several children, relatives and acquaintances whom he had left.

The Druses of the place soon met to inquire into the truth of the matter. The child gave them a full account of his past life among them, of the names of his acquaintances, the property which he had possessed, and the debts which he had left. All was found to be strictly true, except a small sum which he said a certain weaver owed him. The man was called and on the claim being mentioned to him he acknowledged it, pleading his poverty for not having paid it to the children of the deceased.

The child then asked the woman who had been his wife whether she had found a sum of money which he had hid in the cellar; and on her replying in the negative, he went directly to the place, dug up the treasure, and counted it before them.

MASONRY

(RELIGIOUS ASPECTS)

⚜

The deeper students of Masonry have frequently shown a serious interest in reincarnation. E. D. Walker's Reincarnation, a Study of Forgotten Truth, originally published by Houghton Mifflin and Company in 1888, was re-issued in 1926 by Macoy Publishing and Masonic Supply Co. (New York), and distributed by them for over twenty years. The author of Anthony Adverse, Hervey Allen, has some fascinating passages on Masonry with direct allusions to pre-existence and rebirth in his novel Bedford Village, quoted in part at page 266 of this Anthology.

In years past, The New Age, the official Masonic organ of the Supreme Council, 33d degree, in America, has contained numerous articles treating frankly and sympathetically of both rebirth and karma. In the September, 1952 issue of The New Age, under the title "Freemasonry and Reincarnation," C. I. McReynolds, a 32d degree Mason, considers why the founders of Masonry refused to doctrinalize the teaching of reincarnation, and states:

This brings us to the criticism that comparative research shows that ma-sonry is the only esoteric system whose followers have endeavored to carry on their work without some clear-cut doctrine of reincarnation. They say that in every other esoteric organization in history it is taught that man lives on this earth not once but many times, and that each being, in due course and according to his need, will eventually enter upon and be instructed in the secret teachings concerning the soul. This may be true, but the criticism completely overlooks in fact that the reason is that each and every member of the Craft, wherever he may be, is at liberty to decide for himself what he shall believe. . . .

W. L. *Wilmshurst*

PAST MASTER, PAST PROVINCIAL GRAND REGISTRAR (WEST YORKS)

The observant Masonic student is made aware by the formula used at Lodge-closing, that by some great Warden of life and death each soul is called into this objective world to labour upon itself, and is in due course summoned from it to rest from its labours and enter into subjective celestial refreshment, until once again it is recalled to labour. For each the "day," the opportunity for work at self-perfecting, is duly given; for each the "night" cometh when no man can work at that task. . . .

The world-old secret teaching upon this subject, common to the whole of the East, to Egypt, the Pythagoreans and Platonists, and every College of the Mysteries, is to be found summed up as clearly and tersely as one could wish in the *Phædo* of Plato, to which the Masonic seeker is referred as one of the most instructive of treatises upon the deeper side of the science.

It testifies to the great rhythm of life and death above spoken of, and demonstrates how that the soul in the course of its career weaves and wears out many bodies, and is continually migrating between objective and subjective conditions, passing from labour to refreshment and back again many times in its great task of self-fulfillment. . . . until such time as its work is completed and it is "made a pillar in the House of God and no more goes out" as a journey-man builder into this sublunary workshop.

*The Masonic Initiation**

* John M. Watkins, London.

THEOSOPHY

The first widespread movement in the modern Western world to investigate and study the idea of reincarnation and related concepts was inaugurated by the Theosophical Society, founded in New York City in 1875 by Mme. H. P. Blavatsky, Col. H. S. Olcott, William Q. Judge, and others. Their views on the subject are included in this section, although they do not appear to confine their activities to the realm of religion, seeking more for a synthesis of religion, philosophy, science, and psychology.

Theosophists have an approach to the reincarnation theory that is manifestly different from that commonly found in the East, or among the early Jews and Christians. In the Orient the great hope has been to escape as quickly as possible from the wheel of rebirth, and to attain Moksha or Nirvana. Similarly, Western religions usually viewed return to earth life as a penance or as a means of purging oneself of impurities. The Theosophists, however, regard re-embodiment as the universal law of evolutionary progress, holding that in an infinite universe there must be infinite possibilities for growth and development. Hence one would never outgrow the need for fresh experience and new cycles of incarnations, although a long period of rest and assimilation may separate one life from another, as well as one great world-period of activity from another.

A letter to Sean O'Faolain,* written in 1935 by George Russell (Æ), the well-known Irish poet, painter, and editor, tells of the interest in scholarly

---

* Quoted by John Eglinton in his A Memoir of Æ, Macmillan, 1937, p. 164

circles evoked by Mme. Blavatsky's writings (in which reincarnation is a frequent theme):

You dismiss H. P. Blavatsky rather too easily as "hocus pocus." Nobody ever affected the thought of so many able men and women by "hocus pocus." The real source of her influence is to be found in *The Secret Doctrine*, a book on the religions of the world suggesting or disclosing an underlying unity between all great religions. It was a book which Maeterlinck said contained the most grandiose cosmogony in the world, and if you read it merely as a romantic compilation, it is one of the most exciting and stimulating books written for the last hundred years. It is paying a poor compliment to men like Yeats, Maeterlinck, and others, to men like Sir William Crookes, the greatest chemist of modern times, who was a member of her society, to Carter Blake, F.R.S., the anthropologist, and the scholars and scientists in many countries who read H. P. Blavatsky's books, to assume that they were attracted by "hocus pocus."

If you are ever in the National Library, Kildare Street, and have a couple of hours to spare, you might dip into "The Proëm" to *The Secret Doctrine*, and you will understand the secret of the influence of that extraordinary woman on her contemporaries. . . . You should not be misled by popular catchwords about "hocus pocus," but try to find out the real secret of H. P. Blavatsky's influence, which still persists strong as ever, as I have found over here [in London] among many intellectuals and well-known writers.

Helena Petrovna Blavatsky (1831-1891)

A flower blossoms; then withers and dies. It leaves a fragrance behind, which, long after its delicate petals are but a little dust, still lingers in the air. . . . Let a note be struck on an instrument, and the faintest sound produces an eternal echo. A disturbance is created on the invisible waves of the shoreless ocean of space, and the vibration is never wholly lost. Its energy being once carried from the world of matter into the immaterial world will live for ever. And man, we are asked to believe, man, the living, thinking, reasoning entity, the indwelling deity of our nature's crowning masterpiece, will evacuate his casket and be no more! Would the principle of continuity which exists even for the so-called *inorganic* matter, for a floating atom, be denied to the spirit, whose attributes are consciousness, memory, mind, LOVE! Really, the very idea is preposterous. . . .

The doctrine of *Metempsychosis* has been abundantly ridiculed by men of science and rejected by theologians, yet if it had been properly understood in its application to the indestructibility of matter and the immortality of spirit, it would have been perceived that it is a sublime conception. If the Pythagorean metempsychosis should be thoroughly explained and compared with the modern theory of evolution it would be found to supply every "missing link" in the chain of the latter. There was not a philosopher of any notoriety who did not hold to this doctrine, as taught by the Brahmans, Buddhists, and later by the Pythagoreans.

Isis Unveiled*

It is only the knowledge of the constant re-births of one and the same individuality throughout the life-cycle; the assurance that the same MONADS . . . have to pass through the "Circle of Necessity," rewarded or punished by such rebirth for the suffering endured or crimes committed in the former life . . . it is only this doctrine, we say, that can explain to us the mysterious problem of Good and Evil, and reconcile man to the terrible and *apparent* injustice of life.

Nothing but such certainty can quiet our revolted sense of injustice. For, when one unacquainted with the noble doctrine looks around him, and observes the inequalities of birth and fortune, of intellect and capacities; when one sees honour paid fools and profligates, on whom fortune has heaped her favours by mere privilege of birth, and their nearest neighbour, with all his intellect and noble virtues—far more deserving in every way—perishing of want and for lack of sympathy; when one sees all this . . . one's ears ringing and heart aching with the cries of pain around him—that blessed knowledge of Karma alone prevents him from cursing life and men, as well as their supposed Creator. . . . "But who shall dare to tax Eternal Justice?" . . . Verily there is not an accident in our lives, not a misshapen day, or a misfortune, that could not be traced back to our own doings in this or another life. . . .

Those who believe in Karma have to believe in destiny, which, from birth to death, every man is weaving, thread by thread, around himself, as a spider does his cobweb. . . . This law, whether conscious or unconscious, predestines nothing and no one. . . . Karma creates nothing, nor does it design. It is man who plants and creates causes, and Karmic law adjusts the effects, which adjustment is not an act but universal harmony, tending ever to resume its original position, like a bough, which, bent down too forcibly, rebounds with corresponding vigor. . . . Karma has never sought to destroy intellectual and individual liberty. . . . It has not involved its decrees in darkness purposely to perplex man, nor shall it punish him who dares to scrutinize its mysteries. On the contrary, he who unveils through study and meditation its intricate paths, and throws light on those dark ways, in the

* Theosophy Co., Los Angeles 7, Calif.

winding of which so many men perish owing to their ignorance of the laby-rinth of life, is working for the good of his fellow-men. . . .

Intimately, or rather indissolubly, connected with Karma, then, is the law of re-birth, or of the re-incarnation of the same spiritual individuality in a long, almost interminable, series of personalities. The latter are like the various costumes and characters played by the same actor, with each of which that actor identifies himself and is identified by the public, for the space of a few hours. The *inner*, or real man, who personates those characters, knows the whole time that he is Hamlet for the brief space of a few acts, which represent, however, on the plane of human illusion the whole life of Hamlet. And he knows that he was, the night before, King Lear, the transformation in his turn of the Othello of a still earlier preceding night; but the outer, visible character is supposed to be ignorant of the fact. In actual life that ignorance is, unfortunately, but too real. Nevertheless, the *permanent* individuality is fully aware of the fact, though, through the atrophy of the "spiritual" eye in the physical body, that knowledge is unable to impress itself on the consciousness of the false personality. . . . The whole secret of Life is in the unbroken series of its manifestations.

The Secret Doctrine*

Have perseverance as one who doth for evermore endure. Thy shadows [bodies] live and vanish; that which in thee shall live for ever, that which in thee *knows*, for it is knowledge, is not of fleeting life: it is the Man that was, that is, and will be, for whom the hour shall never strike. . . .

The PATH is one Disciple, yet in the end two-fold. . . . The *Open* PATH leads to the changless change—Nirvana, the glorious state of Absoluteness, the Bliss past human thought. . . . Know, O beginner, this is . . . the way to selfish bliss, shunned by the . . . Buddhas of Compassion. . . .

The "Secret Way" leads also to Paranirvanic bliss—but at the close of Kalpas [cycles] without number; Nirvanas gained and lost from boundless pity and compassion for the world of deluded mortals. But it is said: "The last shall be the greatest." Samyak Sambuddha [Gautama, the Buddha], the Teacher of Perfection, gave up his SELF for the salvation of the World, by stopping at the threshold of Nirvana—the pure state. . . . A Saviour of the World is he.

The Voice of the Silence†
Trans. H. P. Blavatsky

* Theosophy Co., Los Angeles 7, Calif.
† Theosophy Co., Los Angeles 7, Calif.

Henry Steel Olcott (1832-1907)

[Col. Olcott rendered considerable assistance to the people of Ceylon. For use in their Buddhist schools he prepared A Buddhist's Catechism, which was widely circulated in the West, and later published in the "Wisdom of the East" series (John Murray, London). Quoting therefrom:]

On this point [of reincarnation] the Western world is for the most part as far from understanding the Oriental conception as it is in mistaking Nirvana for "annihilation." . . . Much of the Western misconception is due to ignorance of the difference between . . . his individuality and his personality at any given period. These two are only temporarily coincident and conjoined. . . . In each birth the personality differs from that of a previous or next succeeding birth. . . . But though personalities ever shift, the one line of life along which they are strung, like beads, runs unbroken; it is ever that *particular line*, never any other. It is therefore individual, an individual vital undulation, which began in Nirvana . . . and leads through many cyclic changes back to Nirvana.

William Q. Judge (1851-1896)

Although reincarnation is the law of nature, the complete trinity of *Atma-Buddhi-Manas* [Spirit-Soul-Mind] does not yet fully incarnate in this race. They use and occupy the body by means of the entrance of *Manas* or Mind, the lowest of the three. . . . This was symbolized in the old Jewish teaching about the Heavenly Man who stands with his head in heaven and his feet in hell. That is, the head *Atma* and *Buddhi* are yet in "heaven,"* and the feet, *Manas*, walk in hell, which is the body and physical life. For that reason man is not yet fully conscious, and reincarnations are needed to at last complete the incarnation of the whole trinity in the body. When that has been accomplished the race will have become as gods. . . . It was so grand a thing in the case of any single person, such as Jesus or Buddha, as to be looked upon as a divine incarnation. . . .

It is because the trinity is not yet incarnate in the race that life has so many mysteries, some of which are showing themselves from day to day in all the various experiments made on and in man. The physician knows not what

---

* [From the context it appears that the term "heaven" is used as a state of consciousness, not as a place. Eds.]

life is nor why the body moves as it does, because the spiritual portion is yet enshrouded in the clouds of "heaven"; the scientist is wandering in the dark, confounded and confused by all that hypnotism and other strange things bring before him, because the conscious man is out of sight . . . thus compelling the learned to speak of the "subconscious mind," the "latent personality," and the like.

*The Ocean of Theosophy**

Man is indeed evolved from lower forms. But *which* man? the physical? the psychical? the intellectual? or the spiritual? *The Secret Doctrine* points where the lines of evolution and involution meet; where matter and spirit clasp hands; and where the rising animal stands face to face with the fallen god; for *all natures* meet and mingle in man. . . .

[The doctrines of Karma and Reincarnation] are beneficent to individuals, not only because they furnish, as they necessarily do, a solid foundation for ethics, or all human conduct, but because they are the very keynotes of the higher evolution of man. Without Karma and Reincarnation evolution is but a fragment; a process whose beginnings are unknown, and whose outcome cannot be discerned; a glimpse of what might be; a hope of what should be. But in the light of Karma and Reincarnation evolution becomes the logic of what *must* be. The links in the chain of being are all filled in, and the circles of reason and of life are complete. Karma gives the eternal law of action, and Reincarnation furnishes the boundless field for its display. Thousands of persons can understand these two principles, apply them as a basis of conduct, and weave them into the fabric of their lives, who may not be able to grasp the complete synthesis of that endless evolution of which these doctrines form so important a part. In thus affording even the superficial thinker and the weak or illogical reasoner a perfect basis for ethics and an unerring guide in life, Theosophy is building toward the future realization of the Universal Brotherhood and the higher evolution of man.

"The Synthesis of Occult Science"
The Path, May 1892

Annie Besant (1847-1933)

Reincarnation is a truth that has . . . moulded the thoughts of the vast majority for uncounted centuries. It dropped out of the European mind during the Dark Ages, and so ceased to influence our mental and moral development. . . . The ignorance that swamped Europe carried away belief in Reincarnation, as it carried away all philosophy, all metaphysics, and all science. Medieval Europe did not offer the soil on which could flourish any wide-sweeping and philosophical view of man's nature and destiny. . . .

The question which arises so naturally in the mind and which is so often asked: "Why do I not remember my past lives?" is really based on a misconception of the theory of reincarnation. "I," the true "I," does remember; but the animal-man, not yet in full responsive union with his true Self, cannot remember a past in which he, personally, had no share. Brain-memory can contain only a record of the events in which the brain has been concerned. . . .

Through thousands of generations the Immortal Thinker patiently toils at his mission of leading the animal-man upwards till he is fit to become one with the Divine. Out of a life, he wins perchance but a mere fragment for his work. . . . On that slightly improved model will be moulded the next man . . . and so on and on . . . with many failures gallantly made good; with many wounds slowly healed; yet on the whole, upward; yet, on the whole forward; the animal lessening, the human increasing: such is the story of human evolution, such the slowly accomplished task of the Ego, as he raises himself to divine manhood.

*Reincarnation**

With reincarnation man is a dignified, immortal being, evolving towards a glorious end; without it, he is a tossing straw on the stream of chance circumstances, irresponsible for his character, for his actions, for his destiny. . . . The Ancient Wisdom teaches, indeed, that the soul progresses through many worlds, but it also teaches that he is born in each of these worlds over and over again, until he has completed the evolution possible in that world. . . . Truly, further evolution lies before us in other worlds, but . . . they are not open to us until we have learned and mastered the lessons our own world has to teach.

The Ancient Wisdom†

A. P. Sinnett (1840-1921)

The human soul, once launched on the streams of evolution as a human individuality, passes through alternate periods of physical and relatively spiritual existence. It passes from the one plane, or stratum, or condition of nature to the other under the guidance of its Karmic affinities . . . it re-

* Theosophical Publishing House, Adyar, Madras, India.
† Theosophical Publishing House, Adyar, Madras, India.

turns to spiritual existence . . . for rest and refreshment and for the gradual absorption into its essence, as so much cosmic progress, of the life's experience gained "on earth." . . .

In truth, no hard-and-fast line separates the varieties of spiritual conditions, that even the spiritual and physical planes . . . are not so hopelessly walled off from one another as materialistic theories would suggest; that all states of nature are all around us simultaneously. . . . We—the souls within us—are not as it were altogether adrift in the ocean of matter. We clearly retain some surviving interest or rights in the shore from which, for a time, we have floated off. The process of incarnation, therefore, is not fully described when we speak of an *alternate* existence on the physical and spiritual planes, and thus picture the soul as a complete entity slipping entirely from the one state of existence to the other. The more correct definitions of the process would probably represent incarnation as taking place . . . by reason of an efflux emanating from the soul. The Spiritual realm would all the while be the proper habitat of the Soul, which would never entirely quit it. . . .

Transactions No. 7, October, 1885
London Theosophical Society

C. Jinarajadasa (1875-1953)

The man is an Ego, an imperishable circle in the sphere of Divinity. . . . He has lived on earth in many a past life, and there thought and felt and acted both good and evil; he has set in motion forces that help or hinder both himself and others. He is bound and not free. But he lives on from age to age to achieve an ideal, which is his Archetype. Just as for plant and animal life there are archetypes of the forms, so are there archetypes for the souls of men. One shall be a great saint of compassion, another a teacher of truth, a third a ruler of men; artist and scientist, doer and dreamer, each has set before him his archetype. . . .

Nations come and nations pass away; but nations are reborn too. By what we do in them now to serve them we earn the right to be their inspirers and leaders in their future transformations. Time may pass us by, and we grow old and "die"; but that is only an illusion. We are immortal souls, and the world's history is only the alphabet of our speech, and we fashion the future as we *will* to fashion it. . . . For this is the power the Divine Wisdom gives to all who love her—to greet life in all time not as the elders of the sunset, but as the children of the dawn.

Theosophy and Modern Thought*

* Theosophical Publishing House, Adyar, Madras, India.

Robert Crosbie (1849-1919)

Man, the invisible being, eternally is; for him there is never for an instant cessation of consciousness. The curtain rings down on one scene to immediately rise on another. . . . Theosophy presents a larger view in showing that man is *not* his body, because the body is continually changing; that man is not his mind, because he is constantly changing his mind; that there is in man a permanency which is the identify throughout all kinds of embodiments. There has been no change in our identity from childhood up to the present day. The body has changed; the surroundings have changed; but the identity remains the same and will not change from now on through all changes of body or mind or circumstance. That in us which is itself unchanging is the only real. . . . It is only the real that perceives change. Change can not see change. . . . However dimly we may perceive it, there is that in us which is eternal and changeless. . . .

All progress goes on in the natural sequence of periods of activity and periods of rest. As after night comes morning again; as after spring, summer, autumn, winter comes spring again; so after birth, youth, manhood, death comes birth again. The process of reincarnation is just as natural as coming into another day which is not yet. This life is; last life was; next life will be. So, as planets or solar systems have their ending, will they and the beings who composed them, have their re-incarnation—a new beginning. . . . We must know that we are all of other peoples. We came through all the civilizations that have been. We have passed through the Eastern, the near East, and the European peoples and now we are here, at the farthest confines of the West, under the law of Karma. . . .

There is always help. . . . Always there are beings greater in evolution than we, who return to this field of physical existence to help us, to wake us up to a perception of our natures. . . . They are our Elder Brothers—Jesus, for example; Buddha for another; and all those who come at different times as Saviours to the many different peoples. . . . They all had a common body of knowledge [and] achieved it through observation and experience. . . . In the far distant past they had to go through similar experiences to those we are now encountering. . . . There was a time when they were sinning and erring mortals like ourselves. But they saw the true path and followed it, as in all time to come must every being.

*The Friendly Philosopher**

* Theosophy Co., Los Angeles 7, Calif.

PRIMITIVE AND TRIBAL RELIGIONS

The famed orientalist, Max Müller, once remarked concerning metempsychosis:

The ancients were convinced that this belief came from the East; they imagined that Pythagoras and others could have got their belief in Metempsychosis from India only, [but] it can easily be shown that a belief in the transmigration of souls sprang up in other countries also, which could not possibly have been touched by the rays of Indian or Greek philosophy.

By consulting such works as Sir Edward Tylor's Primitive Culture (Chap. XII), Hasting's Encyclopedia of Religion and Ethics, and the Encyclopædia Britannica (both under "Metempsychosis"), and Sir J. G. Frazer's The Golden Bough (Vol. III), it will be seen that the tribal groups listed below hold (or if ancient, held) to some concept of rebirth, though often in a distorted form. One naturally wonders who taught the concept to peoples widely scattered over the face of the earth. Or is reincarnation a spontaneous innate idea, not derivative, based as Carl Jung thinks on certain archetypes of the collective unconscious (see p. 299)?

American Tribes

North America:

> Algonquins, Dakotas, Hurons, Iroquois, Koloshes, Mo-
> haves, Moqui (Hopi), Natchez, Nutkas, Powhatans,
> Tacullis, Tlingit
> (Canada:) Ahts of Vancouver Island, Denes, Eskimos,
> Haidas (Alaskan Islands), Montagnais

Central and South America: Caribs, Chiriguanos, Maya and Quiches,
Patagonians, Peruvians, Soutals, Popayans; Powhattans of
Mexico; Icannas and Abysones of Brazil

Charles Eastman's Soul of the Indian: "Many of the Indians believed
that one may be born more than once; and there were some who claimed
to have full knowledge of a former incarnation."

Europe

Finns, Lapps, Danes, Norse, Icelandic peoples, Early Saxons; Celts of Gaul,
Wales, England, and Ireland; Old Prussians and Early Teutonics; Lithua-
nians, Letts; Cheremiss and Gilijacks of Russia.

Middle East

Karaites of Babylonia; Bari of White Nile, and Al-Makhawilahs, both in
Arabia; Nusairis north of Lebanon; Druses of Mt. Lebanon.

Sir Richard Burton's A Pilgrimage to Al-Madinah and Mecca:
There is also a race called Al-Makhawilah . . . about 35,000 in number,
which holds to the Imanship. . . . They believe in a transmigration of the
soul which, gradually purified, is at last orbed into a perfect star.

Asia

India: Andaman Islanders and Santals of Bengal; Dravidians and Nayars
of southern India; Tukarams; Khondas of east India; Garos and
Nagas of Assam; Changs of Naga Hills.
Lusheis of Indo-China; Karens of Burma; Semany of Malay Peninsula.

Africa

East Africa: Suks (Kenya); Wanikas; Akikiyus

West Africa: Negroes of the Gold Coast; Mandingo; Edo; Ibo; Ewes, Yorubas; Old Calabar tribes; Southern Nigerian tribes.

South Africa: Siena, Twi, Zulus, Bantus, Barotse; Maravi Tribes of Madagascar.

In the Hibbert Journal for April, 1957, Dr. E. G. Parrinder of the University College, Ibadan, Nigeria, states in an article "Varieties of Belief in Reincarnation":

In tropical Africa, belief in rebirth is deeply enrooted. The studies made by anthropologists and other serious writers in many different parts of Africa, especially in the last forty years, have revealed deep-seated beliefs in reincarnation held by many different African peoples.

Islands of Pacific and Malay Archipelago

Okinawans; Papuans of New Guinea; Melanesians; Indonesians; Solomon Islanders; Sandwich Islanders; Fijians; Dayaks and Bakongs of Borneo; Poso-Alfures of Celebes.

Australia and Neighboring Islands

Aruntas; Kadhirs; Arunto; Warramunga; Benbenga; Anula; Urabunna; Tasmains; New Zealanders.

The Northern Tribes of Central Australia, by Spencer and Gillen:

In every tribe without exception there exists a firm belief in the reincarnation of ancestors. Emphasis must be laid on the fact that this belief is not confined to the tribes such as the Arunto, Warramunga, Benbenga, and Anula, and others, amongst whom descent is counted on the male line, but is found just as strongly developed in the Urabunna tribe, in which descent, both of class and totem, is strictly maternal.

PART TWO

Western Thinkers on Reincarnation

GREECE

Orpheus

This alone may be depended upon, from general assent, that there formerly lived a person named Orpheus, who was the founder of theology among the Greeks; the first of prophets and the prince of poets; who taught the Greeks their sacred rites and mysteries, and from whose wisdom the divine muse of Homer and the sublime theology of Pythagoras and Plato flowed.

> Mystical Hymns of Orpheus
> Thomas Taylor

Historically it can apparently be demonstrated [that the Greek doctrine of metempsychosis] first appeared in Thrace. . . . To Thrace belongs the legendary figure of the famous singer Orpheus, from whom the mysterious sect of the "Orphici" took their name. Their doctrines are . . . the soul is divine, immortal, and aspires to freedom, while the body holds it in fetters as a prisoner. Death dissolves the compact, but only to re-imprison the liberated soul after a short time: for the wheel of birth revolves inexorably. . . . The Orphic belief seems to have been widely current in the Greek colonies in Southern Italy and Sicily.

> The Transmigration of Souls
> D. Alfred Bertholet*

The doctrine of metempsychosis, seems really to have passed from the theology of the mysteries into Philosophy. . . . In the Orphic theology,

---

* Harpers, 1909. Bertholet was Professor of Theology at the University of Basle.

transmigration is clearly to be found. . . . The doctrine of metempsychosis is ascribed to Pherecydes, and regarded as anterior to Pythagoras, not only by the writers we have quoted, but indirectly by all those who make Pherecydes the teacher of Pythagoras. We have, therefore, every reason to believe that it was taught in the Orphic mysteries prior to the date of Pythagoras.

According to Herodotus, the Orphics obtained it from Egypt. But it is also conceivable that this belief, the affinity of which with Hindoo and Egyptian doctrines indicates an Eastern source, may have originally emigrated from the East with the Greeks themselves, and have been at first confined to a narrow circle becoming afterwards more important and more widely diffused.

A History of Greek Philosophy
Prof. E. Zeller

Pythagoras (582-507 B.C.)

[Pythagoras] was accustomed to speak of himself in this manner: that he had formerly been Aethalides. . . . At a subsequent period, he was reborn as Euphorbus, and was wounded by Menelaus at the siege of Troy, and so died. In that life he used to say that he had formerly been Aethalides; and that he had received as a gift from Mercury [god of Wisdom] the memory of his soul's transmigrations . . . also the gift of recollecting what his own soul and the souls of others had experienced between death and rebirth.

Life of Pythagoras
Diogenes Laertius

What Pythagoras wished to indicate by all these particulars was that he knew the former lives he had lived, which enabled him to begin providential attention to others and remind them of their former existences.

Life of Pythagoras
Iamblichus

NOTE: *Pythagoras has frequently been accused of teaching that human souls could incarnate in animal forms. Even Shakespeare was influenced by this tradition when he wrote in* Twelfth Night *(and similarly in* As You Like it, *III. ii, and* The Merchant of Venice *IV. i):*

What is the opinion of Pythagoras concerning wild-fowl?
That the soul of our grandam might haply inhabit a bird.
What thinkest thou of his opinion?
I think nobly of the soul, and no way approve of his opinion.

Pythagoras himself left no writings, but Dacier in his Life of Pythagoras *points out:*

A sure token that Pythagoras never held the opinion attributed to him lies in the fact that there is not the faintest trace of it in the symbols we have left of him, or in the precepts his disciple, Lysis, collected together and handed down as a summary of the Master's teaching.

Hierocles, a Pythagorean, states in his Commentary of the Golden Verses of *Pythagoras (a view shared by the Neoplatonists regarding Plato's remarks on transmigration in the Timæus; see index under "Proclus"):*

He who believes that he transmigrates, after death, into the body of a beast or a plant is grossly mistaken; he is ignorant of the fact that the essential form of the soul cannot change, that it is and it remains human, and only metaphorically speaking does virtue make of it a god and vice an animal.

Heraclitus of Ephesus (540-475 B.C.)

This world which is the same for all, neither any god nor any man made; but it was always, is, and ever shall be, an ever-living fire. . . . The quick and the dead, the wakers and the sleepers, young and old; all are the same. For the last are moved about to be the first, and the first in turn become the last. They rise again and become watchful guardians of the quick and the dead.

[*Commenting on the above, the German philosopher Georg Misch states in his* The Dawn of Philosophy:]

The "ever-living fire" subsists only in its transmigrations, as that which is perpetually changing, since it is not a fixed quantity that "is," but "lives." This dynamic principle accords very well with the idea of world-cycles of events; indeed periodicity was a self-evident fact to all thinking persons right down to modern times. In connection with these up-down cycles or the "wheel of births," to use the Indian term, he [Heraclitus] says, "The way up and the way down are the same."

Pindar (522-443 B.C.)

LYRIC POET

They who thrice on either side of death have refrained their souls from wickedness, travel on the road of Zeus to the tower of Cronus, where the ocean breezes blow around the island of the blest!

Odes

While the body of all men is subject to over-mastering death, an image of life ["the soul" translator] remaineth alive, for it alone cometh from the gods. But it sleepeth, while the limbs are active. . . . But, as for those from whom Persephone shall exact the penalty of their pristine woe, in the ninth year she once more restoreth their souls to the upper sunlight; and from these come into being august monarchs, and men who are swift in strength and supreme in wisdom; and, for all future time, men call them sainted heroes.

Dirges

Anaxagoras (500-428 B.C.)

Wrongly do the Greeks suppose that aught begins or ceases to be; for nothing comes into being or is destroyed; but all is an aggregation or secretion of pre-existent things.*

Empedocles (490-430 B.C.)

All things doth Nature change, enwrapping souls
In unfamiliar tunics of the flesh.
The worthiest dwellings for the souls of men.

The Purifications

Plato (427-347 B.C.)

Every soul is immortal—for whatever is in perpetual motion is immortal. . . . All that is soul presides over all that is without soul and patrols all

---

* Quoted in *The Religion of Philosophy* by Raymond S. Perrin, p. 34.

heaven, now appearing in one form and now in another. . . . Every man's soul has by the law of his birth been a spectator of eternal truth, or it would never have passed into this our mortal frame, yet still it is no easy matter for all to be reminded of their past by their present existence.

Phædrus
Trans. J. Wright

The soul of the true philosopher . . . abstains as much as possible from pleasures and desires, griefs and fears . . . because each pleasure and pain, having a nail, as it were, nails the soul to the body, and fastens it to it, and causes it to become corporeal, deeming those things to be true whatever the body asserts to be so. For, in consequence of its forming the same opinions with the body, and delighting in the same things . . . it can never pass into Hades in a pure state, but must ever depart polluted by the body, and so quickly falls into another body . . . and consequently is deprived of all association with that which is divine, and pure, and uniform.

Phædo
Trans. Henry Cary

Know that if you become worse you will go to the worse souls, or if better to the better, and in every succession of life and death you will do and suffer what like may fitly suffer at the hands of like.

Laws, Book X

Well, I will tell you a tale . . . of what once happened to a brave man, Er . . . who, according to story, was killed in battle [but his body would not disintegrate]. . . . On the twelfth day after his death, as he lay on the funeral pyre, he came to life again, and then proceeded to describe what he had seen in the other world. . . .

Each soul, as it arrived, wore a travel-stained appearance ; . . and those who had descended from heaven were questioned about heaven by those who had risen out of the earth; while the latter were questioned by the former about the earth. Those who were come from earth told their tale with lamentations and tears, as they bethought them of all the dreadful things they had seen and suffered in their subterranean journey . . . while those who were come from heaven described enjoyments and sights of marvellous beauty. . . .

[*The souls about to enter earth life are thus addressed:*]

"Ye short-lived souls, a new generation of men shall here begin the cycle of its mortal existence. Your destiny shall not be allotted to you, but you shall choose it for yourselves. . . . Virtue owns no master. He who honours her shall have more of her, and he who slights her less. The responsibility lies with the chooser. Heaven is guiltless." . . .

It was a truly wonderful sight, he said, to watch how each soul selected its life—a sight at once melancholy, and ludicrous, and strange. The experience of their former life generally guided the choice. . . . It so happened that the soul of Odysseus had drawn the last lot of all. When he came up to choose, the memory of his former sufferings had so abated his ambition that he went about a long time looking for a quiet retired life, which with great trouble he discovered lying about, and thrown contemptuously aside by the others. As soon as he saw it, he chose it gladly, and said that he would have done the same if he had even drawn the first lot. . . .

Now, when all the souls had chosen their lives . . . they all travelled into the plain of Forgetfulness . . . and took up their quarters by the bank of the river of Indifference. . . . each, as he drinks, forgets everything. When they had gone to rest, and it was now midnight, there was a clap of thunder and an earthquake; and in a moment the souls were carried up to their birth, this way and that, like shooting stars.

The Republic, Book **X**
Trans. J. Wright

Aristotle (384-322 B.C.)

[*Dr. Henry More, in his treatise on the "Immortality of the Soul," writes:*]

We shall evince that Aristotle, that has the luck to be believed more than most authors, was of the same opinion [as to the pre-existence of the soul], in his treatise "De Anima," where he says, "for every art must use its proper instruments, and every soul its body." He speaks something more plainly in his "De Generatione Animae." "There are generated," saith he, "in the earth, and in the moisture thereof, plants and living creatures, and in the whole universe an animal heat; insomuch that in a manner all places are full of souls."

We will add a third place still more clear, out of the same treatise, where he starts that very question of the pre-existency of souls, of the sensitive and rational especially, and he concludes thus: "It remains that the rational or intellectual soul only enters from without, as being only of a nature purely divine; with whose actions the actions of this gross body have no communication." Concerning which point he concludes like an orthodox scholar of his excellent master Plato; to whose footsteps the closer he keeps, the less he ever wanders from the truth. For in this very place he does plainly profess what many would not have him so apertly guilty of, that the soul of man is immortal, and can perform her proper functions without the help of this terrestrial body.

Apollonius of Tyana (first century A.D.)

There is no death of anything save in appearance. That which passes over from essence to nature seems to be birth, and what passes over from nature to essence seems to be death. Nothing really is originated, and nothing ever perishes; but only now comes into sight and now vanishes. It appears by reason of the density of matter, and disappears by reason of the tenuity of essence. But it is always the same, differing only in motion and condition.

Epistle to Valerius

[Philostratus, in his Life of Apollonius of Tyana, reports the following conversation between Apollonius and Iarchas a wise man of Kashmir, India, to whom Apollonius traveled to be instructed in the higher philosophy: Iarchas explained that his own soul had once been in the body of a king, while Apollonius told him that he had once been an Egyptian pilot of a ship.]

"And you must not be surprised at my transformation from one Indian to another; for here is one" and he [Iarchas] pointed to a stripling of about twenty years of age—"who in natural aptitude for philosophy excels everyone . . . yet, in spite of all these advantages, he detests philosophy."

"What, then," said Apollonius, "O Iarchas, is the matter with the youth? For it is a terrible thing to tell me, if one so well adapted by nature to the pursuit refuses to embrace philosophy, and has no love for learning. . . ."

"The truth is this stripling was once Palamedes of Troy, and he found his bitterest enemies in Odysseus and Homer; for the one laid an ambush against him of people by whom he was stoned to death, while the other denied him any place in his Epic; and because neither the wisdom with which he was endowed was of any use to him nor did he meet with any praise from Homer . . . he has conceived an aversion to philosophy, and deplores his ill-luck. And he is Palamedes, for indeed he can write without having learned his letters."

Plutarch (A.D. 46-120)

Every soul . . . is ordained to wander between incarnations in the region lying between the moon and the earth for a term. . . . The genii do not always pass their time upon her [the moon], but they come down hither or take charge of Oracles; they are present at, and assist in, the most advanced of the initiatory rites . . . ; they act, and shine as saviours in battle and at sea; and whatsoever thing in these capacities they do amiss . . . they are punished for it, for they are driven down again to earth and coupled with human bodies.

Morals

When is death in us, when is it not? As Heraclitus says "It is the same thing in us that is alive and dead, awake and asleep, young and old. For the former shift and become the latter, and the latter shift back again and become the former."

Consolation to Appollonius

Ammonius Saccas and the Neoplatonists

Ammonius was the founder in A.D. 193 of the famous Alexandrian School of Neoplatonism in Egypt, sometimes called the Eclectic Theosophical School, or the Philalethians, the "lovers of truth."

His immediate disciples were Origen, Plotinus, Herennius, and Longinus, the counselor of Queen Mab. Philo Judæus, Josephus, Clement of Alexandria, Iamblichus, Porphyry, Proclus, Eratosthenes (the astronomer), Hypatia (the virgin philosopher), the Emperor Julian, and numerous other stars of second magnitude all belonged at various times to these great schools, helping to make Alexandria with its incomparable library one of the greatest seats of learning the world has known.

With the revival of the teachings of Plato, the idea of reincarnation came naturally into prominence, as will be seen from the quotations from the voluminous works of Ammonius' disciples. Ammonius himself left no written record of his thought. Under "Christianity" will be found reincarnation quotations for Origen and Clement; and under "Judaism" for Philo and Josephus, the latter two having belonged to the earlier Alexandrian schools.

The Encyclopædia Britannica (1959) under "Neoplatonism" states:

Pagan Greek philosophy was Neoplatonist till it faded out in the sixth century A.D. Many of the greatest Christian thinkers of this period, the great formative period of Christian theology, were deeply influenced by Neoplatonism, as were later the great Moslem philosophers. The influence of Neoplatonism on the thought of the middle ages was thus very great; and it has continued, through very diverse channels, to influence men's minds down to our own day.

Plotinus (A.D. 205-270)

The soul . . . falling from on high, suffers captivity, is loaded with fetters, and employs the energies of sense. . . . She is reported also to be buried and to be concealed in a cave; but when she converts herself to intelligence she then breaks her fetters and ascends on high, receiving first of all from reminiscence the ability of contemplating real beings. . . .

Souls therefore are necessarily of an amphibious nature, and alternately experience a superior and inferior condition of being; such as are able to enjoy a more intimate converse with Intellect abiding for a longer period in the higher world, and such to whom the contrary happens, either through nature or fortune, continuing longer connected with these inferior concerns. . . .

Thus the soul, though of divine origin, and proceeding from the regions on high, becomes merged in the dark receptacle of body. . . . By this means it receives a knowledge of evil, unfolds its latent powers, and exhibits a variety of operations peculiar to its nature, which, by perpetually abiding in an incorporeal habit, and never proceeding into energy, would have been bestowed in vain. . . . For the experience of evil produces a clearer knowledge of good.

Indeed, if it is proper to speak clearly what appears to me to be the truth . . . the whole of our soul does not enter into body, but something belonging to it always abides in the intelligible . . . world. . . . For every soul possesses something which inclines towards the body, and something which tends upwards toward intellect . . . but the superior part of the soul is never influenced by fraudulent delights, and lives a life always uniform and divine.

The Descent of the Soul
Trans. Thomas Taylor

Iamblichus (died c. A.D. 333)

What appears to us to be an accurate definition of justice does not also appear to be so to the Gods. For we, looking at that which is most brief, direct our attention to things present, and to this momentary life, and the manner in which it subsists. But the powers that are superior to us know the whole life of the Soul, and all its former lives; and in consequence of this, if they inflict a certain punishment in obedience to the entreaties of those that invoke them, they do not inflict it without justice, but looking at the offences committed by souls in former lives: which men, not perceiving, think that they unjustly fall into the calamities which they suffer.

Egyptian Mysteries, Book IV
Trans. Thomas Taylor

Porphyry (A.D. 233-304)

There is an essential opposition between matter and spirit, yet the world of sense has sprung from the world of spirit. The highest power produced one below it, and so on in a downward course, in which multiplicity and evil increase, the further in the scale beings are removed from the great First Cause. . . .

At last the soul which hovers between the two worlds inclines downwards, and produces a lower power akin to the body, which combines with it. Now this descent on the part of the soul is voluntary, just as in Plato it is the souls which are weighted by the corporeal that are dragged down again into the visible world. It is the soul which seeks the body. Nature indeed binds the body to the soul, but the soul binds herself to the body. Nature therefore liberates the body from the soul, but the soul liberates herself from the body.

Porphyry to His Wife Marcella
Trans. Alice Zimmern

Hypatia (died A.D. 415)

NEOPLATONIC PHILOSOPHER AND MATHEMATICIAN

It is only a few more days, in this world, and each shall return to its own fountain; the blood-drop to the abysmal heart, and the water to the river, and the river to the shining sea; and the dewdrop which fell from heaven shall rise to heaven again, shaking off the dust grains which weighed it down, thawed from the earth frost which chained it here to herb and sward, upward and upward ever through stars and suns, through gods, and through the parents of the gods, purer and purer through successive lives, until it enters the Nothing, which is the All, and finds its home at last.*

* Quoted in *The Philosophy of Life* by A. M. Baten, also, with minor changes, in *Hypatia* by Charles Kingsley, chapter 8.

Proclus (A.D. 410-485)

[*In his* Commentaries on the Phædrus, *Proclus endeavored to show by a multitude of arguments that man's soul can never incarnate in an animal, and in his* Commentaries on the Timæus *thus summarized his views:*]

It is usual to inquire how human souls can descend into brute animals. And some, indeed, think that there are certain similitudes of men to brutes, which they call savage lives: for they by no means think it possible that the rational essence can become the soul of a savage animal. . . . In his "Republic" Plato says, that the soul of Thersites assumed an ape, but not the body of an ape; and in the "Phædrus," that the soul descends into a savage life, but not into a savage body. For life is conjoined with its proper soul. And in this place he says it is changed into a brutal nature. For a brutal nature is not a brutal body, but a brutal life.

[*In* Proclus—The Elements of Theology, *E. R. Dodds writes:*]

The question whether the human soul can attain a final release from the "circle of birth," as in the Orphic-Pythagorean and the Indian doctrine, was one on which the Neoplatonists were not unanimous. . . . Porphyry . . . seems to have asserted in *de regressu animae* that the soul, at any rate the soul of the philosopher, will eventually be released for ever. Later we find the contrary opinion, that souls cannot "leave the body once for all and remain through all time in idleness," maintained by Sallustius (who is very probably following Iamblichus here) : he supports it (a) by the argument from function, that souls have their natural citizenship in the body; and (b) by the consideration that . . . the earth would on the Porphyrian theory eventually be depopulated.

Proclus takes the same view as Sallustius, but relies on the more general argument that an eternal life cannot start from, or finish at, a point in time. . . . That which has no temporal beginning will never have an end, and what has no end cannot have had a beginning. He holds with Syrianus that while self-will causes some human souls to descend more often than is necessary, cosmic law requires that each shall descend at least once in every world-period. Consistently with this, he rejects the . . . view that such descent is in itself sinful. . . . He definitely treats the descent as a necessary part of the soul's education or as a necessary cosmic service.

Olympiodorus *(fifth century* A.D.*)*

HISTORIAN

That the living and the dead come each from the other, Plato made out from the testimony of the ancient poets, those I mean who taught us as Orpheus did, when singing "The self-same souls are fathers, sons, and honoured wives and daughters dear." *

---

* Quoted by the Greek scholar C. A. Lobeck in *Aglaophamus.*

ROME

❀

Ennius (239-169 B.C.)

Ennius, the Calabrian poet, is said to have introduced the doctrine of metempsychosis to the Romans. He it is who tells in his Annals how Homer appeared to him in a dream, and told him that their bodies had once been animated by the same soul.

Julius Caesar (100-44 B.C.)

[Caesar, finding the Celts to be redoubtable warriors, especially because of their disregard of death, investigated the reason for their fearlessness. He wrote:]

They wish to inculcate this as one of their leading tenets, that souls do not become extinct, but pass after death from one body to another, and they think that men by this tenet are in a great degree excited to valor, the fear of death being disregarded.

Gallic War, Book VI, Chap. 14

Cicero (106-43 B.C.)

The mistakes and the sufferings of human life make me think sometimes that those ancient seers, or interpreters of the secrets of heaven and the counsels of the Divine Mind, had some glimpses of the truth, when they said that men are born in order to suffer the penalty for some sins committed in a former life.

Treatise on Glory

No one, my dear Scipio, shall ever persuade me that your father, Paulus, and your two grandfathers . . . or the father of Africanus, or his uncle, or many other illustrious men not necessary to mention, would have attempted such lofty deeds as to be remembered by posterity, had they not seen in their minds that future ages concerned them.

*On Friendship**

The soul is of heavenly origin, forced down from its home in the highest, and, so to speak, buried in earth, a place quite opposed to its divine nature and its immortality. . . . Nor is it only reason and argument that have brought me to this belief, but the great fame and authority of the most distinguished philosophers. I used to be told that Pythagoras and the Pythagoreans—almost natives of our country, who in old times had been called the Italian school of philosophers—never doubted that we had souls drafted from the universal Divine intelligence.

I used besides to have pointed out to me the discourse delivered by Socrates on the last day of his life upon the immortality of the soul—Socrates . . . the wisest of men. I need say no more. I have convinced myself, and I hold—in view of the rapid movement of the soul, its vivid memory of the past and its prophetic knowledge of the future, its many accomplishments, its vast range of knowledge, its numerous discoveries—that a nature embracing such varied gifts cannot itself be mortal. And since the soul is always in motion and yet has no external source of motion, for it is self-moved, I conclude that it will also have no end to its motion, because it is not likely ever to abandon itself. . . .

It is again a strong proof of men knowing most things before birth, that when mere children they grasp innumerable facts with such speed as to show that they are not then taking them in for the first time, but remembering and recalling them.

On Old Age

* This and the following excerpt are taken from Vol. 9 of the *Harvard Classics*, published by the P. F. Collier division of the Crowell-Collier Publishing Company, New York; translator E. S. Shuckburgh.

Virgil (70-19 B.C.)

All these souls, after they have passed away a thousand years, are summoned by the divine ones in great array, to the Lethean river. . . . In this way they become forgetful of the former earthlife, and re-visit the vaulted realms of the world, willing to return again into living bodies.

The Aeneid

Ovid (43 B.C.-A.D. 17)

Orace! stricken by the alarms of icy death, why do you dread Styx? . . . Souls are not subject to death; and having left their former abode, they ever inhabit new dwellings and, there received, live on. . . .

Metamorphoses
Trans. H. T. Riley

Then death, so call'd, is but old matter dress'd
In some new figure, and a varied vest:
Thus all things are but alter'd, nothing dies;
And here and there the unbodied spirit flies. . . .
From tenement to tenement though toss'd,
The soul is still the same, the figure only lost:
And, as the soften'd wax new seals receives,
This face assumes, and that impression leaves;
Now call'd by one, now by another name,
The Form is only changed, the wax is still the same.
So death, so call'd, can but the form deface;
The immortal soul flies out in empty space,
To seek her fortune in some other place.

Metamorphoses
Trans. John Dryden

Lucan (A.D. 39-65)

SPANISH-BORN ROMAN POET

From you [the Druids] we learn that the destination of man's spirit is not the grave, nor the Kingdom of the Shades. The same spirit in another world animates a body and, if your teaching be true, death is the centre, not the finish, of a long life.

The Pharsalia

Apuleius (*second century*)

PHILOSOPHER AND RHETORICIAN

The human soul is an immortal God. . . . The soul is born in this world upon leaving the soul of the world (*anima mundi*) in which her existence precedes the one we all know. Thus, the Gods who consider her proceedings in all the phases of various existences and as a whole, punish her sometimes for sins committed during an anterior life.

The God of Socrates

Lucian (*second century*)

SATIRIST

FIRST DEALER: Where do you come from?

PYTHAGOREANISM: From Samos.

FIRST DEALER: Where did you get your schooling?

PYTHAGOREANISM: From the sophists of Egypt.

FIRST DEALER: If I buy you, what will you teach me?

PYTHAGOREANISM: Nothing. I will remind you. . . . You have to learn that you yourself are not the person you appear to be.

FIRST DEALER: What, I am someone else; not the I who am speaking to you?

PYTHAGOREANISM: You are that "you" now: but you have formerly inhabited another body and borne another name. And in course of time you will change once more.

FIRST DEALER: Why, then I shall be immortal and take one shape after another? But enough of this. . . .

The Sale of Creeds

Emperor Julian (A.D. 331-363)

NEPHEW OF CONSTANTINE THE GREAT

Julian was a Neoplatonist, a pupil of Aedesius, who had been taught by Iamblichus. He was initiated at Ephesus, and later into the Eleusinian Mysteries. His reign lasted only 18 months but was renowned for its enlightenment and religious tolerance. Exiled Christian Bishops were returned to their posts. Pagan subjects were granted complete religious liberty.

Julian had reason to believe himself to be the reincarnation of that un-

enviable character called Alexander the "Great." Ibsen dwelt on this theme
in his play "The Emperor and Galilean" (see index under "Ibsen").
Mortally wounded on the battlefield, Julian as he lay dying said:

I have learned from philosophy how much more excellent the soul is than
the body, and that the separation of the nobler substance should be the subject of joy rather than affliction.

Then, turning to the two philosophers Priscus and Maximus, he entered
into a metaphysical discussion as to the nature of the soul. Here, as in the
case of Socrates, we have an illustration of how at the time of death a deep-
seated conviction in immortality leads to philosophic calm and utter fearlessness.

Sallustius (fourth century)
PRETORIAN PREFECT UNDER EMPEROR JULIAN

It is not unlikely that the rejection of God is a kind of punishment: we
may well believe that those who knew the gods and neglected them in one
life may in another be deprived of the knowledge of them altogether.

[Thomas Whittaker in The Neo-Platonists writes:]

Sallust, the friend of Julian, in setting forth . . . a creed for the reformed
paganism, had put only in cryptic language his explanation of the change
that had come over the world. The guilt, he says, that is now punished in
some by total ignorance of the true divine order may be that of having deified their kings in a former life. Thus it appears that in Julian's circle Christianity was regarded as nemesis for the deification of the Emperors.

Macrobius (fifth century)
NEOPLATONIST

The soul is drawn down to these terrene bodies, and is on this account said
to die when it is enclosed in this fallen region, and the seat of mortality. Nor
ought it to cause any disturbance that we have so often mentioned the death
of the soul, which we have pronounced to be immortal. For the soul is not
extinguished by its own proper death, but is only overwhelmed for a time.

Nor does it lose the benefit of perpetuity by its temporal demersion. Since, when it deserves to be purified from the contagion of vice, through its entire refinement from body, it will be restored to the light of perennial life, and will return to its pristine integrity and perfection.

Commentary on the Dream of Scipio

ITALIAN

Dante and the Fideli d'Amore

Secret organizations are reputed to have kept alive the idea of reincarnation during the Middle Ages. Writers of that time necessarily had to veil all such conceptions in obscure symbolism. Dante, one of the important forerunners of the Italian Renaissance, exercised great caution in what he said. It has been demonstrated by such scholars as Gabriel Rossetti, Luigi Valli, Francesca Perez, and Giovanni Pascoli that Dante and the groups of poets known as the Fideli d'Amore (the faithful to Love) used a secret language.

At least thirty words commonly used by these poets were found to have one and sometimes two hidden meanings. Belonging to the cipher were love, madonna, death, life, women, nature, stone, rose, flower—all of which appear repeatedly, often confusing the surface meaning of the author. Characteristically, the "Beloved," be it Rosa, Beatrice, or Savage, always seems to represent Wisdom. This symbolism of the Beloved was also used by Sufi poets, by the Spanish mystics, of whom Raymond Lully was one, by the troubadours of southern Europe, and by the minnesingers (love singers) of Germany.

Dante's use of symbolical language appears to have been a quite deliberate borrowing from Muslim mystics. In The Philosophy of Ibn 'Arabī (the Sufi philosopher and poet quoted in the section on Mohammedanism) Rom Landau writes:

In the Western world, Dante provides one of the most conspicuous examples of Ibn 'Arabī's pervasive influence. Senor Asin y Palacios, the leading authority on the subject, has proved in his remarkable studies published in the volume *Islam and the Divine Comedy* (John Murray, London, 1926) that not only were innumerable ideas in the *Divine Comedy* inspired by Ibn 'Arabī, but the entire geography of heaven and hell was taken over by Dante from Ibn 'Arabī (and other Muslim sources). And to mention but one other Western thinker whose work unmistakably shows Ibn 'Arabī's influence, there is Ramon Lull, the Spanish mystic.

The Divine Comedy *gives a description in allegorical language of the drama of after-death conditions, of purification in purgatory, of sublimation in heaven, and at least one hint of the soul's return to earth. In Canto XX (Paradiso), Dante writes of meeting a Roman emperor in the Heaven of Jupiter and being told:*

He from Hell came back into his bones, and this was the reward of living hope—the living hope which put power into the prayers made to God to raise him up, that his will might be moved.

The glorious soul returning to flesh where it abode awhile, believed in Him who had power to help, and believing, kindled into such a flame of Love that at the second death it was worthy to come into this Joy.

The Renaissance and the Neoplatonic Revival

In the year 529, when the Emperor Justinian closed the Neoplatonic School in Athens and banished the last of the Neoplatonists, the teachings of Plato and the Alexandrian philosophers disappeared from Christian Europe for almost a thousand years. Aristotle, it will be recalled, was the instructor par excellence of the medieval scholastic philosophers. In Spain, Germany, and later in England, efforts were made to revive Neoplatonism. The chief stronghold of the Neoplatonic revival, however, was in the city of Florence, where it reappeared under the protection of the powerful house of Medici.

Cosmo de Medici made the acquaintance of George Gemistus, a celebrated Byzantine Platonic philosopher and scholar who attended the Council of Florence in 1439 as a deputy of the Greek Church. Gemistus gave Cosmo the idea of founding a Platonic academy in Florence. With this end in view, Cosmo selected Marsilio Ficino, the son of his chief physician, for a thorough education in Greek language and philosophy. Ficino's natural aptitude was so great that he completed his first work on the Platonic Institutions when only twenty-three years old. At thirty he began his translation of Plato, later making excellent translations of Plotinus, Iamblichus, Proclus, and Synesius. He also wrote a treatise on the Platonic doctrine of immortality.

When Lorenzo, Cosmo de Medici's grandson, was eight years old, Ficino became his tutor, embuing him with a deep reverence for the Greeks. After Lorenzo (the "Magnificent") became the head of the house he brought his grandfather's plans to completion and going further, founded a university in Pisa, established public libraries for his people, and became a patron of Michelangelo, Botticelli, and Leonardo da Vinci.

Giovanni Pico, son of the Prince of Mirandola, joined forces with Lorenzo and Ficino and through their united efforts the revival of Neoplatonism made rapid headway. Although only a young man, Pico was deeply versed in the learning of the Chaldeans, Hebrews, and Arabians. He is well known today as the author of the Humanist classic An Oration on the Dignity of Man. With the death of these three the Platonic Academy went out of existence, but not without having made a major contribution to the advancement of art, science, and philosophy, and to the spread of Platonism in Germany, England, and other centers.

George Foot Moore in his Ingersoll Lecture on "Metempsychosis" remarked: "It is not surprising . . . that with the revival of Platonism and Plotinianism at the renaissance, the theory of metempsychosis was revived in European philosophy."

George Gemistus (1355-1450)

[This Byzantine Platonic philosopher, known also by the name of Gemistus Pletho, was an important precursor of the Italian renaissance, and therefore is included in this section. "He is . . . chiefly memorable for having been the first person who introduced Plato to the Western world . . . Cardinal Bessarion became his disciple; he produced a great impression upon Cosmo de' Medici; and . . . effectually shook the exclusive domination which Aristotle had exercised over European thought for eight centuries." (Encyclopædia Britannica, 9th edition.) Pletho wrote:]

As to ourselves, our soul, partaking of the divine nature, remains immortal and eternal in the precincts which are the limit of our world. Attached to a mortal envelope, it is sent by the gods now into one body, now into another, in view of the universal harmony, in order that the union of the mortal and immortal elements in human nature may contribute to the unity of the Whole. . . .

If, in man, the immortal nature is united for an instant to the mortal nature, only to abandon it for the rest of time, no permanent bond would be made between these two mortal and immortal elements, but a temporary union which, the mortal element once removed, would immediately dissolve, and dissolve with it the general harmony. It remains to be said that the union of these two natures exists partially, temporarily, and that whenever the body is destroyed each returns to its respective independence, and this process is renewed indefinitely throughout eternity.*

Michelangelo (1475-1564)

ON IMMORTALITY

Heaven-born, the soul a heavenward course must hold; beyond the world she soars; the wise man, I affirm, can find no rest in that which perishes, nor will he lend his heart to aught that doth on time depend.**

Giordano Bruno (1548-1600)

PHILOSOPHER: BURNT AT THE STAKE

Is not thy body for ever transformed, and flows it not ever
Into the river of time? And in ceaseless alteration
Doth it not cast off the old for the new, ever losing and gaining?
Art so mad as to think that thy poor corporeal substance,
Whether in whole or in part, for ever shall be as it has been?
Art so mad as to dream that the bones and the flesh of thy boyhood
Still shall abide with thee now? that thou comes unchanged to
      thy manhood?
Seest thou not how thy limbs, renewed in the process of change,
Take to themselves new form? . . . Yet ever one nature persisting
Ruling within thy heart is forming for ever a being,
Thou thyself, that one and the same abidest unchanging.***

❦

There is an eternal Principle or Substance which is truly the man and no accident derived from Composition. This is the Deity, the hero, the particular God, the intelligence in, from, and through whom different Complexes

* The Ring of Return, comp. Eva Martin (Philip Allan, 1927) p. 107.
** Useful Quotations, comp. Tryon Edwards (Grosset & Dunlap) p. 609
*** Quoted in Bertholet's Transmigration of Souls, p. 100.

and bodies are formed and form themselves, so that it continually reappears in different species, names, and fortunes.

The Expulsion of the Triumphant Beast

I have held and hold souls to be immortal. . . . Speaking as a Catholic, they do not pass from body to body, but go to Paradise, Purgatory or Hell. But I have reasoned deeply, and, speaking as a philosopher, since the soul is not found without body and yet is not body, it may be in one body or in another, and pass from body to body. This, if it be not [proved] true, seems at least likely, according to the opinion of Pythagoras. . . .

From the spirit, then, which is called the life of the universe, I understand, in my philosophy, proceeds life and soul, which, moreover, I understand to be immortal, as also to bodies, which, as to their substance, are all immortal, there being no other death than division and congregation, which doctrine seems expressed in Ecclesiastes, where it is said that "there is nothing new under the sun; that which is is that which was."

From Bruno's profession of faith
before the Inquisition

Tommaso Campanella (1568-1639)

[This celebrated Renaissance philosopher, poet, and Dominican monk, was imprisoned for twenty-seven years, undergoing much torture and misery, though his spirit remained unbroken. Many of his poems and philosophical works were written during this period.]

> I fear that by my death the human race
> Would gain no vantage. Thus I do not die.
> So wide is this vast cage of misery
> That flight and change lead to no happier place.
> Shifting our pains, we risk a sorrier case:
> All worlds, like ours, are sunk in agony:
> Go where we will, we feel; and this my cry
> I may forget like many an old disgrace.
> Who knows what doom is mine? The Omnipotent
> Keeps silence; nay, I know not whether strife
> Or peace was with me in some earlier life.
> Philip in a worse prison has me pent
> These three days past. . . .

A Sonnet on Caucasus

Giuseppe Mazzini (1805-1872)

ITALIAN LIBERATOR

[Mazzini] speaks of memory as the consciousness of the soul's progress up from earlier existences; love would be a mockery, if it did not last beyond the grave; the unity of the race implies a link between the living and the dead; science teaches there is no death but only transformation. He held passionately to his faith in immortality. . . . The individual soul, he thought, progresses through a series of re-incarnations, each leading it to a more perfect development, and the rapidity of the advance depends on its own purifications. And as the individual has his progress through a series of existences, so collective man progresses ever through the human generations.

The Life of Mazzini
Bolton King

SPAIN

Medieval Spain

E. D. Walker writes: "The Gnostic and Manichaean notions of pre-existence perpetuated themselves in many of the medieval sects, especially the Bogomiles, Paulicians, and Priscillians. Seven adherents of the Priscillian heresy were put to death in Spain A.D. 385, as the first instance of the death penalty visited by a Christian magistrate for erroneous belief." Under "Priscillian" in the Encyclopædia Britannica (11th edition) it is stated:

Spanish theologian and the founder of a party which, in spite of severe persecution for heresy, continued to subsist in Spain and in Gaul until the middle of the 6th century. He was a wealthy layman who had devoted his life to a study of the occult sciences and the deeper problems of philosophy. He was largely a mystic. . . . His favourite idea is that which St. Paul had expressed in the words "Know ye not that ye are the temple of God?" . . . Priscillian was made bishop of Avila, and the orthodox party found it necessary to appeal to the Emperor. . . . With six of his companions he was burned alive at Treves in 385. . . . [He was thus] the first martyr burned by a Spanish Inquisition.*

In the 8th century Spain was conquered by the Muslims and for many centuries became an important center of civilization where philosophy, the

* Hasting's Encyclopedia of Religion and Ethics says he was beheaded [Eds.].

arts, and the science of medicine flourished, as indicated in the section "Mohammedanism." Raymond Lully, the great Spanish mystic, appears to have been considerably influenced by the Muslim philosophers (see index under "Lully"). In 1492, the year Columbus discovered America, the last Moorish stronghold, the Kingdom of Granada, fell to the forces of King Ferdinand and Queen Isabella.

Salvador Dali (1904-   )

[The following extract from an article "Dali Greets the World" by Ben Martin appeared in the N.Y. Herald Tribune's magazine Today's Living, for January 24, 1960, being a report of an interview with this famous artist:]

[Dali stated]: "If you will study the entire series of cards [he had painted] you will find one theme runs through almost all—the butterfly. The butterfly is not present only because it is in itself a thing of beauty. It is present because to one of the greatest Spanish mystics, St. Theresa of Avila, the butterfly was the symbol of the soul. The ugly, ungainly caterpillar, our body, enters a form of the grave, the cocoon. Out of this death emerges the butterfly—beautiful, free, no longer earthbound. To me, as to St. Theresa, the butterfly is the soul of man." . . .

"All Spaniards are mystics," he replied [to the query "Are you a mystic?"] "All Spaniards are both Don Quixote, who is pure spirit, and Sancho Panza, who is pure materialism. That is why 'Don Quixote' is the most Spanish of all books. As for me, I am not only a mystic; I am also the reincarnation of one of the greatest of all Spanish mystics, St. John of the Cross. I can remember vividly my life as St. John, of experiencing divine union, of undergoing the dark night of the soul of which he writes with so much feeling. I can remember the monastery and I can remember many of St. John's fellow monks."

BRITISH

✿   ✿

✿

•BRITISH PHILOSOPHERS AND PROSE WRITERS•

Sir Francis Bacon (1561-1626)

And since I have lost much time with this age,
I would be glad, as God shall give me leave,
To recover it with posterity.

Letters

Sir Thomas Browne (1605-1682)

There is surely a piece of Divinity in us, something that was before the Elements, and owes no homage unto the Sun. . . . Whatever hath no beginning may be confident of no end. . . .

One general council is not able to extirpate one single heresy: it may be cancelled for the present: but revolution of time and the like aspects from heaven will restore it, when it will flourish till it be condemned again. For, as though there were a metempsychosis, and the soul of one man passed into another, opinions do find, after certain revolutions, men and minds like those that first begat them. To see ourselves again, we need not look for Plato's year; every man is not only himself: there have been many Diogeneses, and as many Timons, though but few of that name; men are lived over again; the world is now as it was in Ages past; there was none then, but there hath been some one since, that parallels him, and is, as it were, his revived self.

Religio Medici

The Cambridge Platonists

In the seventeenth century, Cambridge University became the center of a movement which attracted considerable attention. Its leaders were known as the Cambridge Platonists, the most prominent of whom were Henry More, Ralph Cudworth, and John Smith.

Of Dr. More, who was a close friend of Addison and John Milton, Hobbes said that if his own philosophy were not true he knew none that he should sooner adopt than Henry More's of Cambridge. Samuel Johnson esteemed him as "one of our greatest divines and philosophers and no mean poet." More's philosophical works, Coleridge declared, "contain more enlarged and elevated views of the Christian dispensation than I have met with in any other single volume; for More had both philosophical and poetic genius supported by immense erudition." Sir Isaac Newton adopted the doctrines expounded by More as the metaphysical foundation for his scientific conceptions. Wise in the science of their day, and schooled in precise Cartesian thinking, the Cambridge Platonists nevertheless rejected the materialism toward which Descartes had directed the awakening Western intellectuality.

The Italian Neoplatonic revival of the Renaissance was a major inspiration of the English group, the great Florentine Platonist Ficino being a frequently cited authority. Continuing the task begun by Philo Judæus, the English Platonists endeavored to reconcile the Platonic doctrines with the Hebrew Bible. In fact, Plato was considered to be Moses speaking Attic Greek!

Cudworth's encyclopedic book, The True Intellectual System of the Universe, appeared in London in 1678. It was subtitled, "A storehouse of learning on the ancient opinions of the nature, origin, pre-existence, transmigration, and future of the soul." Cudworth agreed with the Greek view that in order for the soul to be immortal after death, it must have existed prior to birth. George Berkeley, the Irish bishop and philosopher, became a professed adherent of the Cudworth school. A few extracts from Dr. More's writings on pre-existence now follow. (He is also quoted elsewhere in the Anthology.)

Henry More (1614-1687)

If it be good for the souls of men to be at all, the sooner they are, the better. . . . Wherefore the pre-existence of souls is a necessary result of the wisdom and goodness of God. Again, the face of Providence in the work seems very much to suit with this opinion, there being not any so natural and easy account to be given of those things that seem the most harsh in the affairs of men, as from this hypothesis: that these souls did once subsist in some other state. . . . Which key is . . . able to unlock that recondite mystery of some particular men's almost fatal averseness from all religion and virtue, their stupidity and dullness and even invincible slowness to these things from their very childhood, and their incorrigible propension to all manner of vice. . . .

And as this hypothesis is rational in itself, so has it also gained the suffrage of all philosophers of all ages, of any note, that have held the soul of man incorporeal and immortal. . . . Let us cast our eye, therefore, into what corner of the world we will, that has been famous for wisdom and literature, and the wisest of those nations you shall find the asserters of this opinion.

The Immortality of the Soul

Thomas Vaughan (1621-1665)

(EUGENIUS PHILALETHES)

I look on this life as the progress of an essence royal: the soul but quits her court to see the country. . . . Thus her descent speaks her original. . . . The magicians tell me that the soul passes out of one mode and enters another. . . .

The soul of man, while she is in the body, is like a candle shut up in a dark lanthorn, or a fire that is almost stifled for want of air. Spirits—say the Platonics—when they are "in their own country" are like the inhabitants of green fields who live perpetually amongst flowers, in a spicy, odorous air: but here below "in the circle of generation," they mourn because of darkness and solitude, like people locked up in a pest-house. This makes the soul subject to so many passions, to such a Proteus of humours. Now she flourishes, now she withers—now a smile, now a tear; and when she hath played out her stock, then comes a repetition of the same fancies, till at last she cries out with Seneca: "How long this self-same round?" . . .

Who seeketh to be more than a man, or to know the harmony of the world and be born again?

The Works of Thomas Vaughan
Ed. A. E. Waite

Soame Jenyns (1704-1787)

WRITER AND MEMBER OF PARLIAMENT

The ancient doctrine of transmigration seems the most rational and most consistent with God's wisdom and goodness; as by it all the unequal dispensations of things so necessary in one life may be set right in another, and all creatures serve the highest and lowest, the most eligible and most burdensome offices of life by an equitable rotation; by which means their rewards and punishments may not only be proportioned to their behavior, but also carry on the business of the universe, and thus at the same time answer the purposes both of justice and utility. . . .

That mankind had existed in some state previous to the present was the opinion of the wisest sages of the most remote antiquity. . . . It is confirmed by reason, which teaches us that it is impossible that the conjunction of a male and female can create, or bring into being, an immortal soul: they may prepare a material habitation for it, but there must be an immaterial pre-existent inhabitant ready to take possession. Reason assures us that an immortal soul, which will eventually exist after the dissolution of the body, must have eternally existed before the formation of it.

Disquisition on a Præexistent State

David Hume (1711-1776)

Reasoning from the common course of nature, and without supposing any new interposition of the supreme cause, which ought always to be excluded from philosophy, what is incorruptible must also be ungenerable. The soul, therefore, if immortal, existed before our birth, and if the former existence noways concerns us, neither will the latter. . . . The Metempsychosis is, therefore, the only system of this kind that philosophy can hearken to.

The Immortality of the Soul

Thomas Taylor (1758-1835)

[As the Soul] is *always* moved . . . hence it is necessary that its motions should be periodic. For motion is a certain mutation from some things into others. . . . But every thing which is moved perpetually and participates of time, revolves periodically and proceeds from the same to the same. And hence the soul, from possessing motion and energizing according to time, will both possess periods of motion, and restitutions to its pristine state.

Again, as the human soul, according to Plato, ranks among the number of those souls that *sometimes* follow the mundane divinities . . . hence it possesses a power of descending infinitely into generation, or the sublunary region, and of ascending from generation to real being. For since it does not reside with divinity through an infinite time, neither will it be conversant with bodies through the whole succeeding time. For that which has no temporal beginning, both according to Plato and Aristotle, cannot have an end; and that which has no end, is necessarily without a beginning. It remains, therefore, that every soul must perform periods, both of ascensions from generation, and of descensions into generation; and that this will never fail, through an infinite time.

From all this it follows that the soul, while an inhabitant of earth, is in a fallen condition, an apostate from deity, an exile from the orb of light. . . .

Let not the reader . . . be surprised at the solitariness of the paths through which I shall attempt to conduct him, or at the novelty of the objects which will present themselves in the journey: for perhaps he may fortunately recollect that he has travelled the same road before, that the scenes were once familiar to him, and that the country through which he is passing is his native land.

Introduction to Taylor's Translation
of the Works of Plato

Thomas Carlyle (1795-1881)

Detached, separated! I say there is no such separation: nothing hitherto was ever stranded, cast aside; but all, were it only a withered leaf, works together with all; is borne forward on the bottomless, shoreless flood of Action, and lives through perpetual metamorphoses. . . .

Nay, if you consider it, what is Man himself, and his whole terrestrial Life, but an Emblem; a Clothing or visible Garment for that divine life of his, cast hither, like a light-particle down from Heaven? . . . Are we not Spirits, that are shaped into a body, into an Appearance; and that fade away again into air and Invisibility? . . . Ghosts! There are nigh a thousand million of them walking the earth openly at noontide; some half hundred have vanished from it, some half hundred have arisen in it, ere thy watch tick one. . . . Death and birth are the vesper and matin bells that summon mankind to sleep and to rise refreshed for new advancement.

Sartor Resartus

[In the myth "The Twilight of the Gods"] the Gods and Jötuns, the divine Powers and the chaotic brute ones, after long contest and partial victory by the former, meet at last in universal world-embracing wrestle and duel; World-serpent against Thor, strength against strength; mutually extinctive; and ruin, "twilight," sinking into darkness, swallows the created Universe. The old Universe with its Gods is sunk; but it is not final death: there is to be a new Heaven and a new Earth. . . .

Curious; this law of mutation, which also is a law written in man's inmost thought, had been deciphered by these old earnest Thinkers in their rude style; and how, though all dies, and even gods die, yet all death is but a phoenix fire-death, and new-birth into the Greater and the Better! It is the fundamental Law of Being for a creature made of Time, living in this Place of Hope. All earnest men have seen into it; may still see into it.

Heroes and Hero-Worship

William Knight (1836-1916)

SCOTCH PHILOSOPHER AND PROFESSOR

The absence of memory of any actions done in a previous state cannot be a conclusive argument against our having lived through it. Forgetfulness of the past may be one of the conditions of an entrance upon a new stage of existence. The body which is the organ of sense-perception may be quite as much a hindrance as a help to remembrance. In that case casual gleams of memory, giving us sudden abrupt and momentary revelations of the past, are precisely the phenomena we would expect to meet with. If the soul has pre-existed, what we would *a priori* anticipate are only some faint traces of recollection surviving in the crypts of memory. . . .

Stripped of all extravagance and expressed in the modest terms of probability, the theory [of metempsychosis] has immense speculative interest and great ethical value. It is much to have the puzzle of the origin of evil thrown back for an indefinite number of cycles of lives; to have a workable explanation of *Nemesis*, and of what we are accustomed to call the moral tragedies and the untoward birth of a multitude of men and women.

"Doctrine of Metempsychosis"
Fortnightly Review, Sept. 1878

Walter Pater (1839-1894)

Like all the higher forms of inward life this character is a subtle blending and interpenetration of intellectual, moral, and spiritual elements. . . . It is a mind of taste lighted upon by some spiritual ray within. . . . A magnificent intellectual force is latent within it. It is like the reminiscence of a forgotten culture that once adorned the mind; as if the mind of one . . . fallen into a new cycle, were beginning its spiritual progress over again, but with a certain power of anticipating its stages.

Diaphaneitè

Edward Carpenter (1844-1929)

Here in this perennial, immeasurable consciousness sleeping within us we come again to our Celestial City, our Home from which as individuals we proceed, but from which we are never really separated. . . . Every man feels doubtless that his little mortal life is very inadequate, and that to express and give utterance to all that is in him would need many lives, many bodies. . . .

The important thing . . . is to see that undoubtedly various orders of consciousness do exist, *actually embedded within us*; and that the words I and Thou do not merely cover our bodily forms and the outlines of our minds as we habitually represent them to ourselves, but cover also immense tracts of intelligence and activity lying behind these and only on occasions coming into consciousness. . . . To command these tracts in such a way as to be able to enter in and make use of them at will, and to bring them into permanent relation with the conscious ego, will I think be the method of advance, and the means by which all these questions of the perduration and reincarnation of the ego, will at length be solved.

The Art of Creation

Think not that the love thou enterest into to-day is for a few months or years: The little seed set now must lie quiet before it will germinate, and many alterations of sunshine and shower descend upon it before it become even a small plant.

When a thousand years have passed, come thou again. And behold! a mighty tree that no storms can shake.

Love does not end with this life or any number of lives; the form that thou seekest lies hidden under wrapping after wrapping;

Nevertheless it shall at length appear—more wondrous far than aught thou hast imagined.

Therefore leave time: do not like a child pull thy flower up by the root to see if it is growing;

Even though thou be old and near the grave there is plenty of time.

When a Thousand Years Have Passed

Bernard Bosanquet (1848-1923)

In the doctrine of metempsychosis, when taken in bitter earnest, i.e., giving full weight to the absence of conscious personality connecting any one life with its successor, we have a precisely complementary conception. Here, the bare subject or ego, the naked form of personality, the soul-thing is supposed to persist; but no content of the personality goes with it. We are offered chains of personalities linked together by impersonal transitions. We need only point out in passing the difficulty, which Aristotle put his finger on, in the conception of an identical soul animating wholly different bodies in succession. Our question at present is simply how far and in what sense any such doctrine appears to satisfy our desire of immortality. It has been, of course, of enormous influence in the history of philosophy and religion. It readily lends itself to pessimism, and has roots perhaps in very primitive beliefs; but it is, I am convinced, the form which Plato preferred to give to his working conceptions of human survival, and, in shapes largely borrowed and spiritualised from Oriental tradition, it is exceedingly popular to-day.

Dr. McTaggart's advocacy of it on strict philosophical grounds, is familiar to students. . . . I may draw attention here to a difficulty which Mr. Bradley mentions, nearly following Plato, *Rep.* 611 A. "A constant supply of new souls, none of which ever perished, would obviously land us in an insoluble difficulty" (the universe being held incapable of increase) (*Appearance*, ed. 2, 502). It would follow that some souls must perish, or be used over again as in metempsychosis. . . .

Advocates of this conception [of metempsychosis] point to the fact that character and the principles of knowledge can persist in the soul through intervals of oblivion and unconsciousness, wholly apart from specific memories of the incidents of their acquisition. Why, it is asked, should they not persist from life to life, as they persist from day to day, and from youth to age, unimpaired by intervals of unconsciousness and by the loss of particular memories? Such a conception affords to minds of any elevation, a motive for self-improvement which for them is all the stronger that it is wholly divorced from ideas of a personal self-satisfaction in a future world.

Value and Destiny of the Individual
Gifford Lectures, 1912

H. Fielding Hall (1859-1917)

A man has a soul, and it passes from life to life, as a traveller from inn to inn, till at length it is ended in heaven. But not till he has attained heaven in his heart will he attain heaven in reality. . . . Love does not die with the body . . . it lives for ever and ever, through incarnation after incarnation. . . . Love is stronger than death. Not any dogmas of any religion, not any philosophy, nothing in this world, nothing in the next, shall prevent him who loves from the certainty of rejoining some time the soul he loves. . . .

Many children, the Burmese will tell you, remember their former lives. As they grow older, the memories die away and they forget, but to the young children they are very clear. . . . I have seen many such.

The Soul of a People

How easy now is the belief in transmigration. The increasing life and soul has built itself up by slow degrees a form to show itself in. The imperfect beam showed in the animal, the higher in the man, still the same beam only with additions. It is an evolution of the soul manifested in an evolution of the body. . . . We are the products of an evolution. Yes. Not our bodies only but our souls. As our bodies grew fitter to incarnate the greater life, so the life was added from above. . . .

Was it an Oriental who wrote "The earth is the living garment of God"? . . . That is an universal thought that comes to every one who lives near nature. So with the life before this life, what is there Eastern in that? All the world naturally knows it, that we did not begin at birth. . . . Men have always known it till it was crushed in them. They know it even still, the truth does not die. It will rise again, must rise and burst the tombstones placed on it to keep it down.

The Inward Light

G. Lowes Dickinson (1862-1932)

The whole series of [man's] actions and feelings in one life are determined by those of a previous and determine those of a subsequent life. . . . It is, I think, a really consoling idea that our present capacities are determined by our previous actions, and that our present actions again will determine our future character. It seems to liberate us from the bonds of an external fate and make us the captains of our own destinies. If we have formed here a beautiful relation, it will not perish at death, but be perpetuated, albeit unconsciously, in some future life. If we have developed a faculty here, it will not be destroyed, but will be the starting-point of later developments.

> *"Is Immortality Desirable?"*
> *Ingersoll Lecture, Harvard University, 1909*

Of all the dawns that I have watched in the mountains, never was one like that I saw to-day. I forgot the glacier, and was aware only of the stars. Through the chinks in my prison wall they blazed brighter and brighter, till where they shone it fell away, and I looked out on the Past. I knew myself to be more than myself, an epitome of the generations; and I travelled again, from the source, my life which is the life of Man. I was a shepherd pasturing flocks on star-lit plains of Asia; I was an Egyptian priest on his tower conning the oracles of the sky; I was a Greek sailor with Boötes and Orion for my guides. I was Endymion entranced on mountains of Arcady. I saw the star of Bethlehem and heard the angels sing; I spoke with Ptolemy, and watched the night with Galileo. A thousand times I had died, a thousand times been born. By those births and deaths my course was marked through the night of Time.

> *"Euthanasia; Being Lines from the*
> *Note-Book of an Alpinist"* *

John M. Ellis McTaggart (1866-1925)

I suppose the reward of virtue gained in one life is always just the being able to start fresh as a superior kind of baby when one is born (cf. [Browning's] Rabbi Ben Ezra, "Fearless and Unperplexed"), and so you might go on from innocence through crime, punishment, repentance, virtue, to innocence again, until you had got as high as morality can carry you. And though the way is long, it can be no more wearisome than a single life. For with death we leave behind us memory and old age and fatigue. We may die old, but we shall be born young. And death acquires a deeper and more gracious significance when we regard it as part of the continually recurring rhythm of progress—as inevitable, as natural, and as benevolent as sleep.

> *Studies in Hegelian Cosmology*

Even the best men are not, when they die, in such a state of intellectual and moral perfection as would fit them to enter heaven immediately. . . . This is generally recognised, and one of two alternatives is commonly adopted to meet it. The first is that some tremendous improvement—an improvement

---

* Both of Professor Dickinson's essays are printed in his book *Religion and Immortality*, Houghton Mifflin and Company.

out of all proportion to any which can ever be observed in life—takes place at the moment of death. . . . The other and more probable alternative is that the process of gradual improvement can go on in each of us after the death of our present bodies. . . .

The doctrine of pre-existence does not compel us to deny all influence on a man's character of the characters of his ancestors. . . . But there is no impossibility in supposing that the characteristics in which we resemble the ancestors of our bodies may be to some degree characteristics due to our previous lives. . . . A man whose nature had certain characteristics when he was about to be reborn, would be reborn in a body descended from ancestors of a similar character. . . . It would be the character of the ancestors . . . and its similarity to his character, which determined the fact that he was re-born in that body rather than another. The shape of the head does not determine the shape of the hat, but it does determine the selection of this particular hat for this particular head. . . .

A man who dies after acquiring knowledge—and all men acquire some—might enter his new life, deprived indeed of his knowledge, but not deprived of the increased strength and delicacy of mind which he had gained in acquiring the knowledge. And, if so, he will be wiser in the second life because of what has happened in the first. . . .

We miss much here by our own folly, much by unfavourable circumstances. Above all, we miss much because so many good things are incompatible. We cannot spend our youth both in the study and in the saddle. We cannot gain the benefit both of unbroken health and of bodily weakness, both of riches and of poverty, both of comradeship and of isolation, both of defiance and of obedience. We cannot learn the lessons alike of Galahad and of Tristram and of Caradoc. And yet they are all so good to learn. Would it not be worth much to be able to hope that what we missed in one life might come to us in another? And would it not be worth much to be able to hope that we might have a chance to succeed hereafter in the tasks which we failed in here?

Some Dogmas of Religion

W. *Macneile Dixon* (1866-1946)

[*The following is taken from Professor Dixon's Gifford Lectures, delivered at the University of Glasgow 1935-37, and later published as* The Human Situation,* *a most unusual book that has gone through several editions and has been highly praised on both continents:*]

* St. Martin's Press, New York; Edward Arnold, London.

"The soul is eternal and migratory, say the Egyptians," reports Laertius. In its existence birth and death are events. And though this doctrine [of palingenesis or rebirth] has for European thought a strangeness, it is in fact the most natural and easily imagined, since what has been can be again. This belief, taught by Pythagoras, to which Plato and Plotinus were attached . . . "has made the tour of the world," and seems, indeed, to be in accordance with nature's own favourite way of thought, of which she so insistently reminds us, in her rhythms and recurrences, her cycles and revolving seasons. "It presents itself," wrote Schopenhauer, "as the natural conviction of man whenever he reflects at all in an unprejudiced manner." . . .

Many things are hard to believe, and a future life, some say, is quite incredible, and the mere thought of it a sort of madness. But what hinders if we have already found a present? . . . Well, I should myself put the matter rather differently. The present life is incredible, a future credible. "Not to be twice-born, but once-born is wonderful." To be alive, actually existing, to have emerged from darkness and silence, to be here to-day is certainly incredible. A philosopher friend of mine could never, he told me, bring himself to believe in his own existence. A future life would be a miracle, and you find it difficult to believe in miracles? I, on the contrary, find it easy. They are to be expected. The starry worlds in time and space, the pageant of life, the processes of growth and reproduction, the instincts of animals, the inventiveness of nature . . . they are all utterly unbelievable, miracles piled upon miracles. . . .

Our interest in the future, how strange it is if we can never hope to see the future. That interest rarely seems to desert us, and in itself appears inexplicable were we not possessed of an intuition which tells us that we shall have a part in it, that in some sense it already belongs to us, that we should bear it continually in mind, since it will be ours. So closely are all human ideals associated with futurity that, in the absence of the faith that man is an immortal being, it seems doubtful whether they could ever have come to birth. . . . "In the furthest depth of our being we are secretly conscious of our share in the inexhaustible spring of eternity, so that we can always hope to find life in it again" [Schopenhauer]. . . .

From what we have we should therefore except something in relation to what we shall have. If things as they are have not a feature in common with things as they will be, we have no basis for thought at all regarding that future. . . . As Leibniz said, "a leap from one state to another infinitely different state could not be natural." The experiences of time and of our present condition could, one feels, only be valuable in an existence not wholly unlike it; and any doctrine which insists upon a totally dissimilar existence, an indescribable spiritual life as a sequel to the present, makes of the present an insoluble enigma.

Bertrand Russell (1872-   )

I find my boy still hardly able to grasp that there was a time when he did not exist; if I talk to him about the building of the Pyramids or some such topic, he always wants to know what he was doing then, and is merely puzzled when he is told that he did not exist. Sooner or later he will want to know what "being born" means, and then we shall tell him.

Education and the Good Life

Francis M. Cornford (1874-1943)

PHILOSOPHER; PROFESSOR, CAMBRIDGE UNIVERSITY

[Husband of the poet Frances Cornford. See index for her poem "Preexistence."]

The most primitive of these [cardinal doctrines of mysticism] is Reincarnation (palingenesis). This life, which is perpetually renewed, is reborn out of that opposite state called "death," into which, at the other end of its arc, it passes again. In this idea of Reincarnation . . . we have the first conception of a cycle of existence, a Wheel of Life, divided into two hemicycles of light and darkness, through which the one life, or soul, continuously revolves. . . .

The doctrine can be classed unhesitatingly as "Orphic." The soul is conceived as falling from the region of light down into the "roofed-in cave," the "dark meadow of Ate." . . . Caught in the Wheel of Time, the soul, preserving its individual identity, passes through all shapes of life. This implies that man's soul is not "human"; human life is only one of the shapes it passes through. Its substance is divine and immutable, and it is the same substance as all other souls in the world. In this sense the unity of all life is maintained; but, on the other hand, each soul is an atomic individual, which persists throughout its . . . cycle of reincarnations.

From Religion to Philosophy

C. D. Broad (1887-   )

PHILOSOPHER, CAMBRIDGE UNIVERSITY

In the Thirteenth F. W. H. Myers Memorial Lecture (1958) entitled "Personal Identity and Survival," Prof. Broad stated: "Speaking for myself,

I would say that [reincarnation] *seems to me on general grounds to be much the most plausible form of the doctrine of survival. . . ."* In his book Examination of McTaggart's Philosophy (Cambridge University Press, 1938) Broad remarks that the theory of pre-existence and plurality of lives seems to him to be one *"Which ought to be taken very seriously, both on philosophical grounds and as furnishing a reasonable motive for right action. . . . We shall behave all the better if we act on the assumption that we may survive; that actions which tend to strengthen and enrich our characters in this life will probably have a favorable influence on the dispositions with which we begin our next lives; and that actions which tend to disintegrate our characters in this life will probably cause us to enter on our next life "halt and maimed."* If we suppose that our future lives will be of the same general nature as our present lives, this postulate, which is in itself intelligible and not unreasonable, gains enormously in concreteness and therefore in practical effect on our conduct."*

Alban G. Widgery (1887-   )

[*Professor Widgery was Stanton Lecturer on the Philosophy of Religion at Cambridge University, and later Professor of Philosophy at Duke University in the United States:*]

A contemporary Christian missionary in India is only repeating what has too often been said when he writes that the doctrines of transmigration and of karma have a paralysing influence throughout India, which must be freed from them if it is to progress at all. There can be no doubt that bad consequences may follow, and have indeed followed, misunderstanding of these doctrines. But there have been pernicious results also from the misinterpretation of doctrines regarded by others as important. . . .

The doctrine of Reincarnation involves a particular conception of the continuation of human existence: one that may be favourably compared with other views. Many Jews, Christians, and Muslims have the very vaguest notions as to what they believe (if indeed they believe anything) as to the nature of the existence of the soul after death. . . . Reincarnation affirms a series of lives sufficiently alike and with such continuity that a progress in self-realization may reasonably be conceived in accordance with it. Though the incidents of births and deaths may appear abrupt breaks, continuity is involved, analogous to come extent to going to sleep and waking up in the same room. . . .

The doctrine of karma [is] of fundamental importance for the life of the individual, especially on the ethical side. . . . It does not allow shifting responsibility on to others or accusing others for suffering that comes to the individual himself . . . [it] tends to cultivate self-respect, a central attitude in morality. . . .

The doctrine of reincarnation, bound up as it is with the law of karma, also has implications for the State. And these are contrary to those associated with the [misunderstood] statement previously mentioned from the American Declaration of Independence, that "all men are created equal." For it affirms that men are not born equal . . . and this affirmation appears to be more in accordance with the facts. . . . Men are regarded as different at birth: the differences being due to the manner in which in past lives they have built up their nature through the action of the law of karma. Owing to these differences they are fit for particular positions in the State. . . . Thus there is a basis for a hierarchical form of social organization. . . . This does not necessitate any artificial restrictions and is no justification for the pernicious attitudes and practices too often found in the Indian caste system.

"Reincarnation and Karma, Their Value to the
Individual and the State," Aryan Path, Oct. 1936

John Middleton Murry (1889-1957)

AUTHOR AND JOURNALIST

The doctrine of Reincarnation is one of the great historical solutions to the problems which Life sets to the human imagination. It is an answer to the deep desire of the spiritually awakened soul for divine justice . . . for an order of existence in which the suffering and apparent injustice of this world shall be abolished, and . . . for an opportunity of self-redemption and self-purification, not so much from what is generally called "sin," as from the spiritual lethargy which appears to be a condition of continued physical existence itself. . . .

The doctrine of Reincarnation, as I understand it, is an attempt to declare the final triumph of the spiritual life. If we imagine . . . that no human soul is perdurably doomed, we must needs have a religious system which offers the opportunity of redemption to all, and *continues to offer it until the redemption of all is accomplished.* Those who are now blind to the necessity of the spiritual life must journey on till their eyes are at last opened. And there is no denying that the doctrine of Reincarnation declares this in a form acceptable to the ordinary imagination.

"Reasonableness and Practicality of Reincarnation"
Aryan Path, June 1938

Aldous Huxley (1894-   )

The eschatologists of the Orient affirm that there are certain posthumous conditions in which meritorious souls are capable of advancing from a heaven of happy personal survival to genuine immortality in union with the timeless, eternal Godhead. And, of course, there is also the possibility (indeed, for most individuals, the necessity) of returning to some form of embodied life, in which the advance towards complete beatification, or deliverance through enlightenment, can be continued. . . .

Orthodox Christian doctrine does not admit the possibility, either in the posthumous state or in some other embodiment, of any further growth towards the ultimate perfection of a total union with the Godhead. But in the Hindu and Buddhist versions of the Perennial Philosophy the divine mercy is matched by the divine patience: both are infinite. For oriental theologians there is no eternal damnation; there are only purgatories and then an indefinite series of second chances to go forward towards not only man's, but the whole creation's final end—total reunion with the Ground of all being. . . .

In the Vedanta cosmology there is, over and above the Atman or spiritual self, identical with the divine Ground, something in the nature of a soul that reincarnates in a gross or subtle body, or manifests itself in some incorporeal state. This soul is not the personality of the defunct, but rather the particularized I—consciousness out of which a personality arises. . . . Either one of these conceptions [Hindu or Buddhist] is logically self-consistent and can be made to "save the appearances"—in other words, to fit the odd and obscure facts of psychical research.

The Perennial Philosophy

A. C. Ewing (1899-   )

[*Professor Ewing is well known for his work at Cambridge University, having been Lecturer in Moral Science for many years, and now teaches philosophy there. In an article in* The Aryan Path *for February, 1957, entitled "The Philosophy of McTaggart, with Special Reference to the Doctrine of Reincarnation," Professor Ewing concludes with some of his own ideas on rebirth:*]

A common objection made by Christians to the belief in reincarnation [is] on account of its alleged bad effects. It is said that the belief has commonly induced people . . . to be unsympathetic towards those suffering misfortune and to do little to help them because it was supposed that their misfortune was only a punishment for sins in a former life and that, if one did anything to alleviate it, the victim would only be punished in some other fashion.

Any such evil effects would be due not to the belief in reincarnation as such but to the further belief that one's good or bad fortune was proportioned to one's previous goodness or badness. . . . It may indeed be doubted whether there is any meaning in the conception of an exact proportion between such incommensurables as goodness and happiness, sin and suffering, and whether there is not an unworthy mercantile flavour about the conception. A universe in which there was a strict proportion between moral goodness and happiness, moral badness and unhappiness, would be one in which there could be ultimately no righteous self-sacrifice. . . .

Granting previous lives, it would seem . . . plausible to suppose that the cases where good people live in a specially unhappy environment were either cases of voluntary choice before birth. . . . for the same kind of motives as have made exceptionally altruistic people go to live in slums or work among lepers . . . or cases where it was necessary for his own sake to suffer . . . because his faults . . . were of such a kind as to necessitate a more painful route to salvation.*

· B R I T I S H   P O E T S ·

Taliesin (sixth century)

WELSH BARD

Knowest thou what thou art
In the hour of sleep—
A mere body, a mere soul—
Or a secret retreat of light? . . .
I marvel that in their books

---

* [Two ancient aphorisms on Karma seem appropriate to quote here in connection with several ideas mentioned above: "Karmic causes already set in motion must be allowed to sweep on until exhausted, but this permits no man to refuse to help his fellows and every sentient being." "No man but a sage or true seer can judge another's Karma. Hence while each receives his deserts, appearances may deceive, and birth into poverty or heavy trial may not be punishment for bad Karma, for Egos continually incarnate into poor surroundings where they experience difficulties and trials which are for the discipline of the Ego and result in strength, fortitude, and sympathy." Eds.]

They know not with certainty
The properties of the soul;
Of what form are its members;
In what part, and when, it takes up its abode,
Or by what wind or stream it is supplied.

* * *

I have been in many shapes before I attained a
    congenial form . . .
There is nothing in which I have not been.

* * *

I was with my Lord in the highest sphere
On the fall of Lucifer into the depth of hell;
I have borne a banner before Alexander. . . .
I am a wonder whose origin is not known.
I have been in Asia with Noah in the ark,
I have seen the destruction of Sodom and
    Gomorra. . . .
I shall be until the doom on the face of the
    earth. . . .
I was originally little Gwion,
And at length I am Taliesin.

Edmund Spenser (1552-1599)

So every spirit, as it is more pure,
And hath in it the more of heavenly light,
So it the fairer body doth procure
To habit in, and it more fairly dight
With cheerful grace and amiable sight:
For of the soul the body form doth take:
For soul is form, and doth the body make. . . .
               A Hymn in Honour of Beauty

William Shakespeare (1564-1616)

[See index for other quotations on metempsychosis]

If there be nothing new, but that which is
Hath been before, how are our brains beguiled,

Which laboring for invention, bears amiss
The second burthen [bearing] of a former child!
O, that record could with a backward look,
Even of five hundred courses of the sun,
Show me your image in some antique book,
Since mind at first in character was done!
That I might see what the old world would say
To this composed wonder of your frame;
Whether we are mended, or whether better they,
Or whether revolution be the same.
     O, sure I am, the wits of former days
       To subjects worse have been given admiring praise.

Sonnet 59

    No, no, I am but shadow of myself:
    You are deceiv'd, my substance is not here;
    For what you see is but the smallest part
    And . . . were the whole frame here,
    It is of such a spacious lofty pitch,
    Your roof were not sufficient to contain it.

King Henry VI, Act 2, Scene 3

John Donne (1573-1631)

I sing the progress of a deathless soul,
Whom fate, which God made, but doth not control,
Placed in most shapes. . . .

For though through many straits and lands I roam,
I launch at Paradise, and I sail towards home;
The course I there began, shall here be stay'd,
Sails hoisted there, struck here, and anchors laid
    In Thames, which were at Tigris, and Euphrates weigh'd.

For the great soul which here amongst us now
Doth dwell, and moves that hand, and tongue, and brow. . . .
This soul, to whom Luther and Mahomet were
Prisons of flesh; this soul which oft did tear
And mend the wracks of th' Empire, and late Rome,

And lived when every great change did come,
    Had first in Paradise, a low, but fatal room. . . .
The Progress of the Soul

John Milton (1608-1674)

[Milton imbibed from his college friend Dr. Henry More an early fondness for Plato. In the extracts that follow, the Platonic influence seems evident:]

    The soul grows clotted by contagion,
    Imbodies and embrutes till she quite lose
    The divine property of her first being. . . .
Comus

  Wert thou that just maid who once before
Forsook the hated Earth, O tell me sooth,
And cam'st again to visit us once more?
Or wert thou that sweet smiling youth?
    Or any other of that heavenly brood
Let down in cloudy throne to do the world some good?

Or wert thou of the golden-winged host,
Who, having clad thyself in human weed,
To earth from thy prefixed seat didst post,
And after short abode fly back with speed
As if to show what creatures heaven doth breed;
    Thereby to set the hearts of men on fire,
To scorn the sordid world and unto heaven aspire?
On the Death of a Fair Infant

Andrew Marvell (1621-1678)

    See how the orient dew,
  Shed from the bosom of the morn
    Into the blowing roses. . . .
    Shines with a mournful light,
      Like its own tear,
  Because so long divided from its sphere.
    Restless it rolls and insecure,

Trembling lest it grow impure,
Till the warm sun pities its pain
And to the skies exhales it back again.
So the soul, that drop, that ray
Of the clear fountain of eternal day,
Could it within the human flower be seen,
Lamenting still its former height,
Shuns the sweet flowers and the radiant green,
And recollecting its own light
Does in its pure and circling thoughts express
The greater heaven in the heaven less.

A Drop of Dew

Henry Vaughan (1622-1695)

Happy those early days when I
Shined in my angel-infancy,
Before I understood this place
Appointed for my second race . . .
Oh, how I long to travel back
And tread again that ancient track!
That I might once more reach that plain
Where first I left my glorious train. . . .
But ah! my soul with too much stay
Is drunk and staggers in the way.
Some men a forward motion love,
But I by backward steps would move,
And when this dust falls to the urn,
In that state I came return.

The Retreat

John Dryden (1631-1700)

If thy pre-existing soul
Was form'd at first with myriads more,
It did through all the mighty poets roll
Who Greek or Latin laurels wore,
And was that Sappho last, which once it was before.
If so, then cease thy flight, O heaven-born mind!

Thou hast no dross to purge from thy rich ore:
  Nor can thy soul a fairer mansion find,
Than was the beauteous frame she left behind:
  Return to fill or mend the choir of thy celestial kind.

Ode to the Memory of Mrs. Anne Killigrew

Joseph Addison (1672-1719)

It must be so,—Plato, thou reasonest well!
Else whence this pleasing hope, this fond desire,
This longing after immortality?
Or whence this secret dread, and inward horror
Of falling into naught? Why shrinks the soul
Back on herself, and startles at destruction?
'Tis the divinity that stirs within us. . . .

Eternity—thou pleasing, dreadful thought,
Through what variety of untried being,
Through what new scenes and dangers must we pass?
The wide, th' unbounded prospect lies before me,
But shadows, clouds, and darkness rest upon it.

. . . . I shall never die.
The soul, secure in her existence, smiles
At the drawn dagger, and defies its point.
The stars shall fade away, the sun himself
Grow dim with age, and Nature sink in years;
But thou shall flourish in immortal youth,
Unhurt amidst the war of elements,
The wreck of matter, and the crush of worlds.

Cato, Act V, Scene 1

Edward Young (1683-1765)

Look nature through; 'tis revolution all,
All change; no death. Day follows night, and night
The dying day; stars rise and set, and set and rise.
Earth takes the example. All to reflourish fades

As in a wheel; all sinks to reascend;
Emblems of man, who passes, not expires.

* * *

Seems it strange that thou shouldst live forever?
Is it less strange that thou shouldst live at all?
This is a miracle; and that no more.

Night Thoughts

Alexander Pope (1688-1744)

The strong connections, nice dependencies,
Graduations just, has thy pervading soul
Looked through. . . .
Where all must full or not coherent be
And all that rise, rise in due degree. . . .
All are but parts of one stupendous whole
Whose body Nature is, and God the soul;
That, changed through all, and yet in all the
same. . . .

Essay on Man

William Blake (1757-1827)

In my brain are studies and chambers filled with books and pictures of old which I wrote and painted in ages of eternity before my mortal life; and these works are the delight and study of archangels.

You, O dear Flaxman, are a sublime archangel, my friend and companion from eternity. I look back into the regions of reminiscence and behold our ancient days before this earth appeared and its vegetative mortality to my mortal vegetated eyes. I see our houses of eternity which can never be separated, though our mortal vehicles should stand at the remotest corners of heaven from each other.

Letter to John Flaxman, the Sculptor

[Man] stores his thoughts
As in store-houses in his memory. He regulates the forms
Of all beneath and all above . . . he rises to the sun,
And to the planets of the night, and to the stars that gild

The zodiacs, and the stars that sullen stand to North and South;
He touches the remotest pole, and in the centre weeps
That man should labour and sorrow, and learn and forget,
    and return
To the dark valley whence he came, and begin his labours anew.
In pain he sighs, in pain he labours in his universe. . . .
And in cries of birth and in the groans of death his voice
Is heard throughout the universe. Wherever a grass grows,
Or a leaf buds, the Eternal Man is seen, is heard, is felt,
And all his sorrows, till he reassumes his ancient bliss.

Vala

William Wordsworth (1770-1850)

Our birth is but a sleep and a forgetting;
The soul that rises with us, our life's star,
    Hath had elsewhere its setting,
      And cometh from afar.
    Not in entire forgetfulness
    And not in utter nakedness
But trailing clouds of glory do we come
    From God who is our home.
Heaven lies about us in our infancy;
Shades of the prison house begin to close
    Upon the growing boy;
But he beholds the light, and whence it flows
    He sees it in his joy.
The youth who daily farther from the East
Must travel, still is nature's priest,
    And by the vision splendid
    Is on his way attended.
At length the man perceives it die away
And fade into the light of common day.

Intimations of Immortality from
Recollections of Early Childhood

[An article in the weekly London periodical The Spectator for December 10, 1927, p. 1041, stated: "There did not seem, until recently, to be any definite reference to the belief [of reincarnation] in Wordsworth's poems, for well-known lines, 'Our birth is but a sleep and a forgetting,' are a statement of the soul's pre-existence, rather than of its repeated returns to earth. But the newly discovered poem in [his sister] Dorothy Wordsworth's handwriting (the MS. of which is to be sold at Sotheby's on December 15th) provides remarkable evidence of the poet's interest in this age-old doctrine. The lines are addressed to an infant, and begin as follows:"]

> Oh, sweet new-comer to the changeful earth,
> If, as some darkling seers have boldly guessed,
> Thou hadst a being and a human birth,
> And wert erewhile by human parents blessed,
> Long, long before thy present mother pressed
> Thee, helpless stranger, to her fostering breast. . . .

Samuel Coleridge (1772-1834)

[A 25-page article entitled "Coleridge—Metempsychosis . . ." by Irene H. Chayes, appearing in the Journal of English Literary History (Dec. 1958) published by Johns Hopkins University, traces Coleridge's interest in reincarnation to the works of two authors he was studying when the following poem was written in September, 1796, namely, the writings of Chevalier Ramsay and Thomas Taylor, both of whom are quoted in this Anthology:]

> Oft o'er my brain does that strange fancy roll
>   Which makes the present (while the flash doth last)
>   Seem a mere semblance of some unknown past,
> Mixed with such feelings as perplex the soul
> Self-questioned in her sleep: and some have said
>   We lived, ere yet this fleshy robe we wore.
>   O my sweet Baby! when I reach my door
> If heavy looks should tell me thou art dead
> (As sometimes, thro' excess of hope, I fear)
> I think that I should struggle to believe
> Thou wert a Spirit to this nether sphere
> Sentenc'd for some more venial crime to grieve;
> Didst scream, then spring to meet Heaven's quick reprieve,
> While we wept idly o'er thy little bier.

> *On a Homeward Journey upon*
> *Hearing of the Birth of a Son*

Robert Southey (1774-1843)

POET LAUREATE

I have a strong and lively faith in a state of continued consciousness from this stage of existence, and that we shall recover the consciousness of some lower stages through which we may previously have passed seems to me not impossible. . . . The system of progressive existence seems, of all others, the most benevolent; and all that we do understand is so wise and so good, and all we do or do not, so perfectly and overwhelmingly wonderful, that the most benevolent system is the most probable.

Letters

John Leyden (1775-1811)

> Ah, sure, as Hindoo legends tell,
> When music's tones the bosom swell
>   The scenes of former life return,
> Ere sunk beneath the morning star,
> We left our parent climes afar,
>   Immured in mortal forms to mourn.
> *Ode to Scottish Music*

George Gordon, Lord Byron (1788-1824)

I feel my immortality o'ersweep all pains, all tears, all times, all fears; and peal, like the eternal thunders of the deep, into my ears this truth—thou livest forever!*

Percy Bysshe Shelley (1792-1822)

[In Dowden's Life of Shelley, Vol. I, the following anecdote of the poet is quoted from his friend Hogg:]

---

* *Useful Quotations*, comp. Tryon Edwards (Grosset & Dunlap) p. 278.

One morning we had been reading Plato together so diligently that the usual hour of exercise passed away unperceived. We sallied forth hastily to take the air for half an hour before dinner. In the middle of Magdalen Bridge we met a woman with a child in her arms. Shelley was more attentive at that instant to our conduct in a life that was past or to come than to a decorous regulation of his behavior. . . . With abrupt dexterity he caught hold of the child. The mother . . . held it fast by its long train.

"Will your baby tell us anything about pre-existence, madam?" he asked in a piercing voice and with a wistful look. The mother made no answer, but perceiving that Shelley's object was not murderous, but altogether harmless, she . . . relaxed her hold. "Will your baby tell us anything about pre-existence, madam?" he repeated, with unabated earnestness. "He cannot speak, sir," said the mother seriously.

"Worse, worse," cried Shelley with an air of disappointment. . . . "But surely the babe can speak if he will. . . . He may fancy that he cannot, but it is only a silly whim. He cannot have forgotten the use of speech in so short a time. The thing is absolutely impossible" . . .

Shelley sighed as we walked on. "How provokingly close are these new-born babes! but it is not the less certain, notwithstanding the cunning attempts to conceal the truth, that all knowledge is reminiscence. The doctrine is far more ancient than the times of Plato, and as old as the venerable allegory that the muses are the daughters of memory; not one of the muses was ever said to be the child of invention."

❁

[*Shelley in his brief essay "On a Future State" asks: "Have we existed before birth? It is difficult to conceive the possibility of this." Could there exist "a principle or substance which escapes the observation of the chemist and anatomist" and pre-exists our birth?*]

It certainly *may be*; though it is sufficiently unphilosophical to allege the possibility of an opinion as a proof of its truth. Does it see, hear, feel, before its combination with those organs on which sensation depends? Does it reason, imagine, apprehend . . . ? If there are no reasons to suppose that we have existed before that period at which our existence apparently commences, then there are no grounds for the supposition that we shall continue to exist after our existence has apparently ceased. So far as thought and life is concerned, the same will take place with regard to us individually considered, after death, as had taken place before our birth.

❁

Worlds on worlds are rolling ever
From creation to decay,
Like the bubbles on a river,
Sparkling, bursting, borne away.
But they are still immortal
Who, through birth's orient portal
And death's dark chasm hurrying to and fro,
Clothe their unceasing flight
In the brief dust and light
Gathered around their chariots as they go;
New shapes they still may weave,
New gods, new laws receive:
Bright or dim are they as the robes they last
On Death's bare ribs had cast.

Hellas

[Some of Shelley's other poems on rebirth are "Ariel to Miranda" and
"Queen Mab."]

Elizabeth Barrett Browning (1806-1861)

The cygnet finds the water, but the man
Is born in ignorance of his element,
And feels out, blind at first, disorganized
. . . . Let who says
"The soul's a clean white paper," rather say
A palimpsest, a prophet's holograph,
Defiled, erased, and covered by a monk's—
The apocalypse, by a Longus! poring on
Which obscene text, we may discern perhaps
Some fair, fine trace of what was written once,
Some upstroke of an alpha and omega.

Aurora Leigh

Alfred, Lord Tennyson (1809-1892)

Out of the deep, my child, out of the deep,
Where all that was to be, in all that was,

Whirled for a million aeons thro' the vast
Waste dawn of multitudinous eddying light—
Out of the deep, my child, out of the deep,
Thro' all this changing world of changeless law,
And every phase of every heightening life,
And nine long months of ante-natal gloom,
Thou comest.

De Profundis

As when with downcast eyes we muse and brood
And ebb into a former life, or seem
To lapse far back in a confusèd dream.
To states of mystical similitude,
If one but speaks or hems or stirs a chair
Ever the wonder waxeth more and more,
So that we say, all this hath been before,
All this *hath* been, I know not when or where:—
So, friend, when first I looked upon your face,
Our thoughts gave answer, each to each, so true,
Opposed mirrors each reflecting each—
Although I knew not in what time or place,
Methought that I had often met with you,
And each had lived in other's mind and speech.

Early Sonnet No. 1

Yet how should I for certain hold
Because my memory is so cold,
That I *first* was in human mould?

It may be that no life is found
Which only to one engine bound
Falls off, but cycles always round.

But, if I lapsed from nobler place,
Some legend of a fallen race
Alone might hint of my disgrace.

Or, if through lower lives I came—
Tho' all experience past became
Consolidate in mind and frame—

I might forget my weaker lot;
For is not our first year forgot?
The haunts of memory echo not.
The Two Voices

Richard Monckton Milnes (1809-1885)

(LORD HOUGHTON)

As in that world of Dream whose mystic shades
Are cast by still more mystic substances,
We ofttimes have an unreflecting sense,
A silent consciousness of some things past,
So clear that we can wholly comprehend
Others of which they are a part. . . .

        Thus in the dream,
Our universal Dream, of Mortal Life,
The incidents of an anterior dream
Or it may be, Existence, noiselessly intrude
Into the daily flow of earthly things,
Instincts of good—immediate sympathies,
Places come at by chance, that claim at once
An old acquaintance—single random looks
That bare a stranger's bosom to our eyes;
We *know* these things are so, we ask not why,
But act and follow as the Dream goes on.
Returning Dreams

Martin Tupper (1810-1889)

Have ye not confessed to a feeling, a consciousness
    strange and vague,
That ye have gone this way before, and walk again your
    daily life. . . .
Hath not at times some recent friend looked out, an
    old familiar,
Some newest circumstance or place teemed as with
    ancient memories?

A startling sudden flash lighteth up all for an instant,
And then it is quenched, as in darkness, and leaveth the
    cold spirit trembling.
Proverbial Philosophy: On Memory

Robert Browning (1812-1889)

At times I almost dream
I too have spent a life the sages' way,
And tread once more familiar paths. Perchance
I perished in an arrogant self-reliance
An age ago; and in that act, a prayer
For one more chance went up so earnest, so
Instinct with better light let in by Death,
That life was blotted out—not so completely
But scattered wrecks enough of it remain,
Dim memories; as now, when seems once more
The goal in sight again. . . .
Paracelsus

I shall never, in the years remaining,
Paint you pictures, no, nor carve you statues.
This of verse alone one life allows me;
Other heights in other lives, God willing.
One Word More

Delayed it may be for more lives yet
    Through worlds I must traverse, not a few—
Much is to learn and much to forget
    Ere the time be come for taking you. . . .
Evelyn Hope

There's a fancy some lean to and others hate—
    That, when this life is ended, begins
New work for the soul in another state,
    Where it strives and gets weary, loses and wins:
Where the strong and the weak, this world's congeries,
    Repeat in large what they practised in small,
Through life after life in unlimited series;
    Only the scale's changed, that's all. . . .
Old Pictures in Florence

Philip James Bailey (1816-1902)

Who dreams not life more yearful than the hours
Since first into this world he wept his way
Erreth much, may be. Called of God, man's soul
In patriarchal periods, comet-like,
Ranges, perchance, all spheres successive, and in each
With nobler powers endowed and senses new. . . .
The Mystic

Arthur H. Clough (1819-1861)

E'en after utmost interval of pause,
What revolutions must have passed, before
The great celestial cycles shall restore
The starry sign whose present hour is gone. . . .
If in this human complex there be aught
Not lost in death, as not in birth acquired. . . .
Thou yet, we think, somewhere still art.
Sonnets on the Thought of Death

Matthew Arnold (1822-1888)

And then we shall unwillingly return
Back to this meadow of calamity,
This uncongenial place, this human life;
And in our individual human state
Go through the sad probation all again,
To see if we will poise our life at last,
To see if we will now at last be true
To our own only true deep-buried selves,
Being one with which we are one with the whole
    world;
Or whether we will once more fall away
Into some bondage of the flesh or mind,
Some slough of sense, or some fantastic maze
Forg'd by the imperious lonely Thinking-Power. . . .
Empedocles on Etna

Dante Gabriel Rossetti (1828-1882)

PAINTER AND POET

I have been here before,
But when or how I cannot tell;
I know the grass beyond the door,
The sweet keen smell,
The sighing sound, the lights around the shore.
You have been mine before,—
How long ago I may not know:
But just when at that swallow's soar
Your neck turned so,
Some veil did fall,—I knew it all of yore.

Sudden Light

[*Rossetti has also written a reincarnation story entitled "St. Agnes of Intercession": Rossetti's Collected Works, Vol. I, p. 399.*]

Sir Edwin Arnold (1832-1904)

Tis but as when one layeth
His worn out robes away,
And, taking new ones, sayeth
"These will I wear today!"
So putteth by the Spirit
Lightly its garb of flesh,
And passeth to inherit
A residence afresh. . . .

The Song Celestial
The Bhagavad-Gita

If there has been a boundless Past leading to this odd little present, the individual, it is clear, remembers nothing. Either he was not; or he lived unconscious; or he was conscious, but forgets. It may be he always lived, and inwardly knows it, but now "disremembers;" for it is notable that none of us can recall the first year of our human existence, though we were certainly then alive. . . .

[Quoting a gifted correspondent:] "Such expressions as 'immortality,' [no *death*] as we understand and use them, do not merely fail to cover the

ground; they are but half-thoughts—like the half of a man cloven in two—
unless complemented by corresponding terms like 'in-natality' [no *birth*].
We think of 'eternal life' as something which begins but does not end; but
the fallacy of this becomes evident if we try to think conversely of something
'eternal' which ends though it does not begin."

Death and Afterwards

Sir Lewis Morris (1833-1907)

There is an end
Of Wrong and Death and Hell! When the long wear
Of Time and Suffering has effaced the stain
Ingrown upon the soul, and the cleansed spirit,
Long ages floating on the wandering winds
Or rolling deeps of Space, renews itself
And doth regain its dwelling. . . .

Time calls and Change
Commands both men and gods, and speeds us on
We know not whither; but the old earth smiles
Spring after Spring, and the seed bursts again
Out of its prison mould, and the dead lives
Renew themselves, and rise aloft and soar
And are transformed, clothing themselves with change
Till the last change be done.

The Epic of Hades

Algernon Charles Swinburne (1837-1909)

I am that which began;
Out of me the years roll;
Out of me God and man;
I am equal and whole:
God changes, and man, and the form of them bodily;
I am the soul.

Before ever land was,
Before ever the sea,
Or soft hair of the grass,

Or fair limbs of the tree,
Or the flesh-coloured fruit of my branches, I was,
    and thy soul was in me. . . .

Hertha

By the waters of Babylon we sat down and wept,
    Remembering thee,
That for ages of agony hast endured, and slept,
    and wouldst not see. . . .

Super Flumina Babylonis

F. W. H. Myers (1843-1901)

POET, ESSAYIST, AND PSYCHIC RESEARCHER

The simple fact that [reincarnation] was probably the opinion both of
Plato and of Virgil shows that there is nothing here which is alien to the best
reason or to the highest instincts of men. Nor, indeed, is it easy to realise any
theory of the *direct creation* of spirits at such different stages of advancement as those which enter upon the earth in the guise of mortal man. There
must, one feels, be some kind of continuity—some form of spiritual Past.
Yet for reincarnation there is at present no valid evidence.

Human Personality and Its
Survival of Bodily Death

When from that world ere death and birth
    He sought the stern descending way,
Perfecting on our darkened earth
    His spirit, citizen of day—
Guessed he the pain, the lonely years . . . ?

Sun, star, and space, and dark and day,
    Shall vanish in a vaster glow;
Souls shall climb fast their age-long way,
    With all to conquer, all to know:
But thou, true Heart, for aye shalt keep
    Thy loyal faith, thine ancient flame;
Be stilled an hour, and stir from sleep
    Reborn, rerisen, and yet the same.

To Tennyson

William Ernest Henley (1849-1903)

Or ever the knightly years were gone
    With the old world to the grave,
I was a King in Babylon
    And you were a Christian Slave

I saw, I took, I cast you by,
    I bent and broke your pride. . . .

And a myriad suns have set and shone
    Since then upon the grave
Decreed by the King in Babylon
    To her that had been his Slave.

The pride I trampled is now my scathe,
    For it tramples me again.
The old resentment lasts like death,
    For you love, yet you refrain.
I break my heart on your hard unfaith,
    And I break my heart in vain. . . .
                  To W. A.

Was I a Samurai renowned,
Two-sworded, fierce, immense of bow?
A histrion angular and profound?
A priest? a porter?—Child, although
I have forgotten clean, I know
That in the shade of Fujisan,
What time the cherry-orchards blow,
I loved you once in old Japan. . . .
Dear, 'twas a dozen lives ago;
But that I was a lucky man
The Toyokuni here will show:
I loved you—once—in old Japan.
          Ballade of a Toyokuni Colour-Print

Margaret L. Woods (1856-1945)

I shall return to thee,
Earth, O dearest
Mother of mine!
I who have loved thee with joy everlasting,
Endless discovery, newness diurnal. . . .
Now I depart. . . .
I shall still blindly fumble and wait
Till the true door open, the true voice call again;
And back to the human high estate,
Back to the whole of the soul, resurgent,
O Earth! O dearest! I shall return,
I shall return to thee, Earth, my mother.

Vale Atque Ave

H. W. Nevinson (1856-1941)

There, crumbling o'er a sculptured tomb, he found
    The rusted armour he himself did wear,
Battling, long since at Troy, and underground
    Lay his own body, long since crumbling there. . . .

Why waste a thought on long-forgotten men,
    Or spell the record of those fading lines?
Sweet life is sweeter to me now than then,
    And round my heart a nobler armour shines.

Pythagoras at Argos

William Sharp (1856-1905)

(FIONA MACLEOD), SCOTTISH POET

Old memories are mine once more,
I see strange lives I lived of yore;
With dimmed sight see I far-off things,
I feel the breath of bygone springs,
And ringing strangely in mine ears
I hear old laughter, alien tears. . . .

None sees the slow sure upward sweep
By which the soul from life-depths deep
Ascends—unless, mayhap, when free
With each new death we backward see
The long perspective of our race,
Our multitudinous past lives trace. . . .

Each death is but a birth, a change—
Each soul through myriad by-ways strange,
Through birth and death, doth upward range.

A Record

Students of Gaelic will remember that Tuan [who] gave out the same ancient wisdom as Pythagoras gave . . . or as Empedocles gave . . . remembered his many transformations. . . . In like manner . . . the greatest of Greek mages declared that again and again he had lived in a changed body, as old raiment discarded or new raiment donned. . . . I think the soul knows. I think the soul remembers. I think that intuition is divine and unshakable. . . . I think we have travelled a long way, and have forgotten much, and continually forget more and more. The secret road of the soul is a long road.

The Winged Destiny

A. E. Waite (1857-1942)

'Tis scarcely true that souls come naked down
To take abode up in this earthly town,
Or naked pass—all that they wear denied:
We enter slip-shod and with clothes awry,
And we take with us much that by and by
May prove no easy task to put aside.

Collected Poems

Francis Thompson (1859-1907)

All dies:
Lo how all dies! O Seer,
And all things too arise:
All dies, and all is born;

But each resurgent morn, behold more
near the Perfect Morn. . . .
Night of Forebeing

Laurence Binyon (1869-1943)

POET AND ART HISTORIAN

Where is that world that I am fallen from? . . .
Ah, surely I was rather native there
Where all desires were lovely. . . .
Oh, we go shrouded from ourselves, and hide
The soul from its own splendour, and encrust
The virgin sense with thinking. Then some chance
Moment reveals us: we are deified,
Feeling and seeing; gold gleams from the rust;
And, marvelling at our lost inheritance,
We breathe the air of beauty. . . .

Unsated Memory

John Masefield (1878-   )

POET LAUREATE

I held that when a person dies
His soul returns again to earth;
Arrayed in some new flesh-disguise,
Another mother gives him birth.
With sturdier limbs and brighter brain
The old soul takes the road again.

Such was my belief and trust;
This hand, this hand that holds the pen,
Has many a hundred times been dust
And turned, as dust, to dust again;
These eyes of mind have blinked and shone
In Thebes, in Troy, in Babylon. . . .

I know that in my lives to be
My sorry heart will ache and burn,
And worship unavailingly
The woman whom I used to spurn,

And shake to see another have
The love I spurned, the love she gave.

And I shall know, in angry words,
In gibes, and mocks, and many a tear,
A carrion flock of homing-birds,
The gibes and scorns I uttered here.
The brave word that I failed to speak
Will brand me dastard on the cheek.

And as I wander on the roads
I shall be helped and healed and blessed;
Kind words shall cheer and be as goads
To urge to heights before unguessed.
My road shall be the road I made,
All that I gave shall be repaid.

So shall I fight, so shall I tread,
In this long war beneath the stars;
So shall a glory wreathe my head,
So shall I faint and show the scars,
Until this case, this clogging mould,
Be smithied all to kingly gold.

A Creed

John Drinkwater (1882-1937)

Long ere from immanent silence leapt
Obedient hands and fashioning will,
The giant god within us slept,
And dreamt of seasons to fulfil
The shaping of our souls that still
Expectant earthward vigil kept;
Our wisdom grew from secrets drawn
From that far-off dim-memoried dawn.

The Fires of God

Frances Cornford (1886-   )

I laid me down upon the shore
And dreamed a little space;
I heard the great waves break and roar;
The sun was on my face. . . .

And so my dream began.
How all of this had been before:
How ages far away
I lay on some forgotten shore
As here I lie to-day. . . .

I have forgotten whence I came,
Or what my home might be,
Or by what strange and savage name
I called that thundering sea.

I only know the sun shone down
As still it shines to-day,
And in my fingers long and brown
The little pebbles lay.

Pre-existence

Clifford Bax (1886-   )

[This poem, "The School of Plato," was written after Clifford Bax saw the great fresco, L'Ecole de Platon of Jean Delville:]

While I gaze
I seem to watch unfold
Some long-forgotten life I lived of old
In beauty-worshipping Athenian days. . . .

O godlike voice of wisdom! Master-Sage!
Break from the dream that binds thee now; return
Here to this earth and all the hearts that yearn.
The world is waiting, worn: redeem this age—
Ah, quench the bitter thirst with which we burn;

And with thy wisdom make us re-aspire
  To all things high and beautiful and strong
  Bring back the joy that we have lost so long—
Teach us to love, and with thy spirit of fire
  Cleanse the whole world;—or, if this may not be,
Gather about thyself some ardent few
That seek the Good, the True,
  As in those garden-lawns that here we see,
And once, two thousand years ago, we knew.

[Other reincarnation poems of this poet are "Threnody on the Death of Swinburne," "The Traveller's Tale," and "The Meaning of Man."]

· BRITISH NOVELISTS AND DRAMATISTS ·

Henry Fielding (1707-1754)

Fielding's novel, A Journey from This World to the Next, narrates the tale of one who has just died. En route to heaven numerous souls are met returning to earth life. In heaven he finds several historically famous characters, including Julian, the "Apostate," and is amazed to see the latter there thinking he surely would have been entitled to the bottomless pit.

He told me, that several lies had been raised on him in his former capacity, nor was he so bad a man as he had been represented. However, he had been denied admittance [to Elysium], and forced to undergo subsequent pilgrimages on earth.

A long list of these incarnations is given with details thereof.

Sir Walter Scott (1771-1832)

I cannot, I am sure, tell if it is worth marking down, that yesterday, at dinner time, I was strangely haunted by what I would call the sense of pre-existence, viz. a confused idea that nothing that passed was said for the first time; that the same topics had been discussed and the same persons had stated the same opinions on them. . . . The sensation was so strong as to resemble what is called a *mirage* in the desert. . . . It was very distressing yesterday, and brought to my mind the fancies of Bishop Berkeley about an ideal world. There was a vile sense of unreality in all I said or did.

Diary Entry for Feb. 17, 1828

[*Years earlier, in one of his first novels, the same experience is referred to:*]

Why is it that some scenes awaken thoughts which belong, as it were, to dreams of early and shadowy recollections, such as old Brahmin moonshine would have ascribed to a state of previous existence? How often do we find ourselves in society which we have never before met, and yet feel impressed with a mysterious and ill-defined consciousness that neither the scene nor the speakers nor the subject are entirely new; nay, feel as if we could anticipate that part of the conversation which has not yet taken place.

Guy Mannering

Bulwer-Lytton (1803-1873)

Why cheat ourselves with words so vague as life and death! What is the difference? At most, the entrance in and the departure from one scene in our wide career. How many scenes are left to us! We do but hasten our journey, not close it.

Godolphin

Eternity may be but an endless series of those migrations which men call deaths, abandonments of home after home, ever to fairer scenes and loftier heights. Age after age the spirit may shift its tent, fated not to rest in the dull Elysium of the heathen, but carrying with it evermore its two elements, activity and desire.

Charles Dickens (1812-1870)

We have all some experience of a feeling, that comes over us occasionally, of what we are saying and doing having been said and done before, in a remote time—of our being surrounded, dim ages ago, by the same faces, objects, and circumstances—of our knowing perfectly what will be said next, as if we suddenly remembered it!

David Copperfield

At sunset, when I was walking on alone, while the horses rested, I arrived upon a little scene, which, by one of those singular mental operations of which we are all conscious, seemed perfectly familiar to me, and which I see distinctly now. . . . In the foreground was a group of silent peasant girls, leaning over the parapet of the little bridge [in Ferrara] . . . In the distance a deep dell; the shadow of an approaching night on everything. If I had been murdered there in some former life I could not have seemed to remember the place more thoroughly, or with more emphatic chilling of the blood; and the real remembrance of it acquired in that minute is so strengthened by the imaginary recollection that I hardly think I could forget it.

Pictures from Italy

George Eliot (1819-1880)

Perhaps I lived before
In some strange world where first my soul was shaped,
And all this passionate love, and joy, and pain,
That come, I know not whence, and sway my deeds,
Are old imperious memories, blind yet strong,
That this world stirs within me. . . .

The Spanish Gypsy

Our deeds still travel with us from afar, and what we have been makes us what we are.

George Macdonald (1824-1905)
SCOTCH NOVELIST AND POET

It may be centuries of ages before a man comes to see a truth—ages of strife, of effort, of aspiration. . . . A thousand stages, each in itself all but valueless, are of inestimable worth as the necessary and connected gradations of an infinite progress. . . . We cannot yet have learned all that we are meant to learn through the body. How much of the teaching even of this world can the most diligent and most favoured man have exhausted before he is called upon to leave it! Is all that remains to be lost?

Unspoken Sermons

Mortimer Collins (1827-1876)

WRITER AND MATHEMATICIAN

In 1874 appeared Mortimer Collins' three-volume novel, *Transmigration*, the hero of which, because of his firm belief in reincarnation in a shortly previous life, is represented as having entered this one with his memories of that earlier existence intact.

George Du Maurier (1834-1896)

... that ever-growing Conscious Power ... which is slowly, surely, painfully weaving Itself out of us and the likes of us all through the limitless Universe, and Whose coming we can but faintly foretell by the casting of Its shadow on our own slowly, surely, painfully awakening souls. ...

If anything can keep us well within the thorny path that leads to happiness and virtue, it is the certainty that those who come after us will remember having been ourselves, if only in a dream. ...

Wherefore, O reader, if you be but sound in mind and body, it most seriously behooves you ... to go forth and multiply exceedingly ... to select the very best of your kind in the opposite sex for this most precious, excellent, and blessed purpose; that all your future reincarnations (and hers), however brief, may be many.

Peter Ibbetson

Samuel Butler (1835-1902)

We commonly know that we are going to die, though we do not know that we are going to be born. But are we sure this is so? We may have had the most gloomy forebodings on this head and forgotten all about them.

Death is the dissolving a partnership, the partners to which survive and go elsewhere. It is the corruption or breaking up of that society which we have called Ourself. The corporation is at an end, both its soul and body cease as a whole, but the immortal constituents do not cease and never will.

I must have it that neither are the good rewarded nor the bad punished in a future state, but everyone must start anew quite irrespective of anything they have done here, and must try his luck again, and go on trying it again and again *ad infinitum*. Some of our lives, then, will be lucky and some unlucky.

The Note-Books of Samuel Butler

> Yet for the great bitterness of this grief,
> We three, you and he and I,
> May pass into the hearts of like true comrades hereafter,
> In whom we may weep anew and yet comfort them,
> As they too pass out, out, out into the night,
> So guide them and guard them Heaven and fare them well!

In Memoriam—to H. R. F.

Oscar Wilde (1856-1900)

> How vain and dull this common world must seem
> To such a One as thou, who shouldst have talked
> At Florence with Mirandola, or walked
> Through the cool olives of the Academe: . . .
> Ah! surely once some urn of Attic clay
> Held thy wan dust, and thou hast come again
> Back to this common world so dull and vain,
> For thou wast weary of the sunless day,
> The heavy fields of scentless asphodel. . . .

Phèdre: To Sarah-Bernhardt

Olive Schreiner (1855-1920)

It's my decided opinion that in a pre-state of existence she was a Buddhist philosopher . . . and full of contemplations, and at her rebirth she did not become quite rejuvenised or lose all her old habits; otherwise I can't account for her.

Undine

Marie Corelli (1855-1924)

(MARY MACKAY)

[Queen Victoria's favorite author, Marie Corelli, was at one time enormously popular. Allusions to the mystical and occult abound in her novels.]

I know naught of death—save that it is a heavy, dreamless sleep allotted
to over-weary mortals, wherein they gain brief rest 'twixt many lives—lives
that, like recurring dawns, rouse them anew to labour. . . . Life after
life hast thou lived. . . .

If I were certain that death was no more than a sleep, from which I
should assuredly awaken to another phase of existence—I know well enough
what I would do! . . . I would live a different life *now!* . . . so that when
the new Future dawned for me, I might not be haunted or tortured by the
remembrance of a misspent Past! . . . Thus, if we indeed possessed the
positive foreknowledge of the eternal regeneration of our lives, 'twould be
well to free them from all hindrance to perfection here—while we are still
conscious of Time and Opportunity.

Ardath: The Story of a Dead Self

George Bernard Shaw (1856-1950)

JOAN: And now tell me: shall I rise from the dead, and come back to
you a living woman? . . .

What! Must I burn again? Are none of you ready to receive me? . . .

O God that madest this beautiful earth, when will it be ready to receive
Thy saints? How long, O lord, how long?

Saint Joan

Part I   The Garden of Eden

THE SERPENT: The serpent never dies, Some day you shall see me come
out of this beautiful skin; a new snake with a new and lovelier skin. That
is birth. . . . I made the word "dead" to describe my old skin that I cast
when I am renewed. I call that renewal being born.

EVE: Born is a beautiful word.

THE SERPENT: Why not be born again and again as I am, new and beautiful
every time? . . .

Part II The Twentieth Century

SAVVY: I believe the old people are the new people, reincarnated, Frank. I suspect I am Eve. I am very fond of apples; and they always disagree with me.

CONRAD: You *are* Eve in a sense. The Eternal Life persists; only It wears out Its bodies and minds and gets new ones, like new clothes. You are only a new hat and frock on Eve.

FRANKLYN: Yes. Bodies and minds ever better fitted to carry out Its eternal pursuit.

LUBIN (with quiet scepticism): What pursuit, may one ask, Mr. Barnabas?

FRANKLYN: The pursuit of omnipotence and omniscience. Greater power and greater knowledge: these are what we are all pursuing even at the risk of our lives and the sacrifice of our pleasures. Evolution is that pursuit and nothing else. It is the path to Godhead. A man differs from a microbe only in being further on the path.

Back to Methuselah

Sir Rider Haggard (1856-1925)

The Personality which animates each one of us is immeasurably ancient, having been forged in many fires, and that, as its past is immeasurable, so will its future be . . . Unless we have lived before, or the grotesque incongruities of life are to be explained in some way unknown to us, our present existence, to my mind, resembles nothing so much as a handful of what is know as "printer's pie" cast together at hazard.

The Days of My Life

What is a span of ten thousand years, or ten times ten thousand years, in the history of time? It is as naught—it is as the mists that roll up in the sunlight; it fleeth away like an hour of sleep or a breath of the Eternal Spirit. Behold the lot of man! Certainly it shall overtake us, and we shall sleep. Certainly, too, we shall awake, and live again, and again shall sleep, and so on and on, through periods, spaces and times from aeon unto aeon, till the world is dead, and the worlds beyond the world are dead, and naught liveth save the Spirit that is Life. . . .

Time hath no power against Identity, though sleep the merciful hath blotted out the tablets of our mind, and with oblivion sealed the sorrows that else would hound us from life to life, stuffing the brain with gathered griefs till it burst in the madness of uttermost despair. . . .

She

Sir Arthur Conan Doyle (1859-1930)

When the question is asked, "Where were we before we were born?" we have a definite answer in the system of slow development by incarnation, with long intervals of spirit rest between, while otherwise we have no answer, though we must admit that it is inconceivable that we have been born in time for eternity. Existence afterwards seems to postulate existence before.

As to the natural question, "Why, then, do we not remember such existences?" we may point out that such remembrance would enormously complicate our present life, and that such existences may well form a cycle which is all clear to us when we come to the end of it, when perhaps we may see a whole rosary of lives threaded upon one personality.

The convergence of so many lines of theosophic and Eastern thought upon this one conclusion, and the explanation which it affords in the supplementary doctrine of Karma of the apparent injustice of any single life, are arguments in its favour, and so perhaps are those vague recognitions and memories which are occasionally too definite to be easily explained as atavistic impressions.

A History of Spiritualism

H. A. Vachell (1861-1955)

"Archdale has been endowed with tremendous gifts. If I believed in reincarnation, I should be willing to admit that he is 'one of the best,' that, in short, his amazing pre-eminence would indicate . . . evidence of an accumulation of talents and rewards."

Thellusson laughed and shrugged his shoulders. "You represent accumulations also."

"I do—I do. It's amazing. And if one knew a little more—" . . .

"Happiness is as contagious as influenza; probably more so. But, mind you, I could not have been really happy had I not believed in reincarnation. The doctrine permeates nearly all philosophies and has been accepted by the greater portion of the human race. To me it explains adequately the mysteries of sin and suffering, and the apparent injustice involved in lives widely and cruelly differentiated."

The Other Side

A. E. W. Mason (1865-1948)

[Quoting from an article in The Aryan Path for June, 1938, entitled 'Reincarnation in the English Novel':]

The development of the reincarnation concept in the mind of A.E.W. Mason as reflected in his novels is interesting—from his casual references to it in *The Broken Road* (1907) to its domination of *The Three Gentlemen* (1932). In the latter book old affinities assert themselves irresistibly; the elusive half-memories of an earlier life and lives gleam through now and again like lambent embers glowing fitfully beneath the ashes of forgetfulness. Many of the chapter headings are embroideries of Western thought, in prose and poetry, on the reincarnation *motif*. . . .

Rudyard Kipling (1865-1936)

Strangers drawn from the ends of the earth, jewelled and plumed were we.
I was Lord of the Inca race, and she was Queen of the Sea.
Under the stars beyond our stars where the new forged meteors glow
Hotly we stormed Valhalla, a million years ago. . . .

They will come back, come back again, as long as the red Earth rolls.
He never wasted a leaf or a tree. Do you think He would squander souls?
                    Naulahka (*The Sack of the Gods*)

When earth's last picture is painted, and the tubes are twisted and dried,
When the oldest colors are faded, and the youngest critic has died;
We shall rest, and faith, we shall need it—lie down for an aeon or two,
Till the Master of all Good Workmen shall put us to work anew.
                    When Earth's Last Picture is Painted

❁

Kipling's The Finest Story in the World is a short story in which the hero envisioned writing a tale containing the memories of his past lives and lifting the veils of future ones, but after falling in love with a lady the memory of the past gradually faded, and so the "finest story in the world" was never written.

H. G. Wells (1866-1946)

HISTORIAN AND NOVELIST

"I have had a dream, a whole lifetime, two thousand years ago! . . . I have lived through a whole life in that old world. . . ."

"That tale," said the guest-master stoutly, "was no dream. It was a memory floating up out of the deep darkness of forgotten things into a living brain—a kindred brain." . . .

"Sometimes before this in my dreams I have had a feeling that I lived again forgotten lives. Have none of you felt like that?" . . .

"Maybe life from its very beginning has been spinning threads and webs of memories. Not a thing in the past, it may be, that has not left its memories about us. Some day we may learn to gather in that forgotten gossamer, we may learn to weave its strands together again, until the whole past is restored to us, and life becomes one. . . ."

"It was a life," said Sarnac. "And it was a dream, a dream within this life; and this life too is a dream. Dreams within dreams, dreams containing dreams, until we come at last, maybe, to the Dreamer of all dreams, the Being who is all beings.

The Dream

Arnold Bennett (1867-1931)

And in the ecstatic void the vision of the whole cycle of my existence began to be revealed to me, rolling itself backwards into the unguessed deeps of the past, so that I might learn. I saw the endless series of my lives, recurring and recurring. . . . I ceased to be Morrice Loring, and became a legion. These lives flashed up before me, one anterior to another, mere moments between the vast periods that separated them. . . . And one life was not more important to me than another. All were equally indispensable and disciplinal.

The variety of those imprisonments seemed endless. Some were fevers of desire; others had almost the calmness of a final wisdom. Some were cruel; some were kind. In some the double barriers were so thin that the immortal prisoner shone through them, and men wondered. And in the next the walls might be hopelessly thick again. . . . Undulations in the curve of evolution.

The Glimpse

Walter John De la Mare (1873-1956)

If we do call life a journey, and death the inn we shall reach at last in the evening when it's over; that, too, I feel will be only as brief a stopping-place as any other inn would be. Our experience here is so scanty and shallow—nothing more than the moment of the continual present. Surely that must go on. . . . And so we shall all have to begin again. . . . What worlds we've seen together, you and I. And then—another parting. . . . It has all, my one dear, happened scores of times before—mother and child and friend—and lovers.

The Return

John Buchan (1875-1940)

SCOTTISH AUTHOR, AND GOVERNOR GENERAL OF CANADA

[John Buchan, in his volume of reminiscences Memory Hold-the-Door, remarks:]

I find myself in some scene which I cannot have visited before and which is yet perfectly familiar; I know that it was the stage of an action in which I once took part and am about to take part again.

Talbot Mundy (1879-1940)

We live as long as we are useful, and as long as it is good for us to live. Thereafter we die, which is another form of living, even as ice and water and rain and dew are the same thing in different aspects. When the appointed times comes, we return, as the rain returns to the earth it has left for a season. . . . No man can escape the consequences of his own act, though it take him a million lives to redress the balance.

I, who saw the ruins of Egypt, and of Babylon; of Rome and Greece; of Jerusalem; of Ceylon; of India; I, who have lived for fifty years within a stone's throw of a city ten times older than Babylon; I *knew* that day follows night, and I waited for the dawn, not knowing the hour I waited. I knew there are those who have won merit in their former lives, whose time comes to be born again. I knew that the key to evolution is in character—not in numbers or material increase—in the character of the soul, my Son! I knew that at the right time those would begin to be born whose character would influence the world, as mine could not. And I waited.

Om

Algernon Blackwood (1869-1951)

The antipathies and sympathies of To-day, the sudden affinities like falling in love at sight, and the sudden hostilities that apparently had no sense—all were due to relationship in some buried Yesterday, while those of To-morrow could be anticipated, and so regulated, by the actions of To-day. Even to the smallest things. . . .

Le Vallon lived in eternal life. He knew that it stretched infinitely behind his present "section," and infinitely ahead into countless other "sections." The results of what lay behind he must inevitably exhaust. Be that harvest painful or pleasant, he must reap what he had sown. But the future lay entirely in his own hands, and in his power of decision; chance or caprice had no word to say at all. . . . To Julius Le Vallon the soul was indeed unconquerable, and man master of his fate.

Death lost its ugliness and terror; the sense of broken, separated life was replaced by the security of a continuous existence, whole, unhurried, eternal, affording ample time for all development, accepting joy and suffering as the justice of results, but never as reward or punishment.

Julius Le Vallon

Towards the end of a long life, filled with reading, thinking, searching for its explanation, I have yet to find a solution that solves its problems better than the explanation of reincarnation. No saner solution, covering all the facts, presents itself. A few years ago, talking in the shadow of the pyramids with one of the clearest minds in England, in Europe for that matter, his words come back to me in this connection. . . . My friend said suddenly: "We have no proof, nor ever shall have. Survival must always remain a subject for speculation. . . . Of all the systems the world has yet devised, I know one only that offers a satisfactory explanation of the complex problems of existence—reincarnation It is logical, just, complete. It holds water. . . ."

Souls without a past behind them, springing suddenly into existence, out of nothing, with marked mental and moral peculiarities, are a conception as monstrous as would be the corresponding conception of babies appearing suddenly from nowhere, unrelated to anybody, but showing marked racial and family types.

"On Reincarnation"
Aryan Path, March 1930

Somerset Maugham (1874-   )

[In Maugham's best seller The Razor's Edge (1944) reincarnation is briefly explained and illustrated by the report of a psychic vision from which the visioner surmised that he incarnated four times in the past few hundred years. From Maugham's autobiography, The Summing Up, written six years earlier, we learn that he found only one explanation of the problem of evil "that appealed equally to my sensibility and to my imagination. This is the doctrine of the transmigration of souls." He writes:]

It would be less difficult to bear the evils of one's own life if one could think that they were but the necessary outcome of one's errors in a previous existence, and the effort to do better would be less difficult too when there was the hope that in another existence a greater happiness would reward one. But if one feels one's own woes in a more forcible way than those of others (I cannot feel your toothache, as the philosophers say) it is the woes of others that arouse one's indignation. It is possible to achieve resignation in regard to one's own, but only philosophers obsessed with the perfection of the Absolute can look upon those of others, which seem so often unmerited, with an equal mind. If Karma were true one could look upon them with pity, but with fortitude. Revulsion would be out of place and life would be robbed of the meaninglessness of pain which is pessimism's unanswered argument. I can only regret that I find the doctrine . . . impossible to believe. . . . There is no explanation for evil.

Hugh Walpole (1884-1941)

[A fascinating reincarnation story by Sir Hugh Walpole, entitled "The Adventure of the Imaginative Child,"* appeared in Henry Ford's weekly The Dearborn Independent for February 19 and 26, 1927, from which the following is taken:]

"Good Heavens," I answered, "how old are you?"
"I'm twelve and a half," he said, "by years, but do you ever have that

---

* Published by Macmillan, London, in 1938, in Walpole's volume of stories entitled *Head in Green Bronze*.

funny feeling, Mr. Johnson, as though you'd been a lot older really, and seen everything before, and knew just what was coming next?"

"I have known that," I answered . . . "Once or twice at moments but only for a moment."

"Well, I know it often," he said.

D. L. Murray (1888-   )

DRAMATIC CRITIC AND NOVELIST

"Are you telling me that we have all returned to earth together?"

"But isn't that exactly what it would be reasonable to expect? Those who have incurred mutual debts of love and hatred in one life return to pay off their obligation in another. We call it *Karma*."

"And they are reborn with a physical resemblance also to their former selves?"

"It is the same Self or Ego actually, wearing different fleshly masks. These masks *may* have a common likeness, as is, after all, only natural when you consider how closely soul and body affect each other: but there is no fixed rule about it. Generally speaking, it would seem as if advanced Egos—advanced in good or evil—repeat many of their facial and bodily characteristics in successive incarnations. The more primitive and fluid Egos, who have not yet made their characters very firmly, tend to inhabit differing types of body. . . ."

"You mustn't be carried away by the new light . . . as to suppose that everybody you meet in this existence is an Ego you have known before. You make fresh encounters in each life, as well as renewing old links. You work off the debts you have made in the past, and at the same time create new ones to be paid in the future. That's the rhythm of it."

Come Like Shadows

Rose Macaulay (1889-1958)

[*In her poem "A Door," Rose Macaulay, the novelist, tells of a vision evoked while watching a bonfire, of a friend burning at the stake centuries ago:*]

Through eddying wreaths I saw your eyes
Narrowed, as if you were

In mirth, or pain, or sharp surprise,
  Or fear too keen to bear.

The hazel leaves had a stir and thrill
  As if they watched men die;
And the centuries tumbled at a shrill,
  Sharp, long-forgotten cry.

The lit twigs cracked, the flame put out
  A quivering glutton's tongue;
The cruel beech-trees pressed about
  To see you burn so young. . . .

J. B. Priestley (1894-   )

[*Priestley's play, "I Have Been Here Before," is briefly summarized by Andre Maurois in his article "Tragic Decline of the Humane Ideal" (The N.Y. Times, June 19, 1938):*]

The subject of this play was the Eternal Return, the idea that the same events occur over and over again, that men find themselves, after millions of years, in situations which they have previously encountered, and that, each time, they make the same mistakes which cause the same tragedies. But the author of the play . . . admits that certain men, at the moment when they find themselves on the threshold of their drama, remember confusedly their previous misfortunes and find in this memory the strength to thwart destiny by a free action which breaks the fatal chain.

[*In Priestley's novel The Magicians, the central character, Sir Charles Ravenstreet, is aided by three wise men to see his existence in an entirely new light.*]

Ravenstreet . . . knew again an experience he had long forgotten, one that all children and probably most women know but that men forget. A sense and a feeling into which there enters an obscure conviction of immortality; as if somewhere at the root of it there might be knowledge, buried deep in the heart, that nobody . . . could possibly go away forever, die and turn to dust, be lost in the dark spaces of the universe; as if there stirred in our homeless minds some faint memory of the fields of paradise. And Ravenstreet, recapturing this experience . . . wondered if he might be merely recovering one of childhoods illusions or returning to a wisdom mislaid in the scramble of passing time, becoming aware of a profounder insight into the nature of our life and being.

Nevil Shute (1899-1960)

[Nevil Shute's novel In The Wet returns to the reincarnation theme of an earlier book, An Old Captivity:]

"You'll be all right," I said quietly. "God is very merciful, and he won't judge you too hard."

"You don't know nothing," the old man muttered weakly. "I could tell you things. . . . I ain't done so good. I know it. I'll start lower down next time. But I'll be right. Everyone gets another shot, however low you go, and I'll be right. . . . I ain't afraid of dying . . . that's nothing. It's just going off to sleep and sliding off into the next time. I reckon that I'd rather be there than here."

Joan Grant (1907-   )

[Joan Grant's novels have caused considerable comment and wonder, especially her Winged Pharoah, because without scholarly study she disclosed an unusually accurate knowledge of ancient times. In the prefatory note to her autobiography, Far Memory (Harpers), she wrote:]

During the last twenty years, seven books of mine have been published as historical novels which to me are biographies of previous lives I have known. . . . From early childhood, often to my extreme discomfort, I was sometimes aware beyond the usual range of the five senses. I tried to ignore the implications of this awareness, but it was too insistent; so in an attempt to understand what was happening I laboriously trained the faculty of far memory. This book describes, among other things, how I did so and what happened to me as the result.

·BRITISH MISCELLANY·

Sir William Jones (1746-1794)

["One of the great scholars of England. He was famous in jurisprudence and in oriental languages. . . . Founded the Asiatic Society of Bengal at Calcutta, through which, as well as through his publications, he had a great influence on literature, Oriental study, and philology in Western Europe" (Columbia Encyclopedia). S. Radhakrishnan in The Brahma Sutra (Harper, 1960) quotes from J. A. Arberry's Asiatic Jones the following excerpt from a letter of Sir William Jones to Earl Spencer, dated September 4, 1787, as illustrative of a westerner who looked with favor on the doctrine of rebirth:]

I am no Hindu; but I hold the doctrine of the Hindus concerning a future state to be incomparably more rational, more pious, and more likely to deter men from vice, than the horrid opinions inculcated by Christians on punishments without end.

Isaac D'Israeli (1766-1848)
FATHER OF LORD BEACONSFIELD

If we except the belief of a future remuneration beyond this life for suffering virtue and retribution for successful crimes, there is no system so simple, so little repugnant to our understanding, as that of metempsychosis. The pains and pleasures of this life are by this system considered as the recompense or the punishment of our actions in another state.

Curiosities of Literature

F. Max Müller (1823-1900)
ORIENTALIST AND PHILOLOGIST

I cannot help thinking that the souls towards whom we feel drawn in this life are the very souls whom we knew and loved in the former life, and the souls who repel us here we do not know why, are the souls that earned our disapproval, the souls from whom we kept aloof in a former life.

Vol. 18, Collected Works

[If suffering] is a result for us, it can only be the result of acts done in a former life. You see that the previous, nay the eternal existence of individual souls is taken for granted [in the Vedanta system], as it seems to be likewise in certain passages of the New Testament (St. John ix). But whatever we may think of the premises on which this theory rests, its influence on human character has been marvelous. If a man feels that what, without any fault of his own, he suffers in this life can only be the result of some of his former acts, he will bear his sufferings with more resignation, like a debtor who is paying off an old debt. And if he knows besides that in this life he may by suffering not only pay off his old debts, but actually lay by moral capital for the future, he has a motive for goodness, which is not more selfish than it ought to be. The belief that no act, whether good or bad, can be lost, is only the same belief in the moral world which our belief in the preservation of force is in the physical world. Nothing can be lost.

Three Lectures on the Vedanta Philosophy

David Lloyd George (1863-1945)

PRIME MINISTER

The conventional Heaven, with its angels perpetually singing, etc., nearly drove me mad in my youth and made me an atheist for ten years. My opinion is that we shall be reincarnated.

Lord Riddell's Intimate Diary of the
Peace Conference and After

L. Stanley Jast (1868-   )

CHIEF LIBRARIAN, MANCHESTER, ENGLAND

The basic testimony to the truth of reincarnation is of a purely intellectual order. It rests on the ability of the conception to give significance and meaning to what would otherwise be without either, and this is the only kind of evidence of *any* truth, whether in the world of phenomena or the world of thought, which has ultimate value. It can be deduced from rigorous logic from the most elementary assumption of a moral order in the universe, and without *that* assumption there is not even a universe: there is merely a monstrous futility or a colossal nightmare.

Reincarnation and Karma, a Spiritual
Philosophy Applied to the World of Today

Christmas Humphreys (1901-   )

FOUNDER OF THE BUDDHIST SOCIETY

[*In discussing Karma and Rebirth, in his book of that name, published in the Wisdom of the East series, Christmas Humphreys quotes the following from a Buddhist funeral service:*]

When the day's work is ended, night brings the benison of sleep. So death is the ending of a larger day, and in the night that follows, every man finds rest, until of his own volition he returns to fresh endeavour and to labours new. So has it been with this our brother, so will it be for all of us, until the illusion of a separated self is finally transcended, and in the death of self we reach Enlightenment.

R. S. Bluck

PHILOLOGIST, UNIVERSITY OF LONDON

Dr. Bluck's article, "The Phaedrus and Reincarnation," in the American Journal of Philology, for April, 1958, examines in detail the significance of Plato's exposition of reincarnation in the Phædrus. Looking into his description of the "soul's wanderings," Dr. Bluck suggests that Plato's "10,000-year cycle" of rebirth is not meant to refer to the whole of the soul's history. He shows furthermore that when speaking of the "fall" of the soul, Plato explains that a difficult incarnation is due to "bad training" by the soul of some of its instruments. Therefore the "fall" has none of the connotations associated with the doctrine of original sin. As Dr. Bluck states:

Plato does not commit himself to a doctrine of an original "fall." He may be suggesting, rather, that the human soul may aspire to *promotion* which would enable it to enjoy such happiness as it has never known before. . . . How long it takes to achieve that will depend upon individual effort, and will not be fixed at all.

Loran Hurnscot

(PSEUDONYM)

[*The following is taken from the journal of an English writer published by Viking Press in 1959 under the title A Prison, A Paradise:*]

My first genuine memory is about the Fall. There is darkness before and after it, but the memory itself is clear. A baby in a pram, in a late autumn garden, waking suddenly from sleep, at thirteen or fourteen months old. The fingerless infant-gloves tied rather too tightly round the wrists; the strap of the pram an uncomfortable restraint. And then the overwhelming, terrible discovery: "I'm in a body." I began to wail, to scream, to weep distractedly. In a few moments there were three women standing round the pram, comforting, speculating. "Something must have frightened her—but what?" "Could it have been an insect-sting? No, it's getting too late in the year for that." I sobbed in the helpless prison of before-one-can-talk, understanding telepathically, as it were, the gist of what they said. "It isn't that, it isn't that, it's not the sort of thing you think at all—it's that I've found out I'm locked up in a body, and it's dreadful." . . .

Now and then I become passionately pre-occupied by the idea of reincarnation. Is there evidence? Or is there no evidence? [Several stories are given of acquaintances who seem to remember the past.] . . . Had a rather irritable telephone conversation with my parsonical friend. I said that Buddhism was more christian than Christianity: that in the end it promised salvation to all—it did not look on the multitudes as chaff to be burned eternally. He said that there had to be a certain urgency: that with endless lives in prospect, one would always put off making the effort till the next. I said that to hinge eternal salvation on one single, confused and handicapped lifetime seemed to me a diabolical idea. He didn't agree; he said that everyone had their chance in this life, and if they wouldn't take it, "well, you've had it." If this is orthodoxy, then may God save me from it.

After-Death Views Polled

[In the 1940's Mass-Observation, a British fact-finding organization, conducted "A Study in popular attitudes to religion, ethics, progress and politics in a London Borough." The results of the survey were disclosed in a book entitled Puzzled People (Victor Gollancz, 1948), from which the following extract is taken:]

The conception of life after death was explored at various levels—by long informal conversations and through the written comments of Mass-Observation's National Panel. Perhaps the least expected, and in some ways the most significant, fact which came to light was the extent of belief in reincarnation. Among the interview sample about one person in twenty-five *spontaneously* went into enough detail to show that they held some such belief. That amounts to about one in ten of those who have any definite belief in an afterlife at all, and is almost certainly an underestimate, since no attempt was made by direct questioning to go into the details of people's conception.

According to the London *Daily Telegraph* for June 8, 1960, there is a strong preoccupation today among senior school children with some form of reincarnation, judged by informal talks among them on religious education. Tape recordings of the talks are being used by a research group under Harold Leukes of the Oxford University Education Department, as the basis for a report on religious education. In answer to the question "Is there a heaven?" one young person replied: "I think that you kind of come back into the world again, to live and lead a better life, and you go on coming back until you're perfect, and then, well, there isn't a place, but I think you go to God when you're perfect."

I R I S H

Ancient Celts

In his Literary History of Ireland, Douglas Hyde (former President of the Irish Free State) stated that "the idea of re-birth, which forms part of a half dozen existing Irish sages, was perfectly familiar to the Irish Gael."

Dr. W. Y. Evans-Wentz, who sympathetically yet scientifically reviewed the folklore of the Celts in his book The Fairy-Faith in Celtic Countries (Oxford University Press), quoted from Alfred Nut one of the foremost authorities on the subject:

In Greek Mythology as in Irish, the conception of re-birth proves to be a dominant factor of the same religious system in which Elysium is likewise an essential feature.

Chapters 7 and 12 of Dr. Evans-Wentz's book treat in detail of the Celtic doctrine of reincarnation, and also provide evidence that even to this day the idea is alive amongst some of these peoples.

John Scotus Erigena (A.D. 815-877)

PHILOSOPHER AND THEOLOGIAN

Man is the microcosm in the strictest sense of the word. He is the summary of all existence. There is no creature that is not recapitulated in man. There is nothing in the universe lower than body or higher than soul.

Soul and [the spiritual] body were created together, and the soul therefore precedes the body only in dignity, not in space or in time. But the body as we know it, material and corruptible, came into existence after man's sin, and because of it. It was man, after he had transgressed, who made to himself this fragile and mortal body. This is signified by the fig-leaves, which are a shade, excluding the rays of the sun, as our bodies shade our souls in the darkness of ignorance, and exclude the light of truth.

But where, then, is that spiritual and incorruptible body which belonged to man before his sin? It is hidden in the secret recesses of our nature, and it will reappear in the future, when this mortal shall put on immortality.

The Division of Nature

Thomas Moore (1779-1852)

Stranger, though new the frame
Thy soul inhabits now, I've traced its flame
For many an age, in every chance and change
Of that Existence, though whose varied range—
As through a torch-race, where, from hand to hand
The flying youths transmit their shining brand—
From frame to frame the unextinguished soul
Rapidly passes, till it reach the goal! . . .

Lalla Rookh

He [Plato] spoke of Him
The lone, eternal One, who dwells above,
And of the soul's untraceable descent
From that high fount of spirit, through the grades
Of intellectual being, till it mix
With atoms vague, corruptible and dark;
Nor even then, though sunk in earthly dross,
Corrupted all, nor its ethereal touch
Quite lost, but tasting of the fountain still! . . .

A Vision of Philosophy

William Archer Butler (1814-1848)
IRISH ANGLICAN CLERGYMAN
PROFESSOR OF MORAL PHILOSOPHY, TRINITY COLLEGE, DUBLIN

It must be allowed that there is much in the hypothesis of pre-existence (at least) which might attract a speculator busied with the endeavor to reduce the moral system of the world under intelligible laws. The solution which it at once furnishes of the state and fortunes of each individual, as arising in some unknown but direct process from his own voluntary acts, though it throws, of course, no light on the ultimate question of the existence of moral evil (which it only removes a single step), does yet contribute to satisfy the mind as to the equity of that immediate manifestation of it, and of its physical attendants, which we unhappily witness.

There is internally no greater improbability that the present may be the result of a former state now almost wholly forgotten, than that the present should be followed by a future form of existence in which, perhaps, or in some departments of which, the oblivion may be as complete. And if to that future state there are already discernible faint longings and impulses which to many men have seemed to involve a direct proof of its reality, hopes that will not be bounded by the grave, and desires that grasp eternity, others have found within them, it would seem, faint intimations scarcely less impressive of the past, as if the soul vibrated the echoes of a harmony not of this world. . . .

It may be doubted whether the strangeness and improbability of this hypothesis [of pre-existence] among ourselves arises after all from grounds on which our philosophy has reason to congratulate itself. It may be questioned whether, if we examine ourselves candidly, we shall not discover that the feeling of extravagance with which it affects us has its secret source in materialistic or semi-materialistic prejudices.

*Lectures on the History of
Ancient Philosophy*

The Irish Literary Renaissance

John Eglinton in his biography of George Russell, A Memoir of Æ (Macmillan, 1937), observed:

Probably there has never been in any country a period of literary activity which has not been preceded or accompanied by some stimulation of the religious interest. Anyone in search of this in Ireland at this time may find it if he looks for it. . . . He will find it, unless he disdains to look in that direction, in the ferment caused in the minds of a group of young men by the early activities of the Theosophical Movement in Dublin. The proof is, not only that there was no other religious movement in Ireland at this time, but that Yeats and Russell, who were to be the principal leaders of the Literary Revival, were closely associated with this one.

Ernest Boyd's large volume, Ireland's Literary Renaissance, (Knopf, 1922), contains a chapter "The Dublin Mystics," with subtitle "The Theosophical Movement." He too shows the prominent part played in this awakening by Yeats, Charles Johnston, George Russell, Charles Weekes, and other writers associated with the Dublin Theosophical Society, later reorganized by Russell as the Hermetic Society, and which subsequently attracted many of the younger Irish poets. Æ actively conducted the Society until his departure for London in 1933, two years before his death. Concerning the work of this group, he wrote: "It waxed and waned and waxed again, and I felt inwardly satisfied that they all more or less passed through a bath of Theosophical ideas." Reincarnation, of course, is one of the central themes of Theosophical philosophy.

William Butler Yeats (1865-1939)

Yeats's interest in reincarnation is well known. (See Virginia Moore's The Unicorn, William Butler Yeats' Search for Reality.) The reviewer of the Collected Poems of W. B. Yeats, in Newsweek for April 9, 1956, suggests that his perception of rebirth did not come in intuitive flashes, but was rather the result of study and reflection. The reviewer adds:

Toward the end of his life, Yeats began to find personal strength and a fiery poetic imagery in the realm of the transcendental. . . . His interest in religion was especially confusing to many readers because of the un-orthodox, occult terms in which he expressed it. As a youth, he was fascinated by the Russian theosophist Madame Blavatsky, and he went on to explore other avenues of Eastern mysticism.

George W. Russell (1867-1935)
(PEN NAME Æ)

To those who cry out against romance, I would say, You yourself are romance. You are the lost prince, herding obscurely among the swine. The romance of your spirit is the most marvellous of stories. Your wanderings have been greater than those of Ulysses. . . .

Looking back upon that other life through the vistas of memory, I see breaking in upon the images of this world, forms of I know not what antiquity. I walk out of strange cities steeped in the jewel glow and gloom of evening, or sail in galleys over the silvery waves of the antique ocean. I reside in tents, or in palace chambers, go abroad in chariots, meditate in cyclopean buildings, am worshipper of the Earth-gods upon the mountains, lie tranced in Egyptian crypts, or brush with naked body through the long, sunlit grasses of the prairies. Endlessly the procession of varying forms goes back into remote yesterdays of the world. . . . Were not these. . . . memories of the spirit incarnated many times?

The Candle of Vision

[A *reminiscence of Æ told by Constance Sitwell, and included in John Eglinton's* A Memoir of Æ:]

One evening it was about the intuitions he had had of his own incarnations that he talked. "They tell me that my recollections and visions are ancestral memories—a mere phrase. I talked to Julian Huxley about it once. You tell me, I said, that a man cannot transmit musical knowledge, or a language he has mastered, or a craft, to his children? No, he said, you may transmit a tendency, but everything has to be learnt afresh. And yet you tell me, I said, that when I get a glimpse of strange cities and buildings I have never seen, vivid and alive in every detail, the figures in the streets, the sharp shadows, it has nothing to do with me, but is a memory of some hypothetical ancestor of mine who may have gone on the Crusades? Huxley didn't know what to say. He told me he had sat up all night once trying to find a flaw in one of my arguments, and had to give up!"

[*Claude Bragdon in his book* Merely Players *writes:*]

One story . . . gives a hint of the possible derivation of his pseudonym, Æ.* He said that when he was a boy he was just like other boys. . . . except

* ["Æ" was the result of a printer's difficulty with "Æon," with which Russell had signed an article. Eds.]

that he seemed to have a more vivid imagination, for he was always telling himself wonderful stories of gods and demi-gods, and miraculous happenings in some Valhalla, and to these characters he assigned names. He had no other idea but that he invented these stories and these names.

But one day while waiting at the desk of the village library for the librarian to bring him a story book, he happened to glance at the open page of a book that was lying there, and his eye encountered the word 'Aeon.' He declared that his surprise and excitement were so great that he left the library empty-handed and walked about the streets for two hours before he could muster up sufficient calmness and courage to ask the librarian what book it was, and if he might look at it. For the name Aeon was one which he had given to the hero of one of his own stories, a name which he regarded as peculiarly his own . . . and it was upsetting to discover that such was plainly not the case.

The book proved to be a treatise on Gnostic religion and cosmogony and in it, to his utter amazement, he found recorded, in a mass of legendary lore, those very stories which he thought he had invented—even the names of the characters were the same. This forced him to the conclusion that either his imaginings were recovered memories of things learned or experienced in some antecedent life, or that in some inexplicable manner he had tapped, so to speak, the memory of nature.

James Stephens (1882-1950)

Deep Womb of Promise! Back to thee again
And forth, revivified, all living things
Do come and go,
For ever wax and wane into and from thy garden;
There the flower springs,
Therein does grow
The bud of hope, the miracle to come
For whose dear advent we are striving, dumb
And joyless. . . .
Until our back and forth, our life and death
And life again, our going and return
Prepare the way: until our latest breath,
Deep-drawn and agonized, for him [God] shall burn
A path: for him prepare
Laughter and love and singing everywhere;
A morning and a sunrise and a day!

A Prelude and a Song

GERMAN

Neoplatonism and Kabalism in Germany

In the fifteenth century a revival of Neoplatonism arose through the efforts of Nicolas de Cusa, a Catholic Cardinal of German birth, and a noted ecclesiastical and philosophical writer. Cusa directly opposed the anthropomorphic conception of God. His efforts to revive Neoplatonism were continued in Germany by John Reuchlin, Trithemius, and Cornelius Agrippa. Trithemius, the Abbot of the Benedictine Monastery of Spanheim, was a Kabalist as well as a Platonist. His fame was perpetuated by his two distinguished pupils, Paracelsus and Cornelius Agrippa.

In the middle of the fifteenth century appeared John Reuchlin, the celebrated humanist and teacher. While acting as Imperial Counsellor of Emperor Frederick III, he found time to study Neoplatonism, several oriental languages, and to write books on the Kabala. When he denounced the burning of the Hebrew bibles, the Dominicans caused his expulsion for a time from Germany, and his works were burned. But later when Erasmus, Martin Luther, and Melanchthon (the grandson of Reuchlin's sister, and for a long period under his care) came to him for instruction, Reuchlin set going a ferment of ideas in the Christian world which caused him to be called the "Father of the Reformation." The Encyclopædia Britannica (9th edition) provides some significant details of his interest in Neoplatonism and Kabalism, and of his influence on German culture:

Reuchlin . . . in February 1482 left Stuttgart for Florence and Rome
. . . [and] brought the German scholar into contact with several learned
Italians. . . . Reuchlin's life at Stuttgart was often broken by important
missions, and in 1490 he was again in Italy. Here he saw Pico [the Neoplatonist, see p. 97], to whose Cabbalistic doctrines he afterwards became
heir. . . .

[Later in Heidelberg] Reuchlin's appointed function was to make translations from the Greek authors, in which his reading was already extremely
wide . . . and formed an important element in his efforts to spread a knowledge of Greek. For, though Reuchlin had no public office as teacher, and
even at Heidelberg was prevented from lecturing openly, he was during a
great part of his life the real centre of all Greek teaching as well as of all
Hebrew teaching in Germany. . . . His first Latin comedy *Sergius*, [was] a
satire on worthless monks and false relics which his young Heidelberg friends
were eager to act. . . .

His Greek studies had interested him in philosophy, and not least in those
fantastical and mystical systems of later times with which the Cabbala has
no small affinity. Following Pico, he seemed to find in the Cabbala a profound theosophy which might be of the greatest service for the defence of
Christianity and the reconciliation of science with the mysteries of faith.
. . . The most esoteric wisdom of the rabbins was in his eyes of the greatest
value.

*Reincarnation in the Kabala and Zohar has already been considered in
Part I, under "Judaism."*

Baron Gottfried Wilhelm Leibniz (1646-1716)

[*From the context of the statements that follow, Leibniz does not appear
to limit the term "body" to the physical instrument, but includes the inner
bodies of men and animals, and believing that these invisible constituents
never completely die, he prefers the term "metamorphosis," to "metempsychosis."*]

There is nothing waste, nothing sterile, nothing dead in the universe; no
chaos, no confusions, save in appearance. . . . We must not imagine . . .
that each soul has a mass or portion of matter appropriate or attached to itself for ever. . . . For all bodies are in a perpetual flux like rivers, and parts
are passing in and out of them continually. Thus the soul only changes its

body bit by bit and by degrees, so that it is never despoiled of all its organs all together. . . . neither are there any entirely *separate souls,* nor *superhuman spirits* without bodies.

Monadology

As animals are usually not born completely in conception or *generation,* so neither do they perish completely in what we call *death;* for it is reasonable that what does not begin naturally should not come to an end in the order of nature either. Thus, casting off their masks or their rags, they merely return to a more subtle scene, on which, however, they can be as sensible and as well ordered as on the greater one. . . . Thus not only souls but animals also are ingenerable and imperishable; they are only developed, enveloped, reclad, stripped, transformed; souls never leave the whole of their body, and do not pass from one body to another which is entirely new to them. Thus there is no *metempsychosis,* but there is *metamorphosis.*

Principles of Nature

[*James Ward in his Gifford Lectures,* The Realm of Ends, *thus summarizes Leibniz's views on immortality:*]

According to the pluralistic, as according to the Leibnizian view, all the individuals there are have existed from the first and will continue to exist indefinitely. Birth and death, then, cannot really be what they seem to be. . . . [Leibniz believes] that all souls have preexisted 'always in a sort of organized body,' which at the time of generation undergoes a certain transformation and augmentation. . . . Death, as the more or less complete dissolution of the organism, means that the soul in consequence, so far as it is thus deprived of its *locus standi,* is, to use Leibniz's phrase, in the position of a deserter from the general order. Temporarily it is in a like position during sleep; and death for Leibniz was but a longer and profounder sleep: in neither case did he believe that the continuity of the individual's life was completely broken.

Frederick the Great (1712-1786)

[*Shortly before his death, Frederick the Great said:*]

Well, I feel that soon I shall have done with my earthly life. Now, since I am convinced that nothing existing in nature can be annihilated, so I know for a certainty, that for this reason, the more noble part of me will not cease to live. Though I may not be a king in my future life, so much the better: I shall nevertheless live an active life and, on top of it, earn less ingratitude.

King Frederick's Sayings and Thoughts
Compiler: R. Rehlen

The German Transcendentalists

Alfred Bertholet, professor of theology at the University of Basle, said in his Transmigration of Souls (Harpers, 1909): "During the classical period of German literature metempsychosis attracted such attention that that period may almost be styled the flourishing epoch of the Doctrine."

The classical period had its distinct origin, it appears, in the transcendental philosophy of Immanuel Kant, whose Critique of Pure Reason, published in 1781, opened a new epoch in metaphysical thought. Kant undertook to transfer attention from the objects that engaged the mind to the mind itself. He proposed a revolution in metaphysics comparable to the Copernican revolution in astronomy. As Copernicus, finding it impossible to explain the movements of the heavenly bodies on the supposition of their turning round the earth, posited the sun as the center, so Kant, perceiving the confusion that resulted from making man a satellite of the external world, resolved to place him in the central position. Echoing August Schlegel, Carlyle said that in its probable influence on the moral culture of Europe, Kant's philosophy was as important as the Reformation itself.

Fichte became an enthusiastic interpreter of Kant's teachings, endeavoring to render them intelligible and attractive to minds of ordinary culture. Others whose brilliance added light and ardor to the Kantian revolution were: Shelling, Lessing, Herder, Schleiermacher, Goethe, Schiller, Jean Paul Richter, Novalis, the brothers August and Frederich Schlegel, Hegel, and Schopenhauer.

The transcendental movements in England and America were considerably influenced by these German thinkers, as pointed out by Frothingham in his Transcendentalism in New England.* Carlyle undertook the study of German and championed the cause of German philosophy and literature in the English reviews. He also made excellent translations, e.g., Goethe's Wilhelm Meister. Coleridge commenced the study of German when he was twenty-four, and at twenty-six visited Germany in company with Wordsworth, spending fourteen months there in hard study. Coleridge has been called a pure transcendentalist of the Schelling school.

In America we find Frederic Hedge translating Herder's Dialogues on Metempsychosis, as well as other German works. Margaret Fuller wrote a

* G. P. Putnam, 1876.

remarkable paper on Goethe for The Dial. *In his papers called "Carlyle's Miscellanies," Emerson presented Carlyle's great articles on Kant, Fichte, Novalis, Goethe, and Richter. Through the works of Coleridge the American public was made familiar with the leading ideas of Schelling.*

The influence of oriental thought was pronounced among the German transcendentalists, as will be observed from a number of their statements on reincarnation. August Schlegel published the first German translation of The Bhagavad-Gita, as well as other Sanskrit works, and paid tribute to the author of the Gita in these words:

By the Brahmins, reverence of masters is considered the most sacred of duties. Thee therefore, first, most holy prophet, interpreter of the Deity, by whatever name thou wast called among mortals, the author of this poem, by whose oracles the mind is rapt with ineffable delight to doctrines lofty, eternal, and divine—thee first, I say, I hail, and shall always worship at thy feet.

Beethoven also came under the spell of the Orient. He was fond of copying down mystical sentences from Eastern literature, and permanently framed on his desk this quotation: "I am that which is. I am all that was, that is, and that shall be."

Immanuel Kant (1724-1804)

[*Kant, in his teaching of an* unendlichen progressus (*unending progression*), *opposed static immortality in favor of progressive growth of the soul after death. In an early paper, "General History of Nature and Theory of the Heavens," he speculated that souls start imperfect from the sun, and travel by planet stages farther and farther away to a paradise in the coldest and remotest planet of our system. He wrote:*]

In view of the endless duration of the immortal soul throughout the infinity of time, which even the grave itself does not interrupt . . . shall the soul remain forever attached to this one point of world-space, our earth? Will it never participate in a closer contemplation of the remaining wonders of creation? Who knows but that the intention is for it to become acquainted at close range, some day, with those far distant globes of the cosmic system and the excellence of their institutions, which from this distance already provoke our curiosity? Perhaps for just such a purpose some globes of the planetary system are in a state of preparation as a new dwelling place for us to occupy after we have completed the period of time allotted for our sojourn here. Who knows but that the satellites coursing around Jupiter will some day shine on us?

General History of Nature

Generation in the human race . . . depends on . . . many accidents, on occasion, . . . on the views and whims of government, nay, even on vice, so that it is difficult to believe in the eternal existence of a being whose life has first begun under circumstances so trivial, and so entirely dependent on our own choice. . . . It would seem as if we could hardly expect so wonderful an effect from causes so insignificant. But, in answer to these objections, we may adduce the transcendental hypothesis, that all life is properly intelligible, and not subject to the changes of time, and that it neither began in birth, nor will end in death. . . . If we could see ourselves and other objects *as they really are,* we should see ourselves in a world of spiritual natures, our community with which neither began at our birth nor will end with the death of the body.

*Critique of Pure Reason**

G. E. Lessing (1729-1781)

Is it after all so certain that my soul has only once inhabited the form of man? Is it after all so unreasonable to suppose that my soul, upon its journey to perfection, should have been forced to wear this fleshly veil more than once? Possibly this migration of the soul through several human bodies was based on a new system of thought. Possibly this new system was merely the oldest of all.

*Observations upon Campe's
Philosophical Dialogues*

Is this hypothesis [metempsychosis] ridiculous merely because it is the oldest, because the human intellect adopted it without demur, before men's minds had been distracted and weakened by the sophistry of the schools? . . . On the contrary, the first and earliest opinion in matters of speculation is invariably the most probable, because it was immediately accepted by the sound understanding of mankind. . . .

Why should I not return as often as I am capable of acquiring fresh knowledge and further power? Do I achieve so much in one sojourning as to make it not worth my while to return? Never! Or, is it that I forget my former sojourn? Well for me that I forget. The recollection of my former state

* Part II, Transcendental Doctrine of Method, Chap. 1, Section III. James Ward, who in his Gifford Lectures calls attention to the above passage, states that in Kant's lectures on metaphysics shortly before the publication of the *Critique* he taught both the pre-existence and the immortality of the soul.

would enable me to turn my present condition to but poor account. And have I forgotten forever what I must forget for the time being? Or is it that I should lose so much time? Lose time! What need have I for haste? Is not the whole of eternity mine?

Education of the Human Race

J. G. von Herder (1744-1803)

Do you not know great and rare men who cannot have become what they are at once, in a single human existence? Who must often have existed before in order to have attained that purity of feeling, that instinctive impulse for all that is true, beautiful, and good—in short, that elevation and natural supremacy over all around them? . . . Have you never observed that children will sometimes, of a sudden, give utterance to ideas which makes us wonder how they got possession of them; which presuppose a long series of other ideas and secret self-communings; which break forth like a full stream out of the earth, an infallible sign that the stream was not produced in a moment from a few raindrops, but had long been flowing concealed beneath the ground? . . .

Have you never had remembrances of a former state, which you could find no place for in this life? . . . Have you not seen persons, been in places, of which you were ready to swear that you had seen those persons, or had been in those places before? . . . And such are *we*; we who, from a hundred causes, have sunk so deep and are so wedded to matter, that but few reminiscences of so pure a character remain to us. The nobler class of men who, separated from wine and meat, lived in perfect simplicity according to the order of nature, carried it further, no doubt, than others, as we learn from the example of Pythagoras, of Iarchas, of Apollonius, and others, who remembered distinctly what and how many times they had been in the world before.

If we are blind, or can see but two steps beyond our noses, ought we therefore to deny that others may see a hundred or a thousand degrees farther, even to the bottom of time, into the deep, cool well of the foreworld, and there discern everything, plain and bright and clear? . . .

I am not ashamed of my half-brothers, the brutes! On the contrary as far as they are concerned, I am a great advocate of metempsychosis. I believe, for a certainty, that they will ascend to a higher grade of being, and am unable to understand how anyone can object to this hypothesis, which seems to have the analogy of the whole creation in its favour.

Dialogues on Metempsychosis
Trans. F. H. Hedge

J. W. von Goethe (1749-1832)

> The soul of man is like to water;
> From Heaven it cometh
> To Heaven it riseth
> And then returneth to earth,
> For ever alternating. . . .
> *Song of the Spirits over the Waters*

> Two souls contend
> In me and both souls strive for masterdom,
> Which from the other shall the scepter rend.
> The first soul is a lover, clasping close
> To this world tentacles of corporal flame,
> The other seeks to rise with mighty throes
> To those ancestral meadows whence it came.
> *Faust*

I am certain that I have been here as I am now a thousand times before, and I hope to return a thousand times.

Letter to I. Falk

[Goethe wrote to his close friend Charlotte von Stein: "How well it is that men should die, if only to erase their impressions and return clean washed." One of his poems addressed to her appears below, followed by a letter on the same theme written in 1776 to Christoph Wieland—"the German Voltaire".]

> Tell me, what is Destiny preparing?
> Tell me why we two have drawn so near?
> Aeons since, you were my sister, sharing
> Kin with me, or else my wife most dear.
> Everything I am, my every feature,
> You divined, my every nerve could thrill,
> Read me at a glance—no other creature
> Knows me as you know, nor ever will. . . .
> *Poem to Charlotte von Stein*

I cannot explain the significance to me of this woman or her influence over me, except by the theory of metempsychosis.* Yes, we were once man and

---

* Frau von Stein apparently shared Goethe's views on rebirth, for in a memorial discourse delivered at Zwickau (Saxony) in 1892 by a Professor Keller on the occasion of

wife. Now our knowledge of ourselves is veiled, and lies in the spirit world. I can find no name for us—the past, the future, the All!

Letter to Christoph Wieland

J. C. F. von Schiller (1759-1805)

Were our Beings once together twin'd?
Was it therefore that our bosoms pin'd?
Were we in the light of suns now dead,
In the days of rapture long since fled,
　　　　　　　Into One united?

Aye, we were so!—thou wert link'd with me
In Æone that has ceas'd to be;
On the mournful page of vanish'd time. . . .
The Secret of Reminiscence

[Schiller at the age of 21, upon completion of his studies at the Karlsschule in Stuttgart, wrote a thesis entitled "Concerning the Connection between the Animal and the Spiritual Nature of Man." In section 27, treating of what happens at death, he stated:]

Matter decomposes into its final elements, which now wander through the kingdoms of nature in other forms and conditions. . . . The soul continues to exercise its power of thought and views the universe from other aspects. Of course, one can say, that it has not in the least exhausted this sphere as yet. . . . But is one sure that this earth is lost forever? Do we not lay aside many a book we do not understand, to take it up again years later when we will understand it better?

Johann Peter Hebel (1760-1826)

SWISS-BORN GERMAN POET AND PRELATE

[The following are notes for a Sunday sermon at Karlsruhe where Hebel was prelate (published in Vol. II of Hebel's works), the theme being "Have we lived before?":]

---

the 150th anniversary of her birth, the professor stated: "Frau von Stein considered life as a school into which the human spirit enters, coming from its heavenly home. Laden therein with weakness, sin and doubts, after having overcome this difficult ordeal, grown in knowledge, and been purified, it enters again through the gates of death, its spiritual home, and continues thus in different forms of existence, which are always renewing themselves."

(a) Yes, it is possible; here or elsewhere. . . . We drank from Lethe's sweet bowl and a sweeter one, Mneme's [Memory's] is awaiting us. How much we forget in this life!

(b) Versatility of experience; wisdom is the fruit of experience; but how little one life has to offer!

(c) And have we really no memories at all? Do we not observe: easy developments, certain talents. What if we had possessed those once before? . . . Inexplicable sympathy. Preference for the history of special periods, men, countrysides. Have we been there before, perhaps . . . ?

(d) How attractive the thought: I have lived in the period of the mammoths, the patriarchs, have been an Arcadian herdsman, a Greek adventurer, partaken in Hermann's battle. . . .

Some day, having drunk from the golden cup of Mneme, having finished with many wanderings, preserved my "I" through so many forms and conditions, become acquainted with joys and sorrows, and purified through both; what memories, what bliss, what gain!

J. G. Fichte (1762-1814)

These two systems, the purely spiritual and the sensuous—which last may consist of an immeasurable series of particular lives—exist in me from the moment when my active reason is developed, and pursue their parallel course. The former alone gives to the latter meaning and purpose and value.

I *am* immortal, imperishable, eternal, so soon as I form the resolution to obey the law of reason. After an existence of myriad lives the super-sensuous world cannot be more present than at this moment. Other conditions of my sensuous existence are to come, but these are no more the true life than the present condition is.

Man is not a production of the world of sense; and the end of his existence can never be attained in that world. His destination lies beyond time and space and all that pertains to sense. . . . Even because Nature puts me to death she must quicken me anew. It can only be my higher life, unfolding itself in her, before which my present life disappears; and that which mortals call death is the visible appearing of another vivification.

The Destiny of Man

Jean Paul Richter (1763-1825)

Always employ a language some years in advance of the child (men of genius in their books speak to us from the vantage-ground of centuries) . . . Let the teacher, especially he who is too much in the habit of attributing all learning to teaching, consider that the child already carries half his world, that of mind,—the objects, for instance, of moral and metaphysical contemplation,—ready formed within him; and hence language, being provided only with physical images, cannot give, but merely illumine, his mental conceptions.

Levana; or the Doctrine of Education

Friedrich Schleiermacher (1768-1834)

THEOLOGIAN AND PHILOSOPHER

[*Of his* Reden Ueber Die Religion (*Talks on Religion*), *published in 1799, it is said the whole Western world sat up and took notice. Here is an excerpt from the second talk:*]

History, in its essential meaning, is the highest aspect of religion. . . . For here you observe the return of Spirits and Souls ordinarily regarded as mere tender, poetic imaginings. In more than one sense we have [in this conception of metempsychosis] a wonderful arrangement of the universe, enabling us to compare the different periods of mankind on the basis of a reliable measure. For after a long interval, during which nature could not produce anything comparable, an excellent individual will return, recognized only by the Seers, and from the effect this individual produces they alone can judge the signs of the different cycles.

A single moment of mankind's history will return, and from the various causes leading thereto, you shall discern the course of the universe and the formula of its laws. A genius . . . will awaken from his slumber, appearing on a new scene. His speedier growth, his broader exertions, his more beautiful and powerful body, shall then indicate by how much the climate of mankind has improved, and is better adapted to the nourishing of noble growths.

G. W. F. Hegel (1770-1831)

Change while it imports dissolution, involves at the same time the rise of a *new life*—that while death is the issue of life, life is also the issue of death. This is a grand conception; one which the Oriental thinkers attained, and which is perhaps the highest in their metaphysics. In the idea of *Metempsychosis* we find it evolved in its relation to individual existence; but a myth more generally known, is that of the *Phoenix* as a type of the Life of *Nature*; eternally preparing for itself its funeral pile, and consuming itself upon it; but so that from its ashes is produced the new, renovated, fresh life. . . . Spirit—consuming the envelope of its existence—does not merely pass into another envelope, nor rise rejuvenescent from the ashes of its previous form; it comes forth exalted, glorified, a purer spirit. It certainly makes war upon itself—consumes its own existence; but in this very destruction it works up that existence into a new form, and each successive phase becomes in its turn a material, working on which it exalts itself to a new grade. . . .

Nothing in the past is lost . . . for the Idea is ever present; Spirit is immortal; with it there is no past, no future, but an essential *now*. This necessarily implies that the present form of Spirit comprehends within it all earlier steps. . . . The life of the ever present Spirit is a circle of progressive embodiments, which looked at in one aspect still exist beside each other, and only as looked at from another point of view appear as past. The grades which Spirit seems to have left behind it, it still possesses in the depths of its present.

The Philosophy of History

Johann Heinrich Zschokke (1771-1848)
AUTHOR OF NOVELS, HISTORIES, AND RELIGIOUS WORKS

I know of no reason that would prevent me from believing that the holy magnet which here so wonderfully attracts souls to souls, would not under other transformations continue to operate. And so I hope, one day, in another world, another life, to be united again to those I loved in this life. . . .

The reincarnation idea of high antiquity, branded as folly by the ignorance of later times, will take possession again. . . . And if you think it just a delusion that under diverse coverings I encountered one and the same soul on earth, well, call it a delusion, but an inexplicable feeling within me, an inner voice, calls it a certainty.

Harmonius

Friedrich von Schlegel (1772-1829)

This often astonishes me: Each thought . . . seems finished in itself—single, detached, indivisible—like a person, one crowding out the other, and that which now was very near soon sinks back into obscurity. And then again there are moments of sudden general clarity when several such spirits of the inner world . . . melt into one another; a new light shines on many a long forgotten part of our "I" and penetrates the night-of-the-future with its bright ray.

Now as it is with the small, so I think it is also with the great. That which we call a life is for the immortal inner man but a single thought, an indivisible sensation. For him, too, there are moments of deepest, fullest consciousness, when he remembers all his prior lives; they merge and then differentiate.

Lucinde

Philosophy has to refute preeminently [these] two basic errors: firstly, that the human soul can dissolve into nothingness, and secondly that man, without any effort of his own, is already fully endowed with immortality. . . . Man as he is now is entirely too imperfect, too material, to claim that higher kind of immortality. He will have to enter into other earthly, yet far more refined and transfigured forms and developments, before he could directly partake of the eternal glory of the divine world of light.

The third opinion, that of metempsychosis, embraced by mysticism, is remarkable in itself for its antiquity, and lies in the middle path between the other two. It does not permit the soul to pass to full freedom before it has incarnated in many bodies. Here we view metempsychosis in its most general meaning as continuance of spirit, alternately using organic forms, and not in the sense of . . . an aggravating punishment ever accelerating.

Cologne Lectures (1804-1806)

Inasmuch as the true Indian teaching of metempsychosis, as we now know it correctly from the sources, is too serious and solemn to find much credence and applause in our time, the attempt has been made recently to carry it entirely into the realm of romanticism and to paint the future life in glowing colors as a sort of astronomical excursion from one star to another. . . . Would it not be more advisable and more appropriate to human intellect if man . . . would first turn his gaze upon himself and his own dwelling place, the earth . . . instead of at once disappearing into the starry skies? May not he find that which he seeks so often in the distance far closer at hand than he imagines? Perhaps, too, this planet, our earth, holds enclosed within itself many a hidden chamber and passageway . . . as well as the seed of a resurrection to come.

Vienna Lectures on "The Philosophy of Life," 1827

Novalis (1772-1801)

(PSEUDONYM OF G. F. P. VON HARDENBERG)

Whoever does not reach perfection here, perhaps will reach it over there, or else will have to begin an earthly career over again. Could there not also be a death over there, the result of which would be birth on earth? . . . Do not I myself choose all my destinies from all eternity?

Fragments

[One of Novalis' best-known works is an unfinished novel entitled Heinrich von Ofterdingen. A number of minor references to rebirth are to be found therein, such as:]

The earth lay before him like a dear old home that after a long absence he found again. Thousands of memories awoke in him. . . .
"Since when have you been here?"—"Since I left the grave."—"Did you die once before?"—"How else could I live?" . . . "How does it happen that you know me?"—"Oh, from old times."

F. W. J. von Schelling (1775-1854)

Spirit sleeps in the stone, breathes in the plant, moves in the animal, and wakes up to consciousness in man. . . .
There dwells in us all, a secret, wonderful faculty, by virtue of which we can withdraw from the mutations of time into our innermost disrobed selves, and there behold the eternal under the form of immutability; such vision is our innermost and peculiar experience, on which alone depends all that we know and believe of a supra-sensible world.*

Heinrich von Kleist (1777-1811)

DRAMATIST, NOVELIST, AND POET

Just think, this unending continuation! Myriads of periods of time, each one a life, and for everyone a habitation like this world! . . . Come, let us

---

* Quoted in *General Sketch of the History of Pantheism*, Vol. II, by C. Plumptre.

do some good, and die while doing it, our death being but one of the millions of deaths we have already experienced and shall go through again. Dying is like going from one room into another. The world appears to me like a world within a world; the small resembling the great.

Letter to O. A. Ruehle von Lilienstern, Aug. 31, 1806

Gotthilf Heinrich von Schubert (1780-1860)

NATURALIST AND PHILOSOPHER

As long as the higher spirit, which bridges the abyss between this and a future existence, did not awaken in the animal or even animal-human nature, it would seem, according to an old opinion of the wise men of the world, that the planet has not yet lost its need for existence, and that beings, through death, must enter into new forms.

Views of the Nightside of Natural Science, Lecture 12

That old teaching of heathen nations according to which the soul, before its connection with this body, has been in other bodies more than once, should not this teaching solve the riddle of our present lot? The more or less violent attraction for the baser world of sense . . . in a preceding human life, has led souls to this or that fate; some to inevitable suffering, lasting from the cradle to the grave; others from refreshment to refreshment; some few to the highest unfoldment of the inner powers, others to deepest impotence.

The Story of the Soul

Karl Krause (1781-1832)

PHILOSOPHER

Although each one of us has forgotten his past, and has no insight into the greater individual life plan, yet the characteristics of heart and soul with which we are born link the individual to the several previous life periods. Possibly on entering this life we were still fully conscious of the existence just completed and its relation to the overall plan of the total life-series. . . .

Perhaps, too, death simply means birth to a new day on a higher plane of existence, while at the door of exit therefrom, dying out of that state, we are at the same time newly born here, being then reintroduced into that grand but now vanished reminiscence of the past, and enjoying a comprehensive survey of our future.

Spirit of the History of Mankind

Bettina von Arnim (1785-1859)

[*Frau von Arnim was a correspondent of Goethe, and wife of Achim von Arnim, poet and novelist, who has himself written on reincarnation. In a letter to Goethe's mother, published in Bettina von Arnim's book* Goethe's Correspondence with a Child, *she wrote:*]

No doubt, great secrets of a higher development lie hidden in art; in fact, I believe that all those tendencies which the philistines say serve no useful purpose, belong to those mystic inclinations that carry into our souls the germ of wonderful qualities, although in this life they still remain unintelligible. But in the next incarnation they will burst forth as a higher instinct, appropriate to a more spiritual element.

Arthur Schopenhauer (1788-1860)

The personality disappears at death, but we lose nothing thereby; for it is only the manifestation of quite a different Being—a Being ignorant of time, and, consequently, knowing neither life nor death. . . . When we die, we throw off our personality like a worn-out garment, and rejoice because we are about to receive a new and better one. . . .

Were an Asiatic to ask me for a definition of Europe, I should be forced to answer him: It is that part of the world which is haunted by the incredible delusion that man was created out of nothing, and that his present birth is his first entrance into life.

Parerga and Paralipomena

We find the doctrine of metempsychosis springing from the earliest and noblest ages of the human race, always spread abroad in the earth as the belief of the great majority of mankind. . . . In the succession of births . . . the persons who now stand in close connection or contact with us will also be born along with us at the next birth, and will have the same or analogous relations and sentiments towards us as now, whether these are of a friendly or a hostile description. . . .

What sleep is for the individual, death is for the will. . . . It would not endure to continue the same actions and sufferings throughout an eternity without true gain, if memory and individuality remained to it. It flings them off, and this is Lethe; and through the sleep of death, it reappears refreshed and fitted out with another intellect, as a new being—'a new day tempts to new shores.'

These constant new births, then, constitute the succession of the life-dreams of a will which in itself is indestructible. . . . Every new-born being comes fresh and blithe into the new existence, and enjoys it as a free gift; but there is, and can be, nothing freely given. Its fresh existence is paid for by the old age and death of a worn-out existence which has perished, but which contained the indestructible seed out of which this new existence has arisen: they are *one* being. To show the bridge between the two would certainly be the solution of a great riddle.

The World as Will and Idea

Friedrich Rückert (1788-1866)

POET AND ORIENTALIST

First Nature builds the body, a house with doors of sense,
Wherein a strange child, the Spirit is then born.
Tools he finds and uses at his pleasure,
Leaving finally the house, it crumbles,
But the architect always builds anew
And beckons the heavenly guest again to earthly accommodation.

Wisdom of the Brahmins

Carl Gustav Carus (1789-1869)

PHYSICIAN AND PHILOSOPHER

The oldest views of mankind always embraced some perception [of the need for a series of reembodiments] and expressed it in various, often strange symbols and similies; but always it is the old Indian teaching of the perpetual training of the soul through endless forms of existence, which . . . revealed the truth in transparent garment. . . .

What more beautiful, more important result can . . . the human spirit, who beholds the depth of his innermost being, achieve than the realization of his immortality and divinity and the unfolding within himself bright and irrefutable of that divine one. . . . Through this conviction man is enabled in fullest measure to live with a future life in view just as we expect one day to follow another. . . . Man can, then, be sure of this, that in another existence, too, that which is essentially related between souls must reappear and bring them together again.

Psyche

Karl Leberecht Immermann (1796-1840)

POET, DRAMATIST, NOVELIST

Man is of eternal duration; but I add that heaven is on earth and death does not end all, for everything beings anew. Like fire from above the Psyche takes hold of the clay, fashions it, works it out, and when finished with it, seeks fresh substance to mould. We are all *returnées* and to this reappearance of the spirit no time limit is set.

Epigonen

Heinrich Heine (1797-1856)

May it sound ever so ridiculous, I cannot conceal it; the disproportion between body and soul torments me somewhat . . . and metempsychosis often is the object of my meditation. Who may know in what tailor now dwells the soul of a Plato; in which school master the soul of a Caesar! Who knows! Possibly the soul of Pythagoras occupies the poor candidate who failed in the examination due to his inability to prove the Pythagorean theory. . . .

The North Sea

Richard Wagner (1813-1883)

[In the original version of Wagner's first opera, Rienzi, written and composed when he was twenty-five, the dying Roman hero is made to sing:

> Wretches! You think to destroy me?
> So listen now to my last words:
> As long as Roma's seven hills remain
> As long the eternal city will not pass away,
> You shall see Rienzi return again.

Later, when Wagner came to study Schopenhauer and Buddhism, he felt a strong compulsion to compose a reincarnation opera, Die Sieger (The Victor), based on Buddhistic teachings. Although this opera was never completed, several portions were ultimately incorporated in Parsifal. Of the three quotations from Wagner's writings that follow, the first concerns Die Sieger:]

To the mental eye of Buddha the past life of any being he meets is like an open book. . . . The simple story [of *Die Sieger*] assumed significance by having the previous life of the leading characters merge into the present existence by means of an accompanying musical reminiscence. Having immediately realized how to present clearly this double life through simultaneously sounding music, I applied myself to the execution of the poem with particular devotion.

Collected Writings
Vol. VI, p. 278, Kapp edition

From all time the minds that have attained . . . to a clear perception, have turned to the minds of the multitude still in bondage . . . and, having compassion on them, have sought a means of communication with them. Foremost among these enlightened spirits have been the founders of religions. . . . Certainly the Indian Prince Buddha spoke the language which most nearly gives expression to that lofty enlightenment. . . . If we are to speak in terms understood by the people of this highest perception, it can only be done under the form of pure and primitive Buddhist teaching. Especially important is the doctrine of the transmigration of souls as the basis of a truly human life.

Letter to August Roeckel (1855)

A prose translation of the four pieces, *Hollander, Tannhauser, Lohengrin,* and *Tristan,* is soon to be issued. . . . I have just gone through these translations and in so doing I was obliged to recall clearly to mind all the details of my poems. Yesterday *Lohengrin* touched me very much, and I cannot but hold it to be the most tragic poem of all, since only an immensely wide outlook upon life can provide a reconciliation between Lohengrin and Elsa.

Only the profoundly conceived idea of Reincarnation could give me any consolation, since that belief shows how all at last can reach complete redemption. . . . According to the beautiful Buddhist belief, the spotless purity of Lohengrin finds a simple explanation in the fact that he is the continuation of Parsifal, who had to fight for his purity. Even so Elsa in her rebirth would reach to the height of Lohengrin. . . . Thus all the terrible tragedy of life is seen to be nothing but the sense of Separateness in Time and Space.

Letter to Mathilde Wesendonck, Paris, 1860

Hermann Lotze (1817-1881)

PHILOSOPHER

The idea of transmigation of souls has hitherto remained a dream of the fancy, nor has any one yet succeeded in giving it a higher moral significance for the order of the universe.

Microcosm

Queen Elisabeth of Austria (1837-1898)

GERMAN BORN EMPRESS OF AUSTRIA (1854-1898)

[*Constantin Christomanos, the Queen's Greek tutor, who often accompanied her in her long walks, wrote in his* Tagebuchblaetter (diary leaves):]

Speaking of the difference between culture and civilization, she says: "Civilization is reading, culture is the thoughts. . . . Everyone has culture within himself as heritage of all his pre-existences, absorbs it with every breath and in this lies the great unity."

. . . . Of Dante and other great ones, she says: "They are souls, who, from a time long past have come anew to earth to continue their work and to anticipate the development of those still to come. . . .

"Our innermost being is more valuable than are all titles and honors. Those are colored rags to hang on and with which we try to cover our nudities. Whatever is of value in us we bring from our spiritual pre-existences."

Carl du Prel (1839-1899)

The hypothesis of a transcendental consciousness, which many followers of Darwin might repudiate, is . . . completely compatible with Darwinism . . . . According to Darwin, habits are transmitted to the germ-cells, and so to all later generations, species, and kinds; according to the transcendental psychologist, habits pass as predispositions to the transcendental Subject, and so determine its later phenomenal forms. . . . These two views are not opposed to each other. Those who think the metaphysical Darwinism, tending to Palingenesis, a crude explanation of individuality, should consider that the alternative explanations offered by materialism and pantheism are by no means less crude. . . .

Our transcendental Subject not only introduces us into life and determines our particular individuality, but also leads us through life; but it cares only for our transcendental good. . . . Man is his own heir, the Subject inherits from the person, and what I have acquired morally and intellectually remains with me. The law of the Conservation of Energy . . . avails also for the psychical world.

So should we again arrive at the oldest of philosophical conceptions of man, the migration of souls; but this old theory would be revived in a new and incomparably higher form, which could only be described as Palingenesis.

The Philosophy of Mysticism

Peter Rosegger (1843-1918)

AUSTRIAN POET AND NOVELIST

I boldly believe in the resurrection of the individual. . . . And even though the 'I' knows its present only, and cannot remember its past, I still believe that from one life to the next certain causes and effects connectingly persist. And so, it might well be that the person in a succeeding life has to feel and endure the consequences of a former one. A being who perfects himself in this life, will simply enter the next life in a more perfect condition; if he degrades himself here, he will be reborn in lower status. This may seem discouraging to a base person, but is wonderfully encouraging for one endeavoring to become purer and better. . . .

My Kingdom of Heaven

Carmen Sylva (1843-1916)

PEN NAME OF GERMAN-BORN QUEEN ELISABETH OF ROMANIA

In a letter to a friend, Lina Sommer, published in *Letters of a Lonesome Queen*, Carmen Sylva mentions a book on which she worked daily that she preferred to write on parchment with India ink, using old style lettering, and comments that in all probability she must have been a monk or a nun in a former existence because she so enjoyed occupying herself with cell crafts.

Friedrich Nietzsche (1844-1900)

Our duty is present with us every instant. My doctrine is: Live so that thou mayest desire to live again—that is thy duty; for, in any case, thou wilt live again! And in every one of these cycles of human life there will be one hour where for the first time one man, and then many, will perceive the mighty thought of the eternal recurrence of all things—and for mankind this is always the hour of noon.

Eternal Recurrence

Everything goeth, everything returneth; eternally rolleth the wheel of existence. Everything dieth, everything blossometh forth again; eternally runneth on the year of existence.

Everything breaketh, everything is integrated anew; eternally buildeth itself the same house of existence. All things separate, all things again greet one another; eternally true to itself remaineth the ring of existence.

Behold, we know what thou teachest, that all things eternally return, and ourselves with them, and that we have already existed times without number, and all things with us. . . . Oh, how could I not be ardent for Eternity and for the marriage-ring of rings—the ring of the return?

Thus Spake Zarathustra

The fundamental idea of my work [*Thus Spake Zarathustra*]—namely, the Eternal Recurrence of all things—this highest of all possible formulae for a Yea-saying philosophy, first occurred to me in August 1881. I made a note of the thought on a sheet of paper, with the postscript: 6,000 feet beyond men and time! That day I happened to be wandering through the woods alongside of the lake of Silvaplana, and I halted beside a huge, pyramidal and towering rock. . . . It was then that the thought struck me.

Ecce Homo

Gustav Mahler (1860-1911)

[*Mahler's biographer, Richard Specht, relates of his visit to the composer in Hamburg, in 1895:*]

In the course of the conversation Mahler said very emphatically: "We all return; it is this certainty that gives meaning to life and it does not make the slightest difference whether or not in a later incarnation we remember the former life. What counts is not the individual and his comfort, but the great aspiration to the perfect and the pure which goes on in each incarnation."

Rudolf Steiner (1861-1925)

AUSTRIAN PHILOSOPHER AND EDUCATOR; FOUNDER OF ANTHROPOSOPHY

Those who, by means of meditation, rise to that which unites man with spirit are bringing to life within them the eternal element which is limited by neither birth nor death. Only those who have had no experience of it themselves can doubt the existence of this eternal element. . . . Gnosis and Theosophy tell of the eternal nature of this essential being, and of its reincarnation. The question is often asked: "Why does a man know nothing of those experiences which lie beyond the borders of birth and death?" Not thus should we ask, but rather: "How may we attain to such knowledge?" The entrance to the Path is opened by right meditation.

The Way of Initiation

When a man lived as a being of body and soul in one epoch of culture, he does not vanish from the field of evolution but remains, in order again to take part in what earth-existence has later become. . . . Christian thought has actually lost something which the East has always possessed and knowledge of which has now to be reacquired. The course of evolution is such that certain outworn fragments must be discarded and new elements added; ancient heritages must be rescued again, but in a new form and through a new impulse. In olden times clairvoyance was a natural gift of humanity. It had to fade away and be replaced by thinking based upon purely external observation and perception; this will be enriched by the clairvoyance of the future and will add something of untold significance to human life. The West had to pass through a period during which mankind was split up, as it were, into separate personalities, but now that men stand on the threshold of a deepening of thought and experience, they will themselves be aware of a longing to find the thread uniting the fragments which make their appearance in the life of the human being between birth and death. The light of understanding will thus be shed on forces which flow onward through the stream of spiritual development and human progress.

Earthly and Cosmic Man, Lecture V

Christian Morgenstern (1871-1914)

POET

Mankind long ago received all there is to be received, but must receive and digest it over and over again, and always in a new form. The teaching of reincarnation, for instance, is a case in point. . . . The old cycle has run its course and once more this teaching is permitted to enter the current of Western development. As an immeasurable blessing. . . . it will fructify, enlighten, and save mankind anew.

Diary entry, January 1911

The idea of reincarnation shows us the path of development of the single individual extending through ages of time and space, who from a certain moment on—designated in the Bible as the Fall of Man—was endowed with the freedom to choose good or evil, and who then had the opportunity in ever new human incarnations, with extensive intervening periods for purification, rest and inner development, to work its way upward to the Christ, or downward toward the anti-Christ.

Letter to Elisabeth Morgenstern, Mar, 31, 1910

Albert Schweitzer (1875-   )

By reason of the idea of reincarnation Indian thought can be reconciled to the fact that so many people in their minds and actions are still so engrossed in the world. If we assume that we have but one existence, there arises the insoluble problem of what becomes of the spiritual *ego* which has lost all contact with the Eternal. Those who hold the doctrine of reincarnation are faced by no such problem. For them that non-spiritual attitude only means that those men and women have not yet attained to the purified form of existence in which they are capable of knowing the truth and translating it into action.

So the idea of reincarnation contains a most comforting explanation of reality by means of which Indian thought surmounts difficulties which baffle the thinkers of Europe.

Indian Thought and Its Development

Rainer Maria Rilke (1875-1926)

POET AND WRITER

[The Princess Marie of Thurn und Taxis (a principality in Bavaria), wrote in her Recollections of R. M. Rilke: "Deep down he considered Russia his soul-home, convinced that in a former incarnation he lived in Moscow." Speaking of death and return to earth life, Rilke wrote:]

Perhaps one only seeks a homecoming and welcome, pursues it, till the circle rounds, back to that home, feeling with a strange certainty, dream-like and sad, that he had lost it once before.

Letters and Diaries

Dr. Bruno Walter (1876-   )

Knowing of Dr. Walter's interest in the subject, he was approached for a possible statement on reincarnation for inclusion in this Anthology. The famed conductor replied:

It would have given me particular satisfaction to contribute to the book entitled "A Reincarnation Anthology." Unfortunately I cannot find the time and concentration to do so, but permit me to add to the list Emil Bock's *Wiederholte Erdenleben* [*Repeated Lives on Earth*].

The latter book, an excellent German anthology on reincarnation, records a newspaper interview with Dr. Walter at the time of his visit to Germany after an absence of thirteen years (reported in Die Tat for December 21, 1946). The reporters were surprised to be drawn into the realm of the mystical instead of that of politics, as anticipated. When the discussion focused on the common experience of visiting a new place and feeling one had lived there in another life, Dr. Walter showed special interest: "That is what happened to me when I saw Vienna for the first time; I knew all the streets and squares; I recognized them because I felt this had been my home."

Hans Much (1880-1932)

PHYSICIAN AND WRITER

Can you remember a dark chapter in your bible studies that must have stumped you as much as it did me? I am thinking of original sin. Did you ever understand that? And yet underneath one perceived that it contained a great truth. How illuminating this truth stands out in the light of Buddha! The original sin is my own sin, committed in past existences. All that is obscure and contradictory in Christianity, yet containing a trace of truth, probably has its origin in misunderstood buddhistic truths.

Letter to his wife, July 3, 1917

Count Hermann Keyserling (1880-1946)

The principle . . . is indestructible. It continues to act objectively, from reincarnation to reincarnation, on both sides of the grave, in some unknown sense. The bearers of this principle change, and they do not guess, or, if so, only faintly, that their essence is eternal. The rare man, who succeeds in anchoring his consciousness in true Being, knows himself to be immortal, and death no longer signifies an end to him. . . .

Benares is overflowing with the diseased and the infirm. . . . And yet I have never felt less compassion. These sufferers suffer so little; they have, above all, no fear whatever of death. . . . As to their infirmity—well, that must be endured; it will not take very long anyhow. And some old sin is no doubt scored off in the process. The faith of the Indians is said to be pessimistic. I know of none which is less so.

The Travel Diary of a Philosopher

Franz Werfel (1890-1945)

CZECH-BORN POET, DRAMATIST, NOVELIST

I carry much in me.
The past of former lives
Buried regions,
With traces of star-rays. . . .
The World Friend

In Werfel's novel Star of the Unborn, the comment is made that a hundred thousand years from now a man who has passed through many re-embodiments will have the enormous privilege of learning what happened in the decades, centuries, and milleniums after his death.

DUTCH

Spinoza (1632-1677)

It is impossible for us to remember that we had existence prior to the body, since the body can have no vestige of it, and eternity cannot be defined in terms of time or have any relation to time. But, nevertheless, we have in our experience a perception that we are eternal. For the mind is sensible no less of what it understands than of what it remembers. . . . Although, therefore, we do not remember that we existed before the body, yet we perceive that our mind is eternal, in so far as it involves the body's essence under the category of eternity, and that this its existence cannot be defined by time or interpreted by duration.

Ethics, Book V

Henri Borel (1869-1933)

[Henri Borel received a well-earned prominence among students of oriental literature for his exquisite essays on Taoism, a brief quotation from which is given below. These essays are in the form of a conversation with a Chinese sage. In his book Karma, Borel asks: "Do we not all journey in the caravans of our numerous births toward the Great Light?"]

"No man can annihilate Tao, and there shines in each one of us the inextinguishable light of the soul. Do not believe that the evilness of humanity is so great and so mighty. The eternal Tao dwells in all; in murderers and harlots as well as in philosophers and poets. All bear within them an indestructible treasure, and not one is better than another . . . not one will be banished out of Tao eternally. . . ."

"Father, what you say is clear—and compels belief. But life is still so dear to me, and I am afraid of death; I am afraid too lest my friends should die, or my wife, or my child! Death seems to me so black and gloomy—and life is bright—bright with the sun, and the green and flowery earth!"

"That is because you fail as yet to feel the perfect naturalness of death, which is equal in reality to that of life. You think too much of the insignificant body, and the deep grave in which it must lie; but that is the feeling of a prisoner about to be freed, who is troubled at the thought of leaving the dark cell where he has lived so long. You see death in contrast to life; and both are unreal—both are a changing and seeming. Your soul does not glide out of a familiar sea into an unfamiliar ocean. That which is real in you, your soul, can never pass away, and this fear is no part of her. . . . And passing with calm acceptance through the changes of day and night, summer and winter, life and death, you will one day enter into Tao, where there is no more change, and whence you issued once as pure as you now return."

BELGIAN

❀

Franciscus Mercurius van Helmont (1614-1699)

NATURALIST AND PHILOSOPHER

Van Helmont in his *De Revolutione Animarum*, adduced in two hundred problems all the arguments which may be urged in favor of the return of souls into human bodies according to Jewish ideas. The book as published in London, 1684, bears the title, *Two Hundred Queries moderately Propounded concerning the Doctrine of the Revolution of Human Souls*.

Maurice Maeterlinck (1862-1949)

POET, DRAMATIST, ESSAYIST

Let us return to reincarnation . . . for there never was a more beautiful, a juster, a purer, a more moral, fruitful and consoling, nor, to a certain point, a more probable creed than theirs [the Theosophists]. It alone, with its doctrine of successive expiations and purifications, accounts for all the physical and intellectual inequalities, all the social iniquities, all the hideous injustices of fate. But the quality of a creed is no evidence of its truth. Even though it is the religion of six hundred millions of mankind, the nearest to the mysterious origins, the only one that is not odious and the least absurd of all, it will have to do what the others have not done, to bring unimpeachable testimony; and what it has given us hitherto is but the first shadow of a proof begun.

Our Eternity

We parted, and not a word was spoken, but at one and the same moment had we understood our inexpressible thought. . . . We have never met again. Perhaps centuries will elapse before we do meet again.

> Much is to learn, and much to forget,
> Through worlds I shall traverse not a few

before we shall again find ourselves *in the same movement of the soul* as on that evening: but we can well afford to wait.

The Treasure of the Humble

FRENCH

Voltaire (1694-1778)

Pherecides was the first among the Greeks who believed that souls existed from all eternity, and not the first, as has been supposed, who said that the soul survived the body. Ulysses, long before Pherecides, had seen the souls of heroes in the infernal regions; but that souls were as old as the world was a system which had sprung up in the East, and was brought into the West by Pherecides. I do not believe that there is among us a single system which is not to be found among the ancients. The materials of all our modern edifices are taken from the wreck of antiquity.

Voltaire's Philosophical Dictionary
Section X, under "Soul"

The doctrine of metempsychosis is, above all, neither absurd nor useless. It is not more surprising to be born twice than once; everything in nature is resurrection.*

Louis Claude de St. Martin (1743-1803)

Death ought to be looked upon only as one stage in our journey. We reach this stage with tired, worn-out horses, and we start again with horses

* Quoted in French in *Old Truths in a New Light* by Lady Caithness (London, 1876) p. 394.

that are fresh, and able to take us farther on our road. All the same, we must pay what we owe for the portion of the journey that has been traversed, and until the account is settled, we are not allowed to continue our way.

Oeuvres Postumes, Vol. I

Napoleon Bonaparte (1769-1821)

Here was a man born in the humblest possible condition of life, rising until he dominated empires and sent kings from their thrones at a single word, a man who, in those strange, abnormal conditions into which he sometimes passed, would cry out to his Marshals: "I am Charlemagne. Do you know who I am? I am Charlemagne." Emil Ludwig also quotes him as stating: "*Tell the Pope that I am keeping my eyes open; tell him that I am Charlemagne, the Sword of the Church, his Emperor, and as such I expect to be treated.*" While Prince Talleyrand in his Memoirs (Vol. II, p. 77, The Napoleon Society, N.Y., 1895) writes thus of a stormy meeting between Bonaparte and several dignitaries of the Church:

. . . the phrase which follows, and which he repeated every three or four minutes . . . revealed the depth of his thought. "Messieurs," he exclaimed to them," you wish to treat me as if I were Louis le Débonnaire. Do not confound the son with the father. You see in me Charlemagne. . . . I am Charlemagne, I . . . yes, I am Charlemagne."

François Fourier (1772-1837)

SOCIAL SCIENTIST AND REFORMER

Where is there an old man who would not like to feel certain that he would be born again and bring back into another life the experience he has gained in the present one?. . . . We must recognize that we have already lived before being what we now are, and that many other lives await us, some in this world, and the rest in a higher sphere, with a finer body and more delicate senses.

Theory of Universal Unity

Pierre Ballanche (1776-1847)
PHILOSOPHER AND MYSTIC

Each of us is a reincarnating being, ignorant both of his present and of his former transformations. . . . This life we spend on earth, shut in between an apparent birth and an equally apparent death is, in reality, only a portion of our existence, one manifestation of man in time. . . .

There are men in advance of their century; there are even some in advance of this actual existence, who participate in the future existence. . . . There are men sustained by divine goodness to hasten the accomplishment of its designs, who voluntarily take up the burden in order to lighten it for others. . . . Our former lives belong to astronomical cycles lost in the mighty bosom of previous ages; not yet has it been given to us to know them.

Palingenesis Sociale

Pierre Jean de Beranger (1780-1857)

In philosophic mood, last night, as idly I was lying,
That souls may transmigrate, methought there could be no denying:
So, just to know to what I owe propensities so strong,
I drew my soul into a chat—our gossip lasted long.
"A votive offering," she observed, "well might I claim from thee;
For thou in being hadst remained a cipher, but for me:
Yet not a virgin soul was I when first in thee enshrined."
Ah! I suspected, little soul, thus much that I should find! . . .

La Métempsycose

Jean B. F. Obry (1793-1871)

This old belief [metempsychosis] has been held all round the world, and was spread in the remote antiquity to such an extent that a learned English churchman has declared it to be fatherless, motherless, and without genealogy.

Du Nirvana Indien

Pierre Leroux (1797-1871)

PHILOSOPHER AND JOURNALIST

If we regard the world as a series of successive lives for each creature, we see very well how it comes about that God, to whom there is neither time nor space, and who perceives the final goal of all things, permits evil and suffering as being necessary phases through which creatures must pass, in order to reach a state of happiness.

De l'Humanité

André Pezzani

The earthly sojourn is only a new probation, as was said by Dupont de Nemours [in *The Philosophy of the Universe*], that great writer who, in the eighteenth century, outstripped all modern thought. Now, if this be so, is it not plain that the recollection of former lives would seriously hinder probations, by removing most of their difficulties, and consequently of their deserts, as well as of their spontaneity? . . .

The struggle must be free, voluntary, safe from the influences of the past; the field of combat must seem new, so that the athlete may exhibit and practice his virtues upon it. The experience he has already acquired, the forces he has learned how to conquer, serve him in the new strife; but in such a manner that he does not suspect it, for the imperfect soul undergoes reincarnations in order to *develop* the qualities that it has already manifested, to free itself from the vices and faults which are in opposition to the ascensional law. What would happen if all men remembered their former lives? The order of the earth would be overthrown; at least, it is not now established on such conditions. Lethe, as well as free-will, is a law of the actual world.

The Plurality of the Soul's Existence

Honoré de Balzac (1799-1850)

All human beings go through a previous life in the sphere of Instinct, where they are brought to see the worthlessness of earthly treasures, to amass which they gave themselves such untold pains! Who can tell how many times the human being lives in the sphere of Instinct before he is prepared to enter the sphere of Abstraction, where thought expends itself on erring science, where mind wearies at last of human language? For, when Matter is exhausted, Spirit enters. . . . Then follow other existences —all to be lived to reach the place where Light effulgent shines. Death is the post-house of the journey.

A lifetime may be needed merely to gain the virtues which annul the errors of man's preceding life. . . . The virtues we acquire, which develop slowly within us, are the invisible links which bind each one of our existences to the others—existences which the spirit alone remembers, for Matter has no memory for spiritual things. Thought alone holds the tradition of the bygone life. The endless legacy of the past to the present is the secret source of human genius.

Seraphita

Victor Hugo (1802-1885)

I am a soul. I know well that what I shall render up to the grave is not myself. That which is myself will go elsewhere. Earth, thou art not my abyss! . . . The whole creation is a perpetual ascension, from brute to man, from man to God. To divest ourselves more and more of matter, to be clothed more and more with spirit, such is the law. Each time we die we gain more of life. Souls pass from one sphere to another without loss of personality, become more and more bright. . . .

Victor Hugo's Intellectual Autobiography

I feel in myself the future life. I am like a forest once cut down; the new shoots are stronger and livelier than ever. . . . You say the soul is nothing but the resultant of the bodily powers? Why, then, is my soul more luminous when my bodily powers begin to fail? The nearer I approach the end the plainer I hear around me the immortal symphonies of the worlds which invite me. It is marvelous yet simple. It is a fairy tale and it is history.

For half a century I have been writing my thoughts in prose and in verse; history, philosophy, drama, romance, tradition, satire, ode and song; I have tried all. But I feel I have not said a thousandth part of what is in me. When I go down to the grave I can say like many others "I have finished my day's work," but I can not say, "I have finished my life." My day's work will begin again the next morning. The tomb is not a blind alley; it is a thoroughfare. It closes on the twilight. It opens on the dawn.*

---

* The Philosophy of Life, by A. M. Baten, p. 163.

George Sand (1803-1876)

"Consuelo," he said to her. . . . "I am going to leave you for a time, and then I shall return to earth by means of a new birth. I shall return accursed and despairing if you abandon me now, in my last hour. . . . We are brethren; ere we become lovers, death must once more separate us. But we must be united by the marriage-vow, that I may be re-born calm and strong, and free, like other men, from the memory of past lives which has been my torment and my punishment for so many centuries. Consent to this vow. It will not bind you to me in this life, which I am about to leave, but it will reunite us in eternity. It will be as a seal to help us to recognise one another when the shades of death have effaced the clearness of our memories."

Consuelo

Cast into this life, as it were, into an alembic, where, after a previous existence which we have forgotten, we are condemned to be remade renewed, tempered by suffering, by strife, by passion, by doubt, by disease, by death. All these evils we endure for our good, for our purification, and, so to speak, to make us perfect.

From age to age, from race to race, we accomplish a tardy progress, tardy but certain, an advance of which, in spite of all the skeptics say, the proofs are manifest. If all the imperfections of our being and all the woes of our estate drive at discouraging and terrifying us, on the other hand, all the more noble faculties, which have been bestowed on us that we might seek after perfection, do make for our salvation, and deliver us from fear, misery and even death. Yes, a divine instinct that always grows in light and strength helps us to comprehend that nothing in the whole world wholly dies and that we only vanish from the things that lie about us in our earthly life, to reappear among conditions more favorable to our eternal growth in good.*

Jean Reynaud (1806-1863)

PHILOSOPHER

How glorious the light that would be cast on the present order of things by a knowledge of our former existences! And yet, not only is

* Magazine *Lucifer* (London), April, 1889, p. 89.

our memory helpless regarding the times that preceded birth, it is not even conscious of the whole of the intervening period, often playing us false in the course of a lifetime. . . . Who knows but what our soul, in the unknown secret of its essence, has power some day to throw light on its successive journeyings. . . .

Let us try to conceive the infinite treasures of a mind enriched by the recollections of an innumerable series of existences, entirely different from each other, and yet admirably linked together by a continual dependence.

Earth and Heaven

Alphonse Esquiros (1814-1876)

The question may well be asked whether the talents, the good and evil tendencies man brings with him at birth, may not be the fruit of acquired intelligence, of qualities and vices gained in one or many former existences. . . . From the time when intelligence begins to show itself in children, we faintly discern a general attitude towards things, which is very like a memory thereof. . . . I affirm the perpetual union of the soul to organic bodies.*

Charles Renouvier (1815-1903)

[In the course of the elaboration of his theory of monads, of indestructible germs, and of the origin and destiny of personality, this noted French philosopher wrote:]

But it is not once only that each person must live again on earth owing to the actualization of one of those seminal potencies; it is a certain number of times, we do not know how many. . . .

[The several persons which represent the several lives of one continuing individuality] are not held together by memory, and have no earthly genealogical relationships to each other. They also have no memory of the person whom each of them comes to continue on earth. Such forgetting is a condition of any theory of pre-existence . . . the person, reintegrated in the world of ends, recovers there the memory of its state in the world of origins, and of the diverse lives which it has gone through, in the course of which it has received the lessons and undergone the trials of the life of pain.

Le Personnalisme

---

* *Vie Future au Point de Vue Socialiste*, and *Confession d'un Curé de Village*.

Gustave Flaubert (1821-1880)

I do not have, as you do, that feeling of a life that is but beginning, the stupefication of an existence just commencing. It seems to me, on the contrary, that I have always existed! I see myself in the different ages of history, quite clearly, engaging in different trades and experiencing various fortunes. . . . Many things would be explained if we only knew our real genealogy. . . . Thus heredity is a true principle that has been badly applied.

Letter to George Sand

Edouard Schuré (1841-1929)

The doctrine of the ascensional life of the soul through series of existences is the common feature of esoteric traditions and the crown of theosophy. I will add that it is of the utmost importance to us. For the man of the present day rejects with equal scorn the abstract and vague immortality of philosophy and the childish heaven of an infant religion. And yet he abhors the dryness and nothingless of materialism. Unconsciously he aspires to the consciousness of an *organic immortality* responding at once to the demands of his reason and the indestructible needs of his soul. . . .

Lives follow without resembling one another, but a pitiless logic links them together. Though each of them has its own law and special destiny, the succession is controlled by a general law, which might be called the repercussion of lives. . . . There is not a word or action which has not its echo in eternity, says a proverb. According to esoteric doctrine, this proverb is literally applied from one life to another.

Pythagoras and the Delphic Mysteries

Henri Bergson (1859-1941)

ON IMMORTALITY

How can we help seeing . . . that, if there really is a problem of the soul, it must be posited in terms of experience, and in terms of experience it must be progressively, and always partially, solved? . . . This experimental searching will suggest the possibility and even probability of the survival of the soul, since even here below we shall have observed something of its independence of the body, indeed we shall have almost felt it. . . .

Let us now betake ourselves to the higher plane: we shall find an experience of another type, mystic intuition. And this is presumably a participation in the divine essence. Now, do these two experiences meet? Can the after-life, which is apparently assured to our soul by the simple fact that, even here below, a great part of this activity is independent of the body, be identical with that of the life unto which, even here below, certain privileged souls insert themselves? Only a prolongation and a profound investigation of these two experiences will tell us; the problem must remain open. Still it is something to have obtained, on essential points, a probability which is capable of being transformed into a certainty, and for the rest, for the knowledge of the soul and of its destiny, the possibility of endless progress.

The Two Sources of Morality and Religion

Romain Rolland (1866-1944)

When staff in hand in later years I scoured the roads of thought, I found nothing that was strange in any country. All the aspects of mind that I found or felt were in their origin the same as mine. Outside experience merely brought me the realization of my own mind, the states of which I had noted but to which I had no key. Neither Shakespeare nor Beethoven nor Tolstoy nor Rome, the master that nurtured me, ever revealed anything to me except the "Open Sesame" of my subterranean city, my Herculaneum, sleeping under its lava. And I am convinced that it sleeps in the depths of many of those around us. But they are ignorant of its existence just as I was. . . .

I have just rediscovered the key of the lost staircase. . . . The staircase in the wall, spiral like the coils of a serpent, winds from the subterranean depths of the Ego to the high terraces crowned by the stars. But nothing that I saw there was unknown country. I had seen it all before and I knew it well—but I did not know where I had seen it before. More than once I had recited from memory, though imperfectly, the lesson of thought learned at some former time (but from whom? One of my very ancient selves. . . .)

Prophets of the New India

S W I S S

[See also index under: Paracelsus, Johann Lavater, Charles Bonnett, and Carl Jung]

Johann Georg Sulzer (1720-1779)

PHILOSOPHER

Consequently, after the present life, it [the soul] will proceed to another scene there to continue its activity. . . . If there are laws that unite the soul to a physical body, why should we doubt that under similar laws a second union of the soul with another body could take place?

Miscellaneous Philosophical Writings

Henri Amiel (1821-1881)

POET AND PHILOSOPHER

The degrees of initiation are innumerable. Watch, then, disciple of life, watch and labour towards the development of the angel within thee! For the divine Odyssey is but a series of more and more ethereal metamorphoses, in which each form, the result of what goes before, is the condition of those which follow.

The divine life is a series of successive deaths, in which the mind throws off its imperfections and its symbols, and yields to the growing attraction of the ineffable center of gravitation, the sun of intelligence and love. . . .

Life is only a document to be interpreted, matter to be spiritualized. Such is the life of the thinker. Every day he strips himself more and more of personality. . . . He does not even believe his body his own; he feels the vital whirlwind passing through him—lent to him, as it were, for a moment, in order that he may perceive the cosmic vibrations. . . . He asks nothing from life but wisdom.

Amiel's Journal

Conrad Ferdinand Meyer (1825-1898)
POET AND HISTORICAL NOVELIST

[*In a letter to Friedrich von Wiss, Meyer wrote concerning some inner struggles:*]

In the last few years I have gone through more than I am ever willing to confess. Truly what sustained me was a thought on reincarnation. I told myself: Evidently you did something terrible in a former existence. Said the voice of fate: Just for that the fellow shall go to earth and become a Meyer. Now both have to suffer through honestly before a change for the better may be attained.

❁

Henrik Ibsen (1828-1906)

NORWEGIAN DRAMATIST AND POET

[As already mentioned, the Roman Emperor Julian believed himself to be a reincarnation of Alexander the Great. The following lines from Ibsen's tragedy on Julian point up this idea:]

MAXIMUS: Must I remind you how fortune has borne you, as on mighty pinions, through an agitated and perilous life? Who are you, sire? Are you Alexander born again, not, as before, in immaturity, but perfectly equipped for the fulfillment of the task?

JULIAN: Maximus!

MAXIMUS: There is One who ever reappears, at certain intervals, in the course of human history. He is like a rider taming a wild horse in the arena. Again and yet again it throws him. A moment, and he is in the saddle again, each time more secure and more expert; but off he has had to go, in all his varying incarnations, until this day. Off he had to go as the god-created man in Eden's grove; off he had to go as the founder of the world-empire; off he *must* go as the prince of the empire of God. Who knows how often he has wandered among us when none have recognized him? . . .

JULIAN (*looking far away*): Oh, unfathomable riddle—!

The Emperor Julian

Bjornstjerne Bjornson (1832-1910)

NORWEGIAN POET, NOBEL PRIZE 1902

I seem to be
Sundered from Thee,
Thou harmony of all creation.
Am I disowned
For talents loaned
And useless hid in vain probation? . . .

Honor the springtide life ever adoring,
That all things has made!
Things smallest have some resurrectional morning,
The forms alone fade.
Life begets life,
Potencies higher surprise.
Kind begets kind,
Heedles of time as it flies.
Worlds pass away and arise. . . .

Psalms

Hjalmar Hjorth Bogesen

NORWEGIAN-AMERICAN POET

My spirit wrestles in anguish
With fancies that will not depart;
A ghost who borrowed my semblance
Has hid in the depth of my heart.
A dim, resistless possession
Impels me forever to do
The phantom deeds of this phantom
That liv'd ages ago.

Transmigration

Emanuel Swedenborg (1688-1772)

SWEDISH SCIENTIST, PHILOSOPHER, THEOLOGIAN

[In the following extracts from his essay "Swedenborg; or, the Mystic,"
Ralph Waldo Emerson touches upon Swedenborg's view of reincarnation,

but first suggests how this doctrine might explain the seership of the famous mystics of history, including the Swedish seer:]

The Arabians say, that Abul Khain, the mystic, and Abu Ali Seena, the philosopher, conferred together; and, on parting, the philosopher said, "All that he sees, I know;" and the mystic said, "All that he knows, I see." If one should ask the reason of this intuition, the solution would lead us into that property which Plato denoted as Reminiscence, and which is implied by the Brahmins in the tenet of Transmigration. The soul having been often born, or, as the Hindoos say, "Travelling the path of existence through thousands of births," having beheld the things which are here, those which are in heaven and those which are beneath, there is nothing of which she has not gained the knowledge: no wonder that she is able to recollect, in regard to any one thing, what formerly she knew.

That metempsychosis which is familiar in the old mythology of the Greeks, collected in Ovid and in the Indian Transmigration, and is there *objective*, or really takes place in bodies by alien will,—in Swedenborg's mind has a more philosophic character. It is subjective, or depends entirely upon the thought of the person. All things in the universe arrange themselves to each person anew, according to his ruling love. . . . Everyone makes his own house and state. . . .

I think of [Swedenborg] as of some transmigrating votary of Indian legend, who says "Though I be dog, or jackal, or pismire, in the last rudiments of nature, under what integument or ferocity, I cleave to right, as the sure ladder that leads up to man and to God."

August Strindberg (1849-1912)

SWEDISH DRAMATIST AND NOVELIST

The teacher said: "Life is hard to live, and the destinies of men appear very different. Some have brighter days, others darker ones. It is therefore difficult to know how one should behave in life, what one should believe, what views one should adopt, or to which party one should adhere. This destiny is not the inevitable blind fate of the ancients, but the commission which each one has received, the task he must perform. The Theosophists call it Karma, and believe it is connected with a past which we only dimly remember. . . ."

The pupil asked: "If it is so, why is not one informed of one's Karma from the beginning?"

The teacher answered: "That is pure pity for us. No man could endure life if he knew what lay before him. Moreover, man must have a certain measure of freedom; without that he would be only a puppet. Also the wise think that the voyage of discovery we make to discover our destiny is instructive for us. . . ."

Darwin made it seem probable that men derived their origin from animals. Then came the Theosophists with the opinion that our souls are in process of transmigration from one human body to another. Thence comes this excessive feeling of discomfort, this longing for deliverance, this sensation of constraint, the pain of existence, the sighing of the creature. Those who do not feel this uneasiness, but flourish here, are probably at home here. Their inexplicable sympathy for animals and their disbelief in the immortality of the soul points to a connection with the lower forms of existence of which they are conscious, and which we cannot deny.

Zones of the Spirit

Axel Munthe (1857-1949)
SWEDISH DOCTOR AND PSYCHIATRIST

[*Munthe's memoirs, The Story of San Michele, have been translated into twenty-three languages, the editions in English alone accounting for almost a million copies. Written at the suggestion of Henry James, the book treats, in part, of the reconstruction by Dr. Munthe of the chapel built on the Isle of Capri by the Roman Emperor Tiberius (42 B.C.-A.D. 37), who retired to Capri during the last eleven years of his life.*

Although neither Munthe nor the illiterate peasants who helped him in the building had any knowledge of architectural techniques—the answer to problems often appearing in sleep—the wondrous beauty of the completed work was the envy of kings and queens, who were its frequent visitants. When one reads of the unusual psychic adventures that involved Dr. Munthe from boyhood onward in the project, it is not surprising that friends indulged in speculations that he must be Tiberius returned!* Quoting now from the book itself:]

[*A goblin is depicted as asking Munthe about Time:*] "Do you always carry it about with you in that gold box [Munthe's watch]?"

"Yes, it never rests, it never sleeps, it never ceases to repeat the same word in my ears. . . . It tells me every second, every minute, every hour of

---

* The English sculptor and author, Clare Sheridan, wrote in her autobiography *The Naked Truth* (Harpers, 1928): "I called him Tiberio, the name seemed to belong to him. He had the qualities and faults of Tiberius; his tyranny and kindliness. . . . He might have been, and I believed he was, a reincarnation of the Imperator, drawn back to the scene of his past and doomed in this life to pay back an overburdened Karma."

the day and of the night that I am getting older, and that I am going to die. Tell me, little man, before you go, are you afraid of Death?"

"Afraid of what?"

"Afraid of the day when the beating of your heart will cease, the cogs and wheels of the whole machinery fall to pieces, your thoughts stand still, your life flicker out like the light of that dim tallow candle on the table."

"Who has put all that nonsense in your head? Don't listen to the voice inside the gold box with its silly past, present and future, don't you understand that it all means the same thing! Don't you understand that somebody is making fun of you inside that gold box! . . . Don't believe a word of what it tells you, it is nothing but lies! You will always remain a child, you will never grow old, you will never die. You just lie down and get to sleep for a while! The sun will soon rise again over the fir-tops, the new day will soon look in through the window, you will soon see much clearer than you ever saw by the light of that tallow candle."

* * *

[Pacciale, an old Italian fisherman of Capri] had become my friend, the honour was mine, he was a far better man than I. . . . During the long days and nights we were together alone on the sea he taught me many things I had not read in my books or heard from the lips of other men. . . . His thoughts were few and so much the better for him. But his sayings were full of poetry and the archaic simplicity of his similes were pure Greek. Many of his very words were Greek, he remembered them from the time he had sailed down that very coast as one of the crew in Ulysses' ship.

Selma Lagerlöf (1858-1940)

SWEDISH NOVELIST AND POET, NOBEL PRIZE 1909

[In her novel A Fallen King, Selma Lagerlöf tells of a shoemaker who through a sudden change in his life becomes an evangelist. How explain the poetic flight that now ensouls his words?]

Perhaps once before his spirit tarried in this world of death and change. Perhaps he was then a mighty poet, experienced in the art of touching the strings of the heart. Severe crimes condemned him to renewed earth life, to live by the work of his hands, not recognizing the power of his spirit. But now his grief has burst the prison.

Jean Sibelius (1865-1957)

FINNISH COMPOSER

[The former music critic for the New York Times, Howard Taubman, in a featured article (December 4, 1955) in honor of Sibelius at the time of his ninetieth birthday, wrote:]

The interrelationship between life and art is one of Sibelius' chief concerns. . . . Sibelius' identification with the fields, the woods, the sea and the sky is so profound that it has always permeated his music. . . . As a boy, Sibelius wandered in the wilderness of his native province of Häme. Birds always fascinated him. "Millions of years ago, in my previous incarnations," he once told Jalas [his son-in-law], "I must have been related to swans or wild geese, because I can still feel that affinity."

Johan Ludvig Heiberg (1791-1860)

DANISH AUTHOR

[Heiberg states that his long poem "The Newly Married" is based on reality, the events having transpired on his own honeymoon. The poem depicts, in part, a newlywed couple seeking shelter in the home of a poor widow and her adopted son Fredrik, who as an orphaned child found her in a strange way. The little fellow filled an empty place in her heart, her own son being dead. Fredrik, now grown, falls so passionately in love with the young bride that he secretly schemes to kill the husband on a hunting trip. The mother has a fearful premonition and speaks to Fredrik thus:]

"I have never told you, my son . . . maybe the heart gets rest, when I speak to you of my fate; maybe it becomes easier, when we are two to carry the secret tortures. That son, which was given me in my marriage, oh—you don't know how he died!—He was decapitated and his blood covered the scaffold. Rejected by a young and beautiful maiden, who was deaf and blind to his love, he killed a more lucky lover . . . while hunting.

"That morning, when he was to suffer his horrible doom . . . my son sank to my breast and exclaimed: 'Give me a word, a powerful word, which will comfort me on my last walk alive!' And I said—But Fredrik, you frighten me! . . . You stare at me as white as a corpse."

"Oh mother! stop!!—You said: 'When before your saviour you stand say:

My God and my Brother! Forgive me for your martyr-wounds; for my anger and for my mother!' "

[MOTHER]: "How do you know that?" [FREDRIK]: "It was I! I am your real son, and now he lives the life anew. [MOTHER]: "Fredrik, has insanity overtaken your mind?" [FREDRIK]: "No, mother, don't be afraid! But up to now, I walked as one blind, through all these long years. My consciousness awoke in this hour. Now I see my entire self, now I see the basis of my life and at the same time I hope and I tremble. Ah, I feel again my horrible fear, when my head I laid on the block. But still my thought held the comforting words you spoke."

"When the ax fell my consciousness left me. I woke up in strange places; and on my wanderings my eye rested on a man in white garments. I know not . . . maybe he was my Saviour, but ah! I did not know him, so my prayer to him I did not say, though his eyes were so mild looking . . . his hair was shining light. He said: 'Turn around! Your place is not in here. On earth you suffered death for your crime; here is no punishment, no penalty. So go back, down to earth to live over again your days.' "

"Then I turned back on fearful foot; wandering ever so long. . . . I needed rest and slept a sleep so deep I knew nothing of what happened. But, when I woke up as a child I sensed I was another. Oh, mother, look at me; I need you to console me now. Not another time, that I can promise for certain, shall your son make sad your heart.—She does not answer! . . . What a deep sigh she draws—She is dead!"

Soeren Kierkegaard (1813-1855)
DANISH RELIGIOUS PHILOSOPHER

[*The following is a note from the year 1842 found in Kierkegaard's "Nachlass" (literary remains):*]

"Write," said that voice, and the prophet answered: "For whom?" The voice said: "For the dead, for those you have loved in antiquity." "Will they read me?"—"Yes, for they will come back as posterity."

Sandor Petöfi (1823-1849)

NATIONAL POET AND REVOLUTIONARY

[In America there are a number of Petöfi societies in honor of this lyric poet, who apparently lost his life in the Hungarian revolution of 1848-49.]

> The Soul is immortal—this I believe
> But not into another world it goes
> Instead here on earth remains
> On earth to live and to wander.
>
> Among other things, I remember
> In Rome I was Cassius,
> In Helvetia, William Tell,
> In Paris, Desmoulins Kamill
> Here, too, perhaps, I will become something.
>
> *The Soul Is Immortal*

Geza Gárdonyi (1863-1922)

[In an article "Europe and the Doctrine of Rebirth" published in the Maha-Bodhi Journal for April 1953, Francis Hack-Hortobagy mentions among others embracing the doctrine "the famous Hungarian novelist Geza

*Gárdonyi, who, in the course of his writings, furnished so much evidence
of his Buddhistic thinking and feelings." The quotations below are from
one of Gárdonyi's reputed best works:]*

The Vedantic religion is more logical when it teaches that the suffering
is a consequence, than the Christian religion that says it is a precedent. The
effect cannot be the precedent of the cause. . . . Nobody suffers innocently. Neither the suckling. Just the innocently looking suffering proves
that our life on the earth is the consequence of a former life.

POLISH

Wincenty Lutoslawski (1863-?)

PROFESSOR OF PHILOSOPHY, UNIVERSITY OF WILNO, POLAND

[Professor Lutoslawski's book, The World of Souls, to which William James wrote the preface, also treats of reincarnation.]

If we could gather the wisest men of all countries and ages in order to ask their opinion as to palingenesis, we should easily ascertain that a great majority of them not only believed in their own pre-existence and reincarnation, but had also made the further step of widening their personal belief into a general theory, valid for all men, even for those who are totally unaware of their past and uncertain of their future. . . .

In the nineteenth century the number of those who professed belief in palingenesis increased very considerably all over the world, but in no other country is the unanimity in this respect so complete as in Poland. All the greatest poets of Poland, such as Mickiewicz, Slowacki, Krasinski, Norwid, Wyspianski, mention their past lives as a matter of course, and the greatest masterpiece of Polish literature, the *Spirit-King* of Slowacki, is a mystic autobiography in which the poet narrates his past incarnations. Besides the poets also the famous philosopher Ceiszkowski and the mystic Towianski admit palingenesis.

Pre-Existence and Reincarnation

RUSSIAN

A. K. Tolstoy (1817-1875)
DRAMATIST AND POET

How wonderful it is in Wartburg! [a famous castle in central Germany]. They even have here the instruments of the 12th century. And the way your heart beats faster when you are in the world of Asia, so is my heart beating faster in this world of knights, and I know, that at one time I belonged here.

Letters

Feodor Dostoevsky (1821-1881)

Why, you keep thinking of your *present* earth! But your *present* earth may have been repeated a billion times. Why, it's become extinct, been frozen; cracked, broken to bits, disintegrated into its elements, again "the water above the firmament," then again a comet, again a sun, again from the sun it becomes an earth—and the same sequence may have been repeated endlessly and in exactly the same way in every detail. . . . (Italics ours.)

The Brothers Karamazov

[From a letter of Dostoevsky to N. L. Osmidov, dated Petersburg, February 1878, on the subject of immortality:]

Every single organism exists on earth but to live—not to annihilate itself. . . . Now suppose that there is no God, and no personal immortality (personal immortality and God are one and the same—an identical idea). Tell me then: Why am I to live decently and do good, if I die irrevocably here below? . . . Why should I not kill, rob, steal . . . ? For I shall die, and all the rest will die and utterly vanish! By this road, one would reach the conclusion that the human organism alone is not subject to the universal law; that it lives but to destroy itself—not to keep itself alive. . . .

And then reflect on the "I" which can grasp all this. If the "I" can grasp the idea of the universe and its laws, then that "I" stands above all other things, stands aside from all other things, judges them, fathoms them. In that case, the "I" is not only liberated from the earthly axioms, the earthly laws, but has its own law, which transcends the earthly. Now, whence comes that law? Certainly not from earth, where all reaches its issue and vanishes beyond recall. Is that no indication of personal immortality?

If there were no personal immortality, would you, Nikolay Lukitch, be worrying yourself about it, be searching for an answer, be writing letters like this? So you can't get rid of your "I," you see; your "I" will not subject itself to earthly conditions, but seeks for something which transcends earth, and to which it feels itself akin. But whatever I write falls short altogether —as it must. . . . Remain in your unrest—seek farther—it may be that you shall find.

Apollon N. Maykov (1821-1897)

It is not for the first time that you live,
Garbed in this human form;
Again you will be born, again you will meet death,
With each passing period becoming more enlightened.
Finally, because of these transitions,
You will attain the ultimate perfection of human nature;
Now, as a mature soul you will rise
High above us all,
Suddenly as a new star appears
Among the stars in rank with gods.

Album of Antinoy

Count Leo Tolstoy (1828-1910)

"How quiet you young people are!"

"Yes, we're talking philosophy," said Natasha. . . . "Do you know, I think . . . that one goes on remembering, and remembering; one remembers till one recalls what happened before one was in this world."

"That's metempsychosis," said Sonya, who had been good at lessons. . . . "The Egyptians used to believe that our souls had been in animals, and would go into animals again."

"No, do you know, I don't believe that we were once in animals," said Natasha, . . . "but I know for certain that we were once angels somewhere beyond, and we have been here, and that's why we remember everything." . . .

"If we had been angels, why should we have fallen lower?" said Nikolay. "No, that can't be!"

"Not lower . . . who told you we were lower? . . . This is how I know I have existed before," Natasha replied, with conviction: "The soul is immortal, you know, . . . so, if I am to live for ever, I have lived before too, I have lived for all eternity."

"Yes, but it's hard for us to conceive of eternity," said Dimmler, who had joined the young people, with a mildly condescending smile, but now talked as quietly and seriously as they did.

"Why is it hard to conceive of eternity?" said Natasha. "There will be to-day, and there will be to-morrow, and there will be for ever, and yesterday has been, and the day before."

War and Peace

The deeds of the preceding life give the direction to the present life. This is what the Hindoos call Karma.

*Krug Tchtenia**

How well it would be, could one describe the experiences of a man who in a former life committed suicide. He will ever be meeting the same demands that formerly faced him, and so he will arrive at the awareness that he has to fulfill those demands. Set right by this experience, this man will be wiser than others.

Diary Entry for Nov. 13, 1896

* In 1904 Tolstoy completed an arrangement in four volumes of the thoughts of great men under the title *The Circle of Reading*, grouped to provide reading matter for each day of the year. Frequently he headed a page with a contribution of his own, as was the case for March 12, where the above quotation appeared.

You are asking me about the Buddhist idea of "Karma." . . . Now our whole life, from birth until death, with all its dreams, is it not in its turn also a dream, which we take as the real life, the reality of which we do not doubt only because we do not know of the other more real life? . . .

The dreams of our present life are the environment in which we work out the impressions, thoughts, feelings of a former life. . . . As we live through thousands of dreams in our present life, so is our present life only one of many thousands of such lives which we enter from the other, more real life . . . and then return after death. Our life is but one of the dreams of that more real life, and so it is endlessly, until the very last one, the very real life,—the life of God. . . .

I wish you would understand me; I am not playing, not inventing this: I believe in it, I see it without doubt.

*Letter, Published in The Voice of
Universal Love, No. 40, 1908, Moscow*

A. Apuktin (1849-1893)

[The following extract is taken from Apuktin's story "From Death to Life," in which is depicted a man's death, his reflections and experiences in the after-death world, and his subsequent re-embodiment:]

There is no death, there is eternal life. I was always convinced of this, but could never clearly formulate my belief. It was based on the fact that life must otherwise be a crying absurdity. . . . If matter is indestructible, why should consciousness disappear forever? . . . Now I saw, by my own experience, that consciousness does not die, that I never ceased, and probably never shall cease, to live.

Anton Chekhov (1860-1904)

ON IMMORTALITY

In all the universe nothing remains permanent and unchanged but the spirit. Like a prisoner cast into a deep, empty well I know not where I am and what awaits me. All is hidden from me but that in the cruel, persistent struggle with the devil—the principle of the forces of matter—I am destined to conquer, and, after that, matter and spirit will be blended in glorious harmony and the Kingdom of the Cosmic Will will come. But that will come only little by little, through long, long thousands of years when the moon and the bright Sirius and the earth are changed to dust. . . .

The bodies of living creatures have vanished into dust, and eternal matter has transformed them into rocks, into water, into clouds, while the souls of all have melted into one. That world-soul I am—I. . . . In me is the soul of Alexander the Great, of Caesar, of Shakespeare and of Napoleon, and of the lowest leech. In me the consciousness of men is blended with the instincts of the animals, and I remember all, all, all! And I live through every life over again in myself!

The Sea-Gull

Feodor Sologub (1863-1927)

"Man with a single head and a single soul, recall your past, your primitive experience of those ancient days. . . .

"How many souls have you, and how many consciousness? Can you tell me that? You pride yourself on the amazing differentiation of your organs, you have an idea that each member of your body fulfills its own well-defined functions. But tell me, stupid man, have you anything whereby to preserve the memory of your previous existences? The other head contains the rest of you, your early memories and your earlier existence. You argue subtly and craftily across the threshold of your pitiful consciousness, but your misfortune is that you have only one head." . . .

"Man with one head, recall your remote past. . . ." [A scene from a past incarnation then unfolds.]

The Uniter of Souls

Konstantin Balmont (1867-1943)

I remember, O Fire,
How thy flames once enkindled my flesh,
Among writhing witches caught close in thy flame-woven mesh.
How, tortured for having beheld what is secret,
We were flung to the fire for the joy of our sabbath. . . .

Hymn to Fire

I. A. Bunin (1870-1953)

I remember one of the especially beautiful moonlight nights . . . the sparse bluish stars, and my brothers telling me, that they are all worlds, unknown to us, but undoubtedly happy and beautiful, and that most likely, at some time we too will be there.

I visited many famous castles in Europe, and wandering through them often wondered how could I when I was a mere boy, not different from any other boy from Viselki . . . so accurately felt the ancient life of these castles and so exactly pictured them in my mind. . . . To this world, without a slightest doubt I did belong at some time. In the fields of Tambov . . . with such extraordinary force I recalled all that I now saw, how I lived formerly innumerable lives. And when I went to Egypt, Nubia, and the tropics, I only had to tell myself: yes, yes, all this is precisely so, the way I "remembered" it thirty years ago!

The Life of Arsieniev

Wake up, wake up! Shake from yourself the illusions of Mara,* the dream of this short life! Your peaceful rest will be but of short duration. Again and again, in thousands of incarnations, you will be forced out of your land of Eden.

Brothers

Valery Brusov (1873-1924)

In the land of Ra the flaming, by the shores of Nile's slow
    waters, where the roofs of Thebes were seen,
In the days of yore you loved me, as dark Isis loved Osiris,
    sister, friend and worshipped queen!
And the pyramid its shadow on our evening trysts would lean. . . .
Once before, we knew existence, this our bliss is a remembrance,
    and our love—a memory. . . .

The Tryst

---

* *Mara* (Sanskrit), the god of temptation.

Alexander Blok (1880-1921)

My spirit is old; and some black lot awaits me
    On my long road.
Some dream accurst, inveterate, suffocates me
    Still, with its load.

So young—yet hosts of dreadful thoughts appall me,
    Sick and opprest.
Come! and from shadowy phantoms disenthral me,
    Friend unconfest! . . .

                      My Spirit Is Old

Night: the street, a foolish lamp giving
A dingy light, a druggist's store.
For a quarter of a century go on living,
No escape. All will be as before.

You die: afresh you start life boldly,
Just as of old each detail repeat.
Night, the canal rippling so coldly,
The druggist's store, the lamp, the street.
         Night, Street, Streetlight, Drugstore*

Andrey Biely (1880-1934)

(B. N. BUGAYEV)

[Biely's poem "Bright Sun" is reminiscent of the Hindu view that the
visible sun is but a mask for the true Spiritual Sun, our real home.]

The shining and ponderous goblet
I empty: the earth drops below me,
All things sink away—I am treading
Cold space—the vast void—the dim ether
But constant, in ancient space looming,
My radiant goblet, the Sun. . . .
The end of long wanderings, brother,
Lies here, in your motherland, welcome.

* From Janko Lavrin, *Russian Writers: Their Lives and Literature.* Copyright 1954,
D. Van Nostrand Co., Inc., Princeton, New Jersey.

Slow hour upon hour in procession,
Slow centuries, smiling, pass onward.
In ancient space proudly I lift it,
My radiant goblet: the Sun.

Bright Death

Once I trusted the arrows of gold,
Yet from shafts of the sun I fell.
I had solved the riddle of ages;
Could not solve my life's as well.

Do not scorn the departed poet,
Take a wreath to his grave. . . .
I perhaps have not died,
I perhaps shall return:
From my sleep.

An Epitaph

Pitirim A. Sorokin (1889-   )

DIRECTOR OF RESEARCH IN CREATIVE ALTRUISM, HARVARD UNIVERSITY

[*The following are extracts from two letters translated from the Russian, and published with Dr. Sorokin's permission:*]

As to "reincarnation" in the sense of the simplified belief that Socrates or Sorokin existed eternally, and as the same personality died and in the course of time were reborn—such conception of "reincarnation" I do not accept. And such a concept or belief is not given in the main, actual texts of either Hinduism or Buddhism (including Patanjali's *Yoga*, Bhagavad-Gita, the Upanishads, etc.)

Some years ago I was asked by an outstanding Catholic leader . . . what I thought about immortality (after the death of the body). My answer was this: "The immortal, divine element which is in every man, will not die with the death of the body, but will return into the ocean of cosmic, supremely creative energy (often called "God," "Brahman," "Purusha," "Tao," "Divine No Thing," etc.)

However, I do not know whether this divine element will dissolve itself in this ocean or will live in it, preserving its own individuality. Personally, I prefer to "dissolve," because the prospect of being forever tied to the individual idiosyncrasies of Sorokin (which bothers me even in this life), does not seem to me very attractive.

[NOTE: *The distinction between the personality and the immortal individuality is seldom appreciated by Western thinkers, it appears. In the Bhagavad-Gita the personality is called "Ahankara," the false I, a mere reflection of Kshetrajna, the real I. The word "personality" is an excellent substitute for Ahankara, derived as it is from the Latin "persona," meaning a mask. But behind the mask, the oriental sages appeared to teach, was a very real spiritual entity.*]

Boris Pasternak (1890-1960)

NOBEL PRIZE 1958; DECLINED

She spoke with effort. "They wanted to give me the last sacraments. . . . Death is hanging over me. . . . It may come any moment. . . . When you go to have a tooth out you're frightened, it'll hurt, you prepare yourself. . . . But this isn't a tooth, it's everything, the whole of you, your whole life . . . being pulled out. . . . And what is it? Nobody knows. . . . And I am sick at heart and terrified."

"You want to know my opinion as a scientist? Perhaps some other time? No? Right now? Well, as you wish. . . . Resurrection in the crude form in which it is preached to console the weak, it is alien to me. I have always understood Christ's words about the living and the dead in a different sense. Where could you find room for all these hordes of people accumulated over thousands of years? The universe isn't big enough for them; God, the good, and meaningful purpose would be crowded out. They'd be crushed by these throngs greedy merely for the animal life.

"But all the time, life, one, immense, identical throughout its innumerable combinations and transformations, fills the universe and is continually reborn.* You are anxious about whether you will rise from the dead or not, but you rose from the dead when you were born and you didn't notice it. . . . There is nothing to fear. There is no such thing as death. Death has nothing to do with us. . . . What we need is something new, and that new thing is life eternal. . . . Go to sleep." . . .

Next day Anna Ivanovna was better.

Doctor Zhivago

* From the context of the above quotation it would appear that Dr. Zhivago is theorizing on the survival of the collective consciousness of mankind, rather than upon the reincarnation of the *individual* soul.

• A M E R I C A N   P H I L O S O P H E R S   A N D
P R O S E   W R I T E R S •

Benjamin Franklin (1706-1790)

[Benjamin Franklin's epitaph,* written by himself at the age of twenty-two, called by Carl Van Doren "the most famous of American epitaphs:"]

The Body of B. Franklin,
Printer,
Like the Cover of an Old Book,
Its Contents Torn Out
And
Stripped of its Lettering and Gilding,
Lies Here
Food for Worms,
But the Work shall not be Lost,
For it Will as He Believed
Appear Once More
In a New and more Elegant Edition
Revised and Corrected
By the Author.

* This epitaph, slightly modified, appears in almost a dozen different versions, which is not surprising as Franklin often made copies for friends and did not always confine

[*Franklin thus explained his views:*]

When I see nothing annihilated (in the works of God) and not a drop of water wasted, I cannot suspect the annihilation of souls, or believe that He will suffer the daily waste of millions of minds ready made that now exist, and put Himself to the continual trouble of making new ones. Thus, finding myself to exist in the world, I believe I shall, in some shape or other, always exist; and, with all the inconveniences human life is liable to, I shall not object to a new edition of mine, hoping, however, that the *errata* of the last may be corrected.

Thomas Paine (1737-1809)

ON IMMORTALITY

All other arguments apart, the *consciousness of existence* is the only conceivable idea we can have of another life, and the continuance of that consciousness is immortality. The consciousness of existence, or the knowing that we exist, is not necessarily confined to the same form, nor to the same matter, even in this life. We have not in all cases the same form, nor in any case the same matter that composed our bodies twenty or thirty years ago; and yet we are conscious of being the same persons. . . .

Who can say by what exceedingly fine action of fine matter it is that a thought is produced in what we call the mind? and yet that thought when produced . . . is capable of becoming immortal, and is the only production of man that has that capacity. Statues of brass or marble will perish; and statues made in imitation of them are not the same statues. . . . But print and reprint a thought a thousand times over, and that with materials of any kind—carve it in wood or engrave it on stone, the thought is eternally and identically the same thought in every case. It has a capacity of unimpaired existence, unaffected by change of matter, and is essentially distinct and of a nature different from everything else that we know or can conceive.

If, then, the thing produced has in itself a capacity of being immortal, it is more than a token that the power that produced it, which is the self-same thing as consciousness of existence, can be immortal also; and that as independently of the matter it was first connected with, as the thought

---

himself to the original phraseology. See *The Papers of Benjamin Franklin*, Vol. I, p. 310, edited by Leonard W. Labaree, Yale University Press, and article "B. Franklin's Epitaph" by L. H. Butterfield, in *New Colophon*, Vol. III (1950), pp. 9-30.

is of the printing or writing it first appeared in. The one idea is not more difficult to believe than the other, and we can see that one is true.

The Age of Reason

The American Transcendentalists

The August, 1959, issue of the magazine Sunrise contained a symposium entitled "The Transcendentalists on Reincarnation," and some of the passages by Emerson, Thoreau, Bronson and Louisa May Alcott, George Ripley, James Freeman Clarke, Frederic Hedge, Wm. J. Potter, and Cyrus Bartol are reprinted from this source by permission of the editor. The symposium is prefaced by these informative remarks:

In 1836 a group of younger Unitarians who dared to believe in the inherent worth of man, the divinity of all Nature and the continuity of the soul's life after death, openly revolted against the "corpse-cold Unitarianism" of their Harvard associates and, spearheaded by Emerson, Hedge and Ripley, formed the Transcendental Club of America.

Whereas these ideas so long ago taught in India, Persia and Greece and more currently by Kant and Goethe, Wordsworth, Coleridge and Carlyle, were not at all new, they had for centuries in Europe remained the property of the intellectual élite. Now, germinating in the soil of the New World, they blossomed with extraordinary vigor, taking the form of a practical crusade against every form of tyranny—of soul as well as of body.

The marked influence of the German transcendentalists upon the American movement has already been considered (see p. 174). The contribution of ancient Greece is manifest in Emerson's essay on Plato. The Platonic philosophers, incidentally, were not studied in translations but in the original Greek.

The English transcendentalists also played a prominent part in this revival. Coleridge, Carlyle, and Wordsworth were everywhere read and talked about, while Wordsworth's poem on pre-existence, "The Ode to Immortality," was judged by Emerson, in his last discourse on Immortality, to be "the best modern essay on the subject."

An immeasurable influential contribution to American Transcendentalism came from the Orient. Scarce copies of the first English translations of the Bhagavad-Gita, Upanishads, Vedas, and Puranas somehow found their way into the hands of Emerson, Thoreau and the others. Thoreau translated from the French a Sanskrit story entitled The Transmigration of Seven Brahmins, and had it published. Arthur Christy's The Orient in American Transcen-

dentalism (*Columbia University Press*), devotes 367 pages to exploring this subject.

Thus, with the blending here in America of four streams of transcendental philosophy, each bearing the impress of the reincarnation perspective, it is but natural to find frequent references to rebirth in the writings of the New England group. From the quotations that follow it will be observed how refreshingly original was the viewpoint of these men.

Bronson Alcott (1799-1888)

EDUCATOR AND LECTURER

[The extracts presented below are taken from The Record of a School by Elizabeth P. Peabody, a book that contains her eye-witness reports of actual classes conducted by Alcott while she was his assistant at the Temple School in Boston. In the preface to the third edition (1874), Miss Peabody wrote: "The great interest inspired by Miss Alcott's Little Men has led to the inquiry if ever there was or could be a school like Plumfield; and she has proposed the republication of the Record of a School, which was published thirty-eight years ago, and which suggested some of the scenes described in Little Men. . . . What I witnessed in his schoolroom threw for me a new light into the profoundest mysteries that have been consecrated by the Christian symbols; and the study of childhood made there I would not exchange for any thing else I have experienced in life." That her feeling was shared by the children at their own level of understanding is abundantly evident throughout these remarkable journals. For example, one day Alcott asked the children whether a conversation on "ideas" such as they had just finished, was more interesting than one on steam engines. Many said it was. A little boy exclaimed, "I never knew I had a mind till I came to this school;" and a great many more burst out with the same idea. To quote now from the journals, to be followed by several direct quotations from Alcott's own writings:]

January 15 [1835]. . . . What is the meaning of the word *recollect?* . . . Are you now collecting or re-collecting the impressions of child-hood? Some thought they had begun to re-collect, as well as to collect. Shall I tell you an idea some people have of recollecting, reminiscence, remembrance? Yes, said several of them. Mr. Alcott continued (pointing to the bust of Plato), That man believed that all our feelings and thoughts were the remembrances of another state of existence, before we came into the world in our present bodies. And he (pointing to the cast of Jesus Christ) used to say of himself that he came forth from God; that he had lived before. In the Gospel of St. John there are many passages in which he refers to his pre-existent state. . . .

January 30. . . . What do you mean by *birthday?* . . . Birthday is the day on which the spirit is put into the body, said [one] boy. Did you get that idea in this school? said Mr. Alcott. I never thought of such subjects before I came to this school, said he. . . . One of the boys added, that he had always had an indistinct idea that the soul lived before the body, that there was a transmigration of souls. . . .

February 4. . . . Some expressed the idea that the soul shaped and made the body; others that the body was made, and the soul put into it. Which is right? said one boy. That is more than I can tell, but I incline to the first opinion. You are all nearly right, however; you have the important ideas; birth is not the beginning of the spirit; life is the remembrance, or a waking up of spirit. All the life of knowledge is the waking up of what is already within. [Note: the class had been discussing Wordsworth's "Ode to Immortality."]

The Record of a School

To conceive a child's acquirements as originating in nature, dating from his birth into his body, seems an atheism that only a shallow metaphysical theology could entertain in a time of such marvelous natural knowledge as ours. "I shall never persuade myself," said Synesius, "to believe my soul to be of like age with my body." And yet we are wont to date our birth, as that of the babes we christen, from the body's advent . . . as if time and space could chronicle the periods of the immortal mind.

Concord Days

Life is a current of spiritual forces. In perpetual tides, the stream traverses its vessels to vary its pulsations and perspective of things. . . . Vast systems of sympathies, antedating and extending beyond our mundane experiences, absorb us within their sphere relating us to others worlds of life and light. . . . Memory sometimes dispels the oblivious slumber and recovers for the mind recollections of its descent and destiny. Some relics of the ancient consciousness survive, recalling our previous history and experiences.

Tablets

All life is eternal, there is none other; and all unrest is but the struggle of the soul to reassure herself of her inborn immortality.

"Orphic Sayings"
The Dial, July 1840

George Ripley (1802-1880)

There is a class of persons who desire a reform on the prevailing philosophy of the day. These are called Transcendentalists, because they believe in an order of truths which transcends the sphere of the external senses. Their leading idea is the supremacy of mind over matter. Hence they maintain that the truth of religion does not depend on tradition, nor historical facts, but has an unerring witness in the soul. There is a light, they believe, which enlighteneth every man that cometh into the world; there is a faculty in all—the most degraded, the most ignorant, the most obscure—to perceive spiritual truth when distinctly presented; and the ultimate appeal on all moral questions is not to a jury of scholars, a hierarchy of divines or the prescriptions of a creed, but to the common sense of the human race.

Letter to Unitarian friends, Oct. 1, 1840

Ralph Waldo Emerson (1803-1882)

It is the secret of the world that all things subsist and do not die, but only retire a little from sight and afterwards return again. . . . Nothing is dead; men feign themselves dead, and endure mock funerals and mournful obituaries, and there they stand looking out of the window, sound and well, in some new and strange disguise. Jesus is not dead; he is very well alive: nor John, nor Paul, nor Mahomet, nor Aristotle; at times we believe we have seen them all, and could easily tell the names under which they go.

Nominalist and Realist

We wake and find ourselves on a stair; there are other stairs below us which we seem to have ascended; there are stairs above us, many a one, which go upward and out of sight. But the Genius which according to the old belief stands at the door by which we enter, and gives us the lethe to drink, that we may tell no tales, mixed the cup too strongly, and we cannot shake off the lethargy now at noon day. Sleep lingers all our lifetime about our eyes.

Experience

The soul is an emanation of the Divinity, a part of the soul of the world, a ray from the source of light. It comes from without into the human body, as into a temporary abode, it goes out of it anew; it wanders in ethereal regions, it returns to visit it . . . it passes into other habitations, for the soul is immortal. . . .

Life itself is an interim and a transition; this, O Indur, is my one and twenty thousandth form, and already I feel old Life sprouting underneath in the twenty thousand first, and I know well that he builds no new world but by tearing down the old materials.

Journals

> Perchance not he but Nature ailed,
> The world and not the infant failed.
> It was not ripe yet to sustain
> A genius of so fine a strain. . . .
> They could not feed him, and he died,
> And wandered backward as in scorn
> To wait an aeon to be born. . . .
>
> *Threnody*

We must infer our destiny from the preparation. We are driven by instinct to hive innumerable experiences which are of no visible value, and we may revolve through many lives before we shall assimilate or exhaust them. Now there is nothing in nature capricious, or whimsical, or accidental, or unsupported. Nature never moves by jumps, but always in steady and supported advances. . . . If there is the desire to live, and in larger sphere, with more knowledge and power, it is because life and power are good for us, and we are the natural depositaries of these gifts. The love of life is out of all proportion to the value set on a single day, and seems to indicate a conviction of immense resources and possibilities proper to us, on which we have never drawn. . . .

[Quoting from the Katha Upanishad:] "The soul is not born; it does not die; it was not produced from any one. Nor was any produced from it. Unborn, eternal, it is not slain, though the body is slain; subtler than what is subtle, greater than what is great . . . Thinking the soul as unbodily among bodies, firm among fleeting things, the wise man casts off all grief. The soul cannot be gained by knowledge, nor by understanding, nor by manifold science. It can be obtained by the soul by which it is desired. It reveals its own truths. . . ."

Immortality

Frederic Hedge (1805-1890)

We reach back with our recollection and find no beginning of existence. Who of us knows anything except by report of the first two years of earthly life? . . . We began to exist for others before we began to exist for ourselves. Our experience is not co-extensive with our being, and memory does not comprehend it. We bear not the root, but the root us.

What is the root? We call it soul. *Our* soul, we call it; properly speaking, it is not ours, but we are its. It is not a part of us, but we are a part of it. It is not one article in an inventory of articles which together make up our individuality, but the root of that individuality. It is larger than we are, and other than we are—that is, than our conscious self. The conscious self does not begin until some time after the birth of the individual. It is not aboriginal, but a product,—as it were, the blossoming of an individuality. . . . And the soul which does so blossom exists before that blossom unfolds. . . .

The supposition of pre-existence . . . seems best to match the supposed continued existence of the soul hereafter. Whatever had a beginning in time, it should seem must end in time. The eternal destination which faith ascribes to the soul presupposes an eternal origin. . . . This was the theory of the most learned and acute of the Christian Fathers (Origen). . . . Of all the theories respecting the origin of the soul it seems to me the most plausible, and therefore the one most likely to throw light on the question of a life to come. . . . A new bodily organism I hold to be an essential part of the soul's destination.

Ways of the Spirit, and other Essays

Charles C. Emerson (1808-1836)

BROTHER OF RALPH WALDO EMERSON

The reason why Homer is to me like a dewy morning is because I too lived while Troy was, and sailed in the hollow ships of the Grecians to sack the devoted town. The rosy-fingered dawn as it crimsoned the tops of Ida, the broad seashore covered with tents, the Trojan hosts in their painted armor, and the rushing chariots of Diomede and Idomeneus,—all these I too saw: my ghost animated the frame of some nameless Argive. . . . We forget that we have been drugged by the sleepy bowl of the present.

But when a lively chord in the soul is struck, when the windows for a moment are unbarred, the long and varied past is recovered. We recognize it all; we are not mere brief, ignoble creatures; we seize our immortality and bind together the related parts of our secular beings. . . . Something there is in the spirit which changes not, neither is weary, but ever returns into itself, and partakes of the eternity of God.

"Notes from the Journal of a Scholar"
Published in The Dial

James Freeman Clarke (1810-1888)

That man has come up to his present state of development by passing through lower forms is the popular doctrine of science to-day. What is called evolution teaches that we have reached our present state by a very long and gradual ascent from the lowest animal organizations. It is true that the Darwinian theory takes no notice of the evolution of the soul, but only of the body. But it appears to me that a combination of the two views would remove many difficulties which still attach to the theory of natural selection and the survival of the fittest. If we are to believe in evolution, let us have the assistance of the soul itself in this development of new species.

> For of the soul the body form doth take:
> For soul is form, and doth the body make.

. . . The modern doctrine of the evolution of bodily organisms is not complete, unless we unite with it the idea of a corresponding evolution of the spiritual monad, from which every organic form derives its unity. Evolution has a satisfactory meaning only when we admit that the soul is developed and educated by passing through many bodies.

Ten Great Religions

Francis X. Bowen (1811-1890)

PROFESSOR, PHILOSOPHER, HARVARD UNIVERSITY

Our life upon earth is rightly held to be a discipline and a preparation for a higher and eternal life hereafter. But if limited to the duration of a single mortal body, it is so brief as to seem hardly sufficient for so grand a purpose. Threescore years and ten must surely be an inadequate preparation for eternity. But what assurance have we that the probation of the soul is confined within so narrow limits? Why may it not be continued, or repeated, through a long series of successive generations, the same personality animating one after another an indefinite number of tenements of flesh, and carrying forward into each the training it has received, the character it has formed . . . in the stage of existence immediately preceding? . . . Besides the spiritual meaning of the doctrine of regeneration . . . there may be a literal meaning in the solemn words of the Saviour, "Except a man be born again, he cannot see the kingdom of God." . . .

Everyone would ardently desire a renewal of his earthly experience if assured that he could enter upon it under better auspices, if he believed that what we call death is not the end of all things even here below, but that the soul is then standing upon the threshold of a new stage of earthly existence, which is to be brighter or darker than the one it is just quitting, according as there is carried forward into it a higher or lower purpose. . . . We can easily imagine and believe that every person now living is a re-presentation of some one who lived perhaps centuries ago under another name in another country. . . . He has entered upon a new stage of pro-bation, and in it he has now to learn what the character which he there formed naturally leads to when tried upon a new and perhaps broader theatre.

"Christian Metempsychosis"
Princeton Review, May 1881

Epes Sargent (1812-1880)

AUTHOR AND JOURNALIST

The human soul is like a bird that is born in a cage. Nothing can de-prive it of its natural longings, or obliterate the mysterious remembrance of its heritage.*

Cyrus Augustus Bartol (1813-?)

In some sense, I was born and must die. In some sense, my dwelling holds me; your babe is in the crib, and your sires are in the tomb. But there is an I, by which all these contents and consignments are disallowed. Before Abraham was, I am [John 8:58]; I have power to lay down my life and power to take it up again. I am conscious of Eternal Generation, that I am what never lay in the cradle and no coffin can hold, but that which sits behind smiling at what was brought forth and expires.

Rising Faith

William J. Potter

It is possible, perhaps probable, that the soul will always have some form of body and some material limitation . . . now taking this form, now that—yet always ascending in form as giving larger freedom of nature . . . as the scale of being ascends.

* *Useful Quotations*, comp. Tyron Edwards (Grosset & Dunlap) p. 609.

But over and above all change, independent of all limitations of time and matter, beyond the reach of the accidental and perishing relations of individual existence, there enters into human nature another factor by which it lays hold of a substance that is infinite and everlasting and draws its being therefrom. There is somewhat of the Absolute and Eternal in every human soul . . . something that transcends time and space and organic form and makes eternity for the soul to be the continuous unfolding of a perpetual and indestructible principle of life rather than the infinite multiplication of days and years.

"The Doctrine of Pre-Existence and the Fourth Gospel"
The Radical, April 1868

Henry David Thoreau (1817-1862)

We have settled down on earth and forgotten heaven. . . . That Eternity which I see in nature I predict for myself also. . . . Like last year's vegetation our human life but dies down to its root and still puts forth its green blade into eternity. . . . Methinks the hawk that soars so loftily and circles so steadily and apparently without effort, has earned this power by faithfully creeping on the ground as a reptile in a former state of existence. . . .

I am conscious of the presence and criticism of a part of me, which, as it were, is not a part of me, but spectator, sharing no experience, but taking note of it and that is no more I than it is you. When the play, it may be the tragedy, of life is over, the spectator goes his way. It was a kind of fiction, a work of the imagination only, so far as he was concerned. . . .

Walden, and miscellaneous writings

I lived in Judea eighteen hundred years ago, but I never knew that there was such a one as Christ among my contemporaries. . . .

And Hawthorne, too, I remember as one with whom I sauntered in old heroic times along the banks of the Scamander amid the ruins of chariots and heroes. . . . As the stars looked to me when I was a shepherd in Assyria, they look to me now a New-Englander. . . . As far back as I can remember I have unconsciously referred to the experiences of a previous state of existence.

Letters and Journals

June 26 [1851]. . . . Visited a menagerie this afternoon. . . . What constitutes the difference between a wild beast and a tame one? How much more human the one than the other! Growling, scratching, roaring, with whatever beauty and gracefulness, still untamable, this royal Bengal tiger or this leopard. They have the character and the importance of another order of men. The majestic lions, the king of beasts,—he must retain his title. . . . It is unavoidable, the idea of transmigration; not merely a fancy of the poets, but an instinct of the race.

Journals

Louisa May Alcott (1832-1888)

[In a letter to a friend:] I think immortalty is the passing of a soul through many lives or experiences; and such as are truly lived, used, and learned, help on to the next, each growing richer, happier and higher, carrying with it only the real memories of what has gone before. . . . I seem to remember former states and feel that in them I have learned some of the lessons that have never since been mine here and in my next step I hope to leave behind many of the trials I have struggled to bear here and begin to find lightened as I go on. This accounts for the genius and great virtue some show here. They have done well in many phases of this great school and bring into our class the virtue or the gifts that make them great or good. We don't remember the lesser things. They slip away as childish trifles, and we carry on only the real experiences.

Robert G. Ingersoll (1833-1899)

AGNOSTIC, WRITER, LECTURER

We cannot say that death is not a good. We do not know whether the grave is the end of this life, or the door of another, or whether the night here is not somewhere else a dawn. . . . I had rather live and love where death is king than have eternal life where love is not. Another life is nought, unless we know and love again the ones who love us here. . . . The dead do not suffer. If they live again, their lives will surely be as good as ours. . . . We [the Agnostics], too, have our religion, and it is this: Help for the living—hope for the dead.

"At a Child's Grave"

John Muir (1838-1914)

This grand show is eternal. It is always sunrise somewhere; the dew is never all dried at once; a shower is forever falling; vapor is ever rising.

Eternal sunrise, eternal sunset, eternal dawn and gloaming, on sea and continents and islands, each in its turn, as the round earth rolls. . . .

Trees towering in the sky, braving storms of centuries, flowers turning faces to the light for a single day or hour, having enjoyed their share of life's feast—all alike pass on and away under the law of death and love. Yet all are our brothers and they enjoy life as we do, share heaven's blessings with us, die and are buried in hallowed ground, come with us out of eternity and return into eternity. "Our little lives are rounded with a sleep." . . . Death is a kind nurse saying, "Come, children, to bed and get up in the morning"—a gracious Mother calling her children home.

John of the Mountains;
The Unpublished Journal of John Muir

Lafcadio Hearn (1850-1904)

[*Lafcadio Hearn is difficult to classify as to nationality. Born on a Greek island of Greek mother and English father, in later years he became in all ways a Japanese. As he lived in the United States for over twenty years as a writer, he is included in this section.*]

I seemed to understand as never before, how the mystery that is called the Soul of me must have quickened in every form of past existence, and must as certainly continue to behold the sun for other millions of summers, through eyes of other countless shapes of future being. . . . For thousands of years the East has been teaching that what we think or do in this life really decides—through some inevitable formation of atom-tendencies or polarities—the future place of our substance, and the future state of our sentiency. . . . Acts and thoughts, according to Buddhist doctrines, are creative. . . . What we think or do is never for the moment only, but for measureless time; it signifies some force directed to the shaping of worlds—to the making of future bliss or pain. . . . And when all the stars of the visible Night shall have burnt themselves out, those atoms will doubtless again take part in the orbing of Mind—and will tremble again in thoughts, emotions, memories—in all the joys and pains of lives still to be lived in worlds still to be evolved. . . . The very delusion of delusions is the idea of death as loss.

Kotto

Great music is a psychical storm, agitating to unimaginable depth the mystery of the past within us. Or we might say that it is a prodigious incantation—every different instrument and voice making separate appeal to different billions of prenatal memories. There are tones that call up all ghosts of youth and joy and tenderness; there are tones that evoke all phantom pain of perished passion; there are tones that resurrect all dead sensation of majesty and might and glory—all expired exultations, all forgotten magnanimities. Well may the influence of music seem inexplicable to the man who idly dreams that his life began less than a hundred years ago! But the mystery lightens for whomsoever learns that the substance of Self is older than the sun. . . . To every ripple of melody, to every billow of harmony, there answers within him, out of the sea of Death and Birth, some eddying immeasureable of ancient pleasure and pain.

Ghostly Japan

Hopeless . . . any attempt to tell the real pain of seeing my former births. I can say only that no combination of suffering possible to *individual* being could be likened to such pain,—the pain of countless lives interwoven. It seemed as if every nerve of me had been prolonged into some monstrous web of sentiency spun back through a million years. . . . For, as I looked backward, I became double, quadruple, octuple;—I multiplied by arithmetical progression;—I became hundreds and thousands,—and feared with the terror of thousands,—and despaired with the anguish of thousands . . . yet knew the pleasure of none. . . .

Then in the moment when sentiency itself seemed bursting into dissolution, one divine touch ended the frightful vision, and brought again to me the simple consciousness of the single present. Oh! how unspeakably delicious that sudden shrinking back out of the multiplicity into unity!— that immense, immeasurable collapse of self into the blind oblivious numbness of individuality!

"To others also," said the voice of the divine one who had thus saved me—"to others in the like state it has been permitted to see something of their pre-existence. But no one of them ever could endure to look far. Power to see all former births belongs to those eternally released from the bonds of self. Such exist outside of illusion,—outside of form and name; and pain cannot come nigh them. But to you, remaining in illusion, not even the Buddha could give power to look back more than a little way. . . .

"Within the Circle"
Gleanings in Buddha-Fields

Felix Adler (1851-1933)

EDUCATOR; FOUNDER OF ETHICAL CULTURE SOCIETY

There is a story that a spark of fire from heaven fell into the ocean, and this accounts for its ever restless seething and surging. Surely it is true to say that a spark of divine fire has fallen into the breast of man. It flows through his veins like a flood, it glows at his heart, now scorching it, now warming it with generous heat. It mounts to his brain and kindles his intellectual powers. By the sheen of that light which burns within, and by it alone, do we catch glimpses of the eternal verities that dwell at the heart of things.

Lectures

Ernest Thompson Seton (1860-1946)

NATURE WRITER, AND FORMER HEAD OF BOY SCOUTS OF AMERICA

[*In the foreword to* The Gospel of the Red Man,* *by Ernest Thompson Seton and his wife, Julia M. Seton, she writes:*]

In March, 1905, we were in Los Angeles on a lecture tour. The morning after the lecture, we were met at the Van Nuys Hotel by some Eastern friends who, addressing the Chief,† said: "We have a message for you. There is a strange woman in the Hills who wishes to see you." Accordingly, we took the tram to the end of the track, then set out on foot to climb what, I think, are now called the Beverly Hills. On the green slope higher up was a small white cottage; in front of this, a woman dressed like a farmer's wife. . . .

She was introduced to us as a Mahatma from India, although born in Iowa. She had left her home as a small child, had spent many years studying under the Great Masters, and was now back on a mission to America. She was a strange-looking person. We could not tell whether she was thirty or a hundred and thirty years old. . . . Her eyes had the faraway veiled looked of a mystic. Her talk was commonplace as she served coffee and cakes. We wondered why she had sent the summons. Finally, after an hour, we rose to leave.

Then, suddenly, she turned on the Chief with a total change of look and demeanour. Her eyes blazed as she said, in tones of authority: "Don't you know who you are?"

We were all shocked into silence as she continued: "You are a Red Indian Chief, reincarnated to give the message of the Redman to the White race, so much in need of it. Why don't you get busy? Why don't you set about your job?"

* Seton's books are available at Seton Village, Sante Fe, New Mexico.
† Julia Seton: "Ernest Thompson Seton was known the world over as 'The Chief,' a title bestowed originally when he headed the Boy Scouts of America" [from the inception of that organization in 1910 until 1915].

The Chief was moved like one conscience-stricken. He talked not at all on the road back, and the incident was not mentioned for long after. But I know that the strange woman had focussed his thoughts on the mission he had been vaguely working on for some years. He has never since ceased to concentrate on what she had termed "his job."

C. J. Ducasse (1881-   )

FORMER CHAIRMAN, DEPARTMENT OF PHILOSOPHY, BROWN UNIVERSITY
PAST PRESIDENT OF AMERICAN PHILOSOPHICAL ASSOCIATION

Whether or not survival as plurality of lives on earth is a fact, it is at least coherently thinkable and not incompatible with any facts known to us today. Of all the conceptions of the significance of human life on earth the reincarnation hypothesis, which regards each life of a person as being like a day in school, is the only one that makes any sense.

How come one person is born a genius and another a boob; one is born beautiful and another ugly; one is born healthy and another crippled? The concept of rebirth on earth, perhaps after an interval occupied by the individual in distilling out of memories of a life just ended such wisdom as his reflective powers enabled him to extract, would enable us to believe there is justice in the universe.

Providence Evening Bulletin, June 26, 1958

In what a human being is at a given time we may distinguish two parts, one deeper and more permanent, and another more superficial and transient. The latter consists of everything he has acquired since birth: habits, skills, memories, and so on. This is his personality. The other part, which, somewhat arbitrarily for lack of a better name we may here agree to call his individuality, comprises the aptitudes and dispositions which are native in him. . . . There can be no doubt that each of us, on the basis of his same individuality—that is, of his same stock of innate latent capacities and incapacities—would have developed a more or less different empirical mind and personality if, for instance, he had been put at birth in a different family, or had later been thrust by some external accident into a radically different sort of environment.

Reflection on this fact should cause one to take his present personality with a large grain of salt, viewing it no longer humorlessly as his absolute self, but rather, in imaginative perspective, as but one of the various personalities which his individuality was equally capable of generating had it happened to enter phenomenal history through birth in a different environment.

Thus, to the question: What is it that could be supposed to be reborn? an intelligible answer may be returned by saying that it might be the core of positive and negative aptitudes and tendencies which we have called man's individuality, as distinguished from his personality. And the fact might further be that, perhaps as a result of persistent striving to acquire a skill or trait he desires, but for which he now has but little gift, aptitude for it in future births would be generated and incorporated into his individuality.

Nature, Mind and Death
Paul Carus Lectures, 1951

The relation between the man who sows in one life and the man who reaps in a later one is of essentially the same kind as that between the child and the adult. The two are the "same" person not in the sense that any item, physical or mental, in the infant's makeup has persisted unchanged and is identically present in the mature man, but only in the sense that the former has changed into the latter by a gradual transformation from hour to hour, day to day, year to year. The sameness of the two is thus sameness in the sense only of continuousness of becoming.

*A Philosophical Scrutiny of Religion**

[NOTE: *In his latest book,* A Critical Examination of the Belief in a Life After Death (*C. C. Thomas, Springfield, Illinois, 1961*), *Professor Ducasse devotes seven chapters to the reincarnation hypothesis. Also of especial interest is the chapter entitled "Lamont's Attack on Mind-Body Dualism," in which Ducasse analyzes point by point the basic objections to all theories of soul survival raised by Corliss Lamont in his book* The Illusion of Immortality (*Philosophical Library, New York, 1950*).]

Joseph Wood Krutch (1893-)

CRITIC, ESSAYIST, AND NATURALIST

[*Somehow it comes as no surprise to encounter passing but suggestive references to the possibility of rebirth in Krutch's writing. He is one who has truly absorbed the philosophic tone set by the "transcendentalists" Thoreau and Emerson, and also seems to have a special affinity for Wordsworth—and to all these men the idea of reincarnation had meaning. Speaking, in* The Desert Year, *of his first associations with the "austere" yet inspiring desert, Krutch writes:*]

* C. J. Ducasse, *A Philosophical Scrutiny of Religion.* Copyright 1953, The Ronald Press Company.

For three successive years following my first experience I returned with the companion of my Connecticut winters to the same general region, pulled irresistibly across the twenty-five hundred miles between my own home and this world which would have been alien had it not almost seemed that I had known and loved it in some previous existence.

Pierre van Paassen (1895-   )

AUTHOR, JOURNALIST, AND CLERGYMAN

Why not own up to it? We have all, at certain moments, skirted those unknown regions wherein the shades flutter and vanish. . . . Tell me, have you never on a mystic evening of the autumn, when the rain fell softly in the sand and rustled on the trees, come upon a house on the rim of a forest that immediately evoked the memory of other times and another life? You really believe you know that house—you would swear you had lived in it. . . .

How can I explain that on my first visit to London, as an immigrant boy in passage to Canada, I knew (and said so to my traveling companions with whom I was strolling about) that around the next corner we would see the Guild-hall and, in that obscure passage in Threadneedle Street, we would find the church of the Austin [Augustine] Friars in the English capital? Still, I had never been to the city before, nor had I ever studied its street plan.

And then, this small park with the royal mausoleum where I now paused a moment, why, of all the parks in Paris, had it always drawn me so ineluctably? Why did it always bring back a vision of a patio where olive-skinned women with large golden earrings and necklaces of gold walked about exchanging confidences in a low voice? How often have I not looked up from a book or a newspaper in that garden, thinking I heard the sound of bare little feet pattering on cool paving stones, only to find that the hatchet-faced keeper was merely making his rounds. Whence had come that silvery children's laughter I heard?

That Day Alone

Heredity, Environment, and the "Soul"

Some twenty years ago a professor of logic and ethics, who now heads the Department of Philosophy in one of the world's largest universities, made an astounding admission to a senior class. In those days the professor referred to himself as a "Naturalist," which connoted a particular atmosphere of pragmatism, and on this occasion he had been involved in explaining human behavior in terms of environmental conditions, erecting the structure of naturalist ethics in the John Dewey frame of reference. . . .

But near the close of the course, this professor deviated from his accustomed lecture program to make, as he said, a confession of confusion. He would *like*, he said, to think that human behavior could be completely explained in the terms he had been using, but that in all honesty he must not brush aside a nagging thought that often came to him—that every human being seemed to be *born with* something that neither heredity nor environment would adequately account for, and that among the children of a single family the contrasts that seemed to be of essential character were particularly arresting.

This leads us to a favorite "metaphysical" thesis regarding the origin of what might well be called the "soul"—the hypothesis of palingenesis or rebirth. Most arguments about immortality seem to focus on the desire of the individual to believe that his present personality is indestructible, and therefore opponents of all doctrines of immortality like to discount such beliefs on the ground of wishful thinking. It seems to us, as it did to the Greeks, that this is clearly going at the question in the wrong way. As Plato makes plain in the *Phædo*, the Greek thinkers, though cautious on the subject of immortality as an extension of the present life, were convinced of the pre-existence of the soul—this because, as men of natural philosophic temperament, they were trying to find a reasonable explanation for the remarkable diversities of human individuality. Further, philosophic concern with any teaching regarding a plurality of lives becomes especially interesting in the context of education, where unique differences are greatly in need of understanding. Here we find conjunction of everything expressed in the terms of heredity, environment, and the "soul," and it is here that the philosophy of pre-existence, incidentally involving further successive rebirths of the same essential individuality, becomes especially provocative. . . .

Magazine Manas, July 20, 1960

· A M E R I C A N   P O E T S ·

Nathaniel Parker Willis (1806-1867)

[Willis once wrote a story of himself as the reincarnation of an Austrian artist, and how he discovered his previous personality. The tale is to be found *in Dashes at Life under the title "A Revelation of a Previous Exist-ence."*]

> But what a mystery this erring mind?
> It wakes within a frame of various powers
> A stranger in a new and wondrous world.
> It brings an instinct from some other sphere. . .
> Of well trained ministers, the mind goes forth
> To search the secrets of its new found home.
>
> *A Poem Read at Brown University*

Henry Wadsworth Longfellow (1807-1882)

> Thus the seer,
> With vision clear,
> Sees forms appear and disappear,
> In the perpetual round of strange,
> Mysterious change
> From birth to death, from death to birth;
> From earth to heaven, from heaven to earth;
> 'Til glimpses more sublime,
> Of things unseen before,
> Unto his wondering eyes reveal
> The Universe, as an immeasurable wheel
> Turning forevermore
> In the rapid and rushing river of Time.
>
> *Rain in Summer*

> Tell me not, in mournful numbers,
> Life is but an empty dream!—
> For the soul is dead that slumbers,
> And things are not what they seem.
> Life is real! Life is earnest!
> And the grave is not its goal,
> Dust thou art, to dust returnest,
> Was not spoken of the soul. . . .
>
> *A Psalm of Life*

John Greenleaf Whittier (1807-1892)

The river hemmed with leaving trees
    Wound through its meadows green,
A long blue line of mountain showed
    The open pines between. . . .

No clue of memory led me on,
    But well the ways I knew,
A feeling of familiar things
    With every footstep grew. . . .

A presence strange at once and known
    Walked with me as my guide,
The skirts of some forgotten life
    Trailed noiseless at my side. . . .

                                    A *Mystery*

We shape ourselves the joy or fear
    Of which the coming life is made
And fill our Future's atmosphere
    With sunshine or with shade.

The Tissue of the Life to be
    We weave with colors all our own,
And in the field of Destiny
    We reap as we have sown.

Still shall the soul around it call
    The Shadows which it gathered here,
And painted on the eternal wall
    The Past shall reappear.

Think ye the notes of holy song
    On Milton's tuneful ear have died?
Think ye that Raphael's angel throng
    Has vanished from his side?

Oh, no!—We live our life again:
    Or warmly touched or coldly dim

The pictures of the Past remain,—
Man's works shall follow him!

Raphael

Oliver Wendell Holmes (1809-1894)

Year after year beheld the silent toil
That spread his lustrous coil;
Still, as the spiral grew,
He left the past year's dwelling for the new,
Stole with soft step its shining archway through,
Built up its idle door,
Stretched in his last-found home, and knew the old
    no more. . . .

Build thee more stately mansions, O my soul!
As the swift seasons roll!
Leave thy low-vaulted past!
Let each new temple, nobler than the last,
Shut thee from heaven with a dome more vast,
Till thou at length art free,
Leaving thine outgrown shell by life's unresting sea!

The Chambered Nautilus

Walt Whitman (1819-1892)

I know I am deathless,
I know this orbit of mine cannot be swept by a carpenter's
    compass. . . .
And whether I come to my own to-day or in ten thousand or
    ten million years,
I can cheerfully take it now, or with equal cheerfulness I can
    wait. . . .
To be in any form, what is that?
(Round and round we go, all of us, and ever come back
    thither). . . .
Believing I shall come again upon the earth after
    five thousand years. . . .

The clock indicates the moment—but what does eternity indicate?
We have thus far exhausted trillions of winters and summers,
There are trillions ahead, and trillions ahead of them.
Births have brought us richness and variety,
And other births will bring us richness and variety. . . .
I am an acme of things accomplished, and I an encloser
    of things to be. . . .
Rise after rise bow the phantoms behind me,
Afar down I see the huge first Nothing, I know I was even
    there. . . .
Immense have been the preparations for me,
Faithful and friendly the arms that have help'd me. . . .

I tramp a perpetual journey (come listen all!). . . .
This day before dawn I ascended a hill and look'd at the crowded
    heaven,
And I said to my spirit, When we become enfolders of those orbs,
    and the pleasure and knowledge of everything in them,
    shall we be fill'd and satisfied then?
And my spirit said, No, we but level that lift to pass and
    continue beyond. . . .
And as to you, Life, I reckon you are the leavings of many deaths.
(No doubt I have died myself ten thousand times before.) . . .

                                 Song of Myself

[*In the leading article of the Saturday Review for October 31, 1959, en-titled "Walt Whitman's Buried Masterpiece," Malcolm Cowley wrote:*]

Whitman believed . . . that there is a distinction between one's mere personality and the deeper Self. . . . By means of metempsychosis and karma we are all involved in a process of spiritual evolution that might be compared to natural evolution. Even the latter process, however, was not regarded by Whitman as strictly natural or material. He believed that animals have a rudimentary sort of soul ("They bring me tokens of myself"), and he hinted or surmised, without directly saying, that rocks, trees, and planets possess an identity, or "eidolon," that persists as they rise to higher states of being. The double process of evolution, natural and spiritual, can be traced for ages into the past, and he believed that it will continue for ages beyond ages. . . . All men are divine and will eventually be gods. . . . The universe was an eternal becoming for Whitman, a process not a structure, and it had to be judged from the standpoint of eternity.

James Russell Lowell (1819-1891)

Sometimes a breath floats by me
    An odor from Dreamland sent,
Which makes the ghost seem nigh me
    Of a something that came and went,
Of a life lived somewhere, I know not
    In what diviner sphere. . . .
A something too vague, could I name it,
    For others to know:
As though I had lived it and dreamed it,
As though I had acted and schemed it
    Long ago. . . .

             The Twilight

John Townsend Trowbridge (1827-1916)

From her own fair dominions
Long since, with shorn pinions
My spirit was banished.
But above her still hover in vigils and dreams
Ethereal visitants, voices and gleams
That forever remind her
Of something behind her
Long vanished.

             Beyond

Emily Dickinson (1830-1886)

Afraid? Of whom am I afraid?
Not death; for who is he?
The porter of my father's lodge
As much abasheth me.

Of life? 'Twere odd I fear a thing
That comprehendeth me

In one or more existences
At Deity's decree.

Of resurrection? Is the east
Afraid to trust the morn . . . ?

        *   *   *

Death is a dialogue between
The spirit and the dust
"Dissolve," says Death. The Spirit, "Sir,
I have another trust."

Death doubts it, argues from the ground.
The Spirit turns away,
Just laying off, for evidence,
An overcoat of clay.

Paul Hamilton Hayne (1830-1886)

One sails toward me o'er the bay,
And what he comes to do and say
I can foretell. A prescient lore
Springs from some life outlived of yore.
O swift, instructive, startling gleams
Of deep soul-knowledge: not as dreams
For age ye vaguely dawn and die,
But oft with lightning certainty
Pierce through the dark oblivious brain
To make old thoughts and memories plain
Thoughts which perchance must travel back
Across the wild bewildering track
Of countless aeons. . . .

Pre-existence

Thomas Bailey Aldrich (1836-1907)

I know my own creation was divine. . . .
I was ere Romulus and Remus were;
I was ere Nineveh and Babylon;

I was, and am, and evermore shall be,
Progressing, never reaching to the end. . . .

A century was as a single day.
What is a day to an immortal soul?
A breath, no more. And yet I hold one hour
Beyond all price,—that hour when from the sky
I circled near and nearer to the earth. . . .

We weep when we are born, not when we die!
So was it destined; and thus came I here,
To walk the earth and wear the form of Man,
To suffer bravely as becomes my state,
One step, one grade, one cycle nearer God.

The Metempsychosis

Joaquin Miller (1839-1913)

White reindeer's milk is yellow gold
And he who drinks it lives for aye;
He will not drown, he cannot die,
Nor hunger, thirst, nor yet grow cold,
But live and live a thousand lives—
Ten thousand deer, two thousand wives.

Song of Creation

How her heart beat! Three thousand years
Of weary, waiting womanhood. . . .
But now at last to meet once more
Upon the bright all shining shore
Of earth, in life's resplendent dawn. . . .

With Love to You and Yours

Edwin Markham (1852-1940)

Perhaps we are led, and our loves are fated,
  And steps are counted, one by one.
Perhaps we shall meet, and our souls be mated,
  After the burnt out sun.

There are more lives yet; there are more worlds waiting,
　For the Way climbs up to the eldest sun.

The Crowning Hour

William Vaughn Moody (1869-1910)

We have felt the ancient swaying
　Of the earth before the sun,
On the darkness marge of midnight heard sidereal rivers playing;
　Rash it was to bathe our souls there, but we plunged and
　　all is done.
That is lives and lives behind us—lo, our journey is begun.

Road Hymn for the Start

Robert Frost (1874-   )

I'd like to get away from earth awhile
And then come back to it and begin over.
May no fate wilfully misunderstand me
And half grant what I wish and snatch me away
Not to return. Earth's the right place for love:
I don't know where it's likely to go better. . . .

Birches

Sarcastic Science she would like to know,
In her complacent ministry of fear,
How we propose to get away from here
When she has made things so we have to go
Or be wiped out. Will she be asked to show
Us how by rocket we may hope to steer
To some star off there say a half light-year
Through temperature of absolute zero?
Why wait for science to supply the how
When any amateur can tell it now?
The way to go away should be the same
As fifty million years ago we came—
If anyone remembers how that was,
I have a theory, but it hardly does.

Why Wait for Science

Vachel Lindsay (1879-1931)

Do you remember, ages after,
At last the world we were born to own?
You were the heir of the yellow throne—
The world was the field of the Chinese man,
And we were the pride of the sons of Han.
We copied deep books and we carved in jade,
And wove blue silks in the mulberry shade. . . .

The Chinese Nightingale

Don Marquis (1878-1937)

JOURNALIST AND HUMORIST

I say that I think for myself, but what is this Self of mine
But a chance, loose knot in the skein of life where myriad
    selves entwine? . . .
Dust that was flesh of mine moulders in many a tomb.
Ghosts that were sires of mine circles me here in the gloom.
I have heard cries through the night in a tongue I cannot
    speak,
And they knocked on my heart and blanched my cheek. . . .

Heir and Serf

Kahlil Gibran (1883-1931)

SYRIAN-BORN SYMBOLIST POET AND PAINTER

Brief were my days among you, and briefer still the words I have spoken. But should my voice fade in your ears, and my love vanish in your memory, then I will come again, and with a richer heart and lips more yielding to the spirit will I speak. Yes, I shall return with the time, and though death may hide me and the greater silence enfold me, yet again will I seek your understanding. . . . Know, therefore, that from the greater silence I shall return. . . . Forget not that I shall come back to you. . . . A little while, a moment of rest upon the wind, and another woman shall bear me.

The Prophet *

Louis Untermeyer (1885-   )

In what great struggles was I felled,
    In what old lives I laboured long,
Ere I was given a world that held
    A meadow, butterflies and song?

But oh, what cleansings and what fears,
    What countless raisings from the dead,
Ere I could see her, touched with tears,
    Pillow the little weary head.
                How Much of Godhood

Robert Hillyer (1895-   )

Forget not Memphis and the evening lights
    Along the shore, the wind in the papyrus,
The sound of water through the glass-green nights,
    The incense curling upward to Osiris.
Forget not Athens and the starry walks
    Beside Ilissus under the cool trees,
The Master's garden, and the quiet talks
    Of Gods and life to come. Forget not these.
And in the after years, forget not this:
    How in a withered world allied to death,
When love was mocked and beauty deemed amiss,
    We met and pledged again the ancient faith.
For this, of all our loves the loneliest
    So thwarted and so strong, will seem the best.
                Sonnet from "The Halt in the Garden"

·AMERICAN NOVELISTS·
·AND DRAMATISTS·

Our attention is confined to writers who have shown a philosophic or psychological interest in reincarnation. (Quotations from British novelists *and dramatists will be found at pages 144-159.) The numerous novels, plays, and motion pictures that have played up the idea chiefly from the romantic viewpoint are not here considered. More than sixty years ago, Lafcadio Hearn wrote in his book* Kokoro: Hints and Echoes of Japanese Inner Life:

Proof that a reconstruction of the problem of the Ego is everywhere forcing itself upon Occidental minds, may be found not only in the thoughtful prose of the time, but also in its poetry and romance. . . . Creative art, working under larger inspiration, is telling what absolutely novel and exquisite sensations, what hitherto unimaginable pathos, what marvellous deepening of the emotional power, may be gained in literature with the recognition of the idea of pre-existence. Even in fiction we learn that we have been living in a hemisphere only, that we have been thinking but half-thoughts, that we need a new faith to join past with future over the great parallel of the present, and so to round out our emotional world into a perfect sphere.

Edgar Allan Poe (1809-1849)

We walk about, amid the destinies of our world existence, accompanied by dim but ever present memories of a Destiny more vast—very distant in the bygone time and infinitely awful. . . . We live out a youth peculiarly haunted by such dreams, yet never mistaking them for dreams. As *memories* we know them. During our youth the distinctness is too clear to deceive us even for a moment. But the doubt of manhood dispels these feelings as illusions. Existence—self-existence—existence from all Time and to all Eternity —seems, up to the epoch of Manhood, a normal and unquestionable condition,—*seems, because it is.*

Eureka

It is mere idleness to say that I had not lived before—that the soul has no previous existence. You deny it—let us not argue the matter. Convinced myself, I seek not to convince. There is, however, a remembrance of aerial forms—of spiritual and meaning eyes—of sounds, musical yet sad; a remembrance which will not be excluded; a memory like a shadow—vague, variable, indefinite, unsteady; and like a shadow, too, in the impossibility of my getting rid of it while the sunlight of my reason shall exist.

Berenice

Mark Twain (1835-1910)

[Mark Twain's true story "My Platonic Sweetheart" tells of an unusual dream that recurred in manifold forms over a period of forty years. Therein he meets a girl of fifteen for whom he has a deep, reverent, chaste love. Frequently in the dreams she, as well as he, has a new name, her appearance and facial characteristics changing radically. The locus of the vision also varies: it might be India, or England, or America. In "Hawaii" he saw her die a terrible death, and the pain, the grief, and the misery of it transcended many sufferings he had known in waking life. Of his next meeting her in Greece he writes:]

What now follows occurred while I was asleep. . . . I was in Athens—a city which I had not then seen, but I recognized the Parthenon from the pictures, although it had a fresh look and was in perfect repair. I passed by it and climbed a grassy hill toward a palatial sort of mansion which was built of red terra cotta and had a spacious portico, whose roof was supported by a rank of fluted columns with Corinthian capitals. . . . I passed into the house and entered the first room. It was very large and light, its walls were of polished and richly tinted and veined onyx, and its floor was a pictured pattern in soft colors laid in tiles. I noted the details of the furniture and the ornaments . . . and they took sharp hold and remained in my memory; they are not really dim yet, and this was more than thirty years ago.

There was a person present—Agnes. I was not surprised to see her, but only glad. She was in the simple Greek costume, and her hair and eyes were different as to color from those she had had when she died in the Hawaiian Islands half an hour before. . . . I remembered her death. . . . I was grateful to have her back, but there was no realizable sense that she had ever been gone, and so it did not occur to me to speak about it, and she made no reference to it herself. It may be that she had often died before, and knew that there was nothing lasting about it, and consequently nothing important enough in it to make conversation out of. . . .

While Agnes and I sat talking in that grand Athens house, several stately Greeks entered from another part of it, disputing warmly about something or other, and passed us by with courteous recognition; and among them was Socrates. I recognized him by his nose. . . . . When I think of that house and its belongings, I recognize what a master in taste and drawing and color and arrangement is the dream-artist who resides in us. In my waking hours, when the inferior artist in me is in command, I cannot draw even the simplest picture. . . . In our dreams—I know it!—we do make the journeys we seem to make; we do see the things we seem to see; the people, the horses, the cats . . . are real, not chimeras; they are living spirits, not shadows; and they are immortal and indestructible. . . . My Dreamland sweetheart . . . to me . . . is a real person, not a fiction. . . .

Everything in a dream is more deep and strong and sharp and real than is ever its pale imitation in the unreal life which is ours when we go about awake and clothed with our artificial selves in this vague and dull-tinted artificial world. When we die we shall slough off this cheap intellect, perhaps, and go abroad into Dreamland clothed in our real selves, and aggrandized and enriched by the command over the mysterious mental magician who is here not our slave, but only our guest.

My Platonic Sweetheart

David Belasco (1854-1931)

[Editors:] *The legend of the Flying Dutchman has been considered by many to be a reincarnation drama. The genius of Richard Wagner (himself a staunch reincarnationist) first awakened, it is said, in the composing of the poem and music to the opera of that name. The motion picture Pandora and the Flying Dutchman also vividly dramatized the theme. Few, however, may recall that in 1916 David Belasco produced the story under the title Van Der Decken in which the famed David Warfield played the leading role. A reviewer wrote:*

Mr. Belasco has taken the familiar legend of the Flying Dutchman; fired it with his marvelous imagination; touched it with romance; dominated it with tremendous faith in reincarnation, saturated it with symbolism. . . .

The typewritten script of this play, available for perusal at the Central Public Library in New York, gives direction to print in the theater program nine quoted lines from John Masefield's reincarnation poem "A Creed" (see Anthology index). In the drama itself are to be found these words:

Ay, God above us! There's his curse! What he's seen . . . the Dutchman! . . . The whole world die and born again. . . . And he's seen it all—all— the only man in the world to see it. All his friends die and come back— Hans is Peter and Peter re-named Hans—with new Mothers—all young again. And he must live on and meet them all as—strangers. Why, he's drank with dead shipmates—heard the laughter o' the drowned. And *he* knew them!

Charles Kelsey Gaines (1854-?)

PROFESSOR OF GREEK PHILOSOPHY, ST. LAWRENCE UNIVERSITY

[*Professor Gaines's once widely read novel Gorgo; a Romance of Old Athens, was acclaimed by some reviewers as one of the best historical novels ever written. His stories therein of Socrates teaching a child are truly priceless. Quoting now from the prologue to Gorgo:*]

I stopped short; I flung down the book. "It is a lie," I cried bitterly, "a cruel, hateful lie," I almost shouted,—and the whole class stared at me in amazement.

A strange outburst was that for the dingy, drowsy Greek-room of the little New England college. I was as much surprised as any; I stood confused at myself. For then it was that I remembered. The passage which I was translating seemed innocent enough—to all the rest. We were reading at sight—the professor's particular hobby; and he was exploiting upon us the Twelfth Oration of Lysias. . . .

" 'And although he has been the author of all these and still other disasters and disgraces, both old and new, both small and great, some dare to profess themselves his friends; although it was not for the people that Theramenes died, but because of his own villainy—' "

Then I choked and stopped. Tears swam in my eyes, and a hot flush scalded my cheeks. . . . "It is a lie," I burst forth. "A cruel, hateful lie. . . . I will not read it—I will not read another line," I cried. For the past had opened like a darkness lightning-cleft; all in one moment I felt the injustices of ages; the shame of an aeon of scorn—and they asked me to read against myself the lying record. . . . After that they nicknamed me Theramenes: I was nicknamed after myself, and none suspected. . . .

Forget! I have far too much to remind me. What is this seething democracy in which we live but Athens renewed? In a thousand ways I am reminded—but I forbear. Yet—do you imagine that I alone among living men have walked those ancient streets? Not so: but the rest do not remember.

Mary Johnston (1870-1936)

As Curtin rode he thought that he faintly remembered all the forests of the world. . . . "Is it because I have been—and surely I *have* been—in all the forests of the world?" . . .

A sense of hut and cave, so often, so long, in so many lands, that there was a feeling of eternity about it. Rain and the cave and the fire, and the inner man still busied with his destiny! There was something that awed in the perception that ran from one to another, that held them in a swift, shimmering band. "How old—how old! How long have we done this?" The rhythm of the storm, the rhythm of the room, the rhythm of the fire, passed into a vast, still sense of ordered movement. "Of old, and now, and tomorrow—everywhere and all time—until we return above time and place, and division is healed."

Sweet Rocket

Jack London (1876-1916)

[*The note of reincarnation resounds on almost every page of Jack London's novel The Star Rover (published in London as The Jacket). Some sample quotations are:*]

All my life I have had an awareness of other times, and places. I have been aware of other persons in me. . . . I, whose lips had never lisped the word "king," remembered that I had once been the son of a king. More—I remembered that once I had been a slave and a son of a slave, and worn an iron collar round my neck. . . .

I, like any man, am a growth. I did not begin when I was born nor when I was conceived. I have been growing, developing, through incalculable myriads of millenniums. All these experiences of all these lives have gone to the making of the soul-stuff or the spirit-stuff that is I. . . .

I am all of my past, as every protagonist of the Mendelian law must agree. All my previous selves have their voices, echoes prompting in me. . . . I am man born of woman. My days are few, but the stuff of me is indestructible. I have been woman born of woman. I have been a woman and borne my children. And I shall be born again. Oh, incalculable times again shall I be born; and yet the stupid dolts about me think that by stretching my neck with a rope they will make me cease.

Joseph Egan (1879-?)

Joseph Egan's book Donn Fendler is on the surface simply a detailed history of a lost twelve-year-old's wandering for nine days in a mountainous area of Maine. However, the author's development of the story should be correlated with his view that every human soul passes, like Ulysses, through many terrors and difficulties in the pursuit of self-reliance and deeper understanding. Mr. Egan has thus expressed his own convictions in a reply to a reader:

By the way: I believe in reincarnation and have just completed a poem "The Flight of Dust Towards Deity." It gives a rational explanation of man's position on this cinder pile as a being in process of becoming perfected to the place where companionship on an equal level with Deity is not only a possibility but a certainty.

Hervey Allen (1889-1949)

The accounts of the good and evil of a lifetime cannot be balanced by explanations and the books closed. The balance is carried forward into other lives; into actions and reactions until equilibrium results. Only time can liquidate it in full.

Anthony Adverse

In North America, especially in the newer settlements, Masonry in sundry and various ways filled vital and long-felt wants. . . . To many a simple frontier youth, in particular, the experience of initiation was frequently overwhelming. . . . For, instead, of arriving in some rude loft . . . the new initiates would now seem to have been translated into the finished cavernlike abode of some powerful magician or spiritual personage, a being superior to and aloof from the wild self-planted nature without. Only a missing password had been needed—and they had at last gained entrance to his very house.

"At last"—because this place and the spirit that dwelt there must after all have always been quite close by. . . . In the recesses of their lonely minds they had sought this dwelling through forests of dream-afflicted nightmare. Somehow, somewhere it had been lost. Now they had suddenly come upon it—again! . . . "Why, this was not a garret! No, this was that old place!"

They would be astonished. But that was not what would astonish them most. It was this:

Each would suddenly feel that he had been alive for ages. He would instantly "remember" that he had often and often seen this familiar place before.

Bedford Village

Louis Bromfield (1896-1956)

There have been moments in my experience when I have been sharply aware of the "strange intimations" of which Dr. Alexis Carrel writes—intimations which have scarcely been touched upon in the realms of science—"strange intimations," of worlds which I had known before, of places which in the spirit I had touched and heard and smelled.

France was one of the places I had always known. From the time I was old enough to read, France had a reality for me, the one place in all the world I felt a fierce compulsion to see. Its history fascinated me, its pictures, its landscapes, its books, its theatre. It was, during all my childhood and early youth, the very apotheosis of all that was romantic and beautiful. And finally when, the morning before we were allowed ashore, the gray landscape of Brittany appeared on the horizon, there was nothing strange about it. I had seen those shores before, when I do not know. And afterward during all the years I lived there, during the war when I served with the French army and in the strange melodramatic truce between wars, it was always the same. Nothing ever surprised or astonished me; no landscape, no forest, no chateau, no Paris street, no provincial town ever seemed strange. I had seen it all before. It was always a country and its people a people whom I knew well and intimately.

Pleasant Valley (Nonfiction)

William Faulkner (1897-   )

NOBEL PRIZE, 1949

[*Faulkner's views on immortality, contained in his Nobel prize acceptance address, reported in the* Saturday Review of Literature *for February 3, 1951:*]

I decline to accept the end of man. It is easy enough to say that man is immortal simply because he will endure; that when the last ding-dong of doom has clanged and faded from the last worthless rock hanging tideless in the last red and dying evening, that even then there will still be one more sound: that of his puny inexhaustible voice, still talking. I refuse to accept this. I believe that man will not merely endure: he will prevail. He is immortal, not because he alone among creatures has an inexhaustible voice, but because he has a soul, a spirit capable of compassion and sacrifice and endurrance. The poet's, the writer's duty is to write about these things. . . . The poet's voice need not merely be the record of man, it can be one of the props, the pillars to help him endure and prevail.

Mildred McNaughton

Harry Gregg walked quickly toward the ancient sundial in the center of the garden. . . . "*In memoria aeterna erit justus,*" he read, then said, "Do you know what that means?"

"The Just shall be in eternal memory. . . . Where does it come from?" John asked.

"The Psalms. I forget which. But there's a deeper meaning to it than the obvious one. That is that the just, or evolved, soul remembers its past lives. The memory is a sign of spiritual attainment. Few have anything of it; almost none have it with any clarity." . . .

"Do you believe we've lived before?" John asked.

"Certainly. It's not an original idea, you know. About two thirds of the human race accept it absolutely. It is woven into all the Eastern religions, and was taught, or at least accepted, by the Christian Church until the third or fourth century. There is pretty clear evidence all through the Gospels that Jesus knew of the belief and did not rebuke it."

John felt that this strange thought was so tremendous in its implications that he did not want to think about it now. It shed a blinding white light upon all that had been dark and obscure to him since he had come into the valley.

Four Great Oaks

J. D. Salinger (1919-   )

Author of Catcher in the Rye, Salinger is well known for his stories in The New Yorker, one of which, called "Teddy" (January 31, 1953), revolves around a phenomenal ten-year-old who matter-of-factly recalls his previous incarnations in India. Brought before a panel of distinguished but skeptical scholars, who are soon confounded by his knowledge, Teddy confides to one professor that in the boy's last incarnation he wasn't a holy man; just a person making nice spiritual advancement. Then he met a lady and sort of stopped meditating. Even had this not occurred he wasn't so spiritually enlightened that he would have gone straight to Brahma, never to return; but he wouldn't have had to incarnate in an American body if he had not met that lady. "It's very hard to meditate and live a spiritual life in America. People think you are a freak if you try to."

James Jones (1921-   )

"Some day they will rank Joe Hill right up alongside old John the Baptist. He must have done something great, back a long time ago before he was ever Joe Hill, to have earned a chance at a ticket like that one." When Prewitt asked what he meant, he said, "In one of his previous lives." . . .

Jack Malloy believed in reincarnation, because to his logical mind, it was the only logical explanation. And it was for this same reason that he worshipped the memory of Joseph Hillstrom so. "He was a saint. He had to be one, to have been given the life he was allowed to have."

* * *

He [Prewitt] remembered one day for no good reason how Jack Malloy had always talked about Jack London all the time, and how he had worshipped him almost as much as Joe Hill. . . . So he started to [read London's books] in earnest. Of them all, he liked *Before Adam* and *The Star Rover* the best because for the first time they gave him a clear picture of what Malloy had meant by reincarnation of souls. He thought he could see now, how there could just as easily be an evolution of souls in different bodies, just like there had been an evolution of bodies in different souls from . . . prehistoric times. . . . It seemed to be logical.

From Here to Eternity

Tom T. Chamales (1924-1960)

"You believe in reincarnation, don't you?" she asked pointedly. . . . "Can you explain why it wasn't mentioned in the Bible?" . . .

"It was mentioned," Con said. "At least according to Danny. It's a matter of interpretation I guess. Danny thinks that when Christ said 'the last shall come first and the first last' he was speaking of reincarnation. I'm not sure.

He also believes that the Emperor Constantine had all references to reincarnation stricken from the Bible at the Council of Nicea. That the actual testimony lies in the ashes of the Alexandrian libraries that were ordered burned."

"If there is such a thing as reincarnation," she said, . . . "Why can't we remember anything of our past lives?" . . .

"Suppose we could remember everything about our past lives exactly as we remember this one. Being what we are, the way we are, we would carry all our strengths and weaknesses, hopes and prejudices, from our former lives into this one. We'd make a bigger mess of this living, over our now active concern of the mess we made of other livings. We wouldn't advance. We wouldn't be putting ourselves to any new test. Would we? The conscious mind is the record of a single life. The subconscious of all lives. . . . What you are really, the character of you shines through as much from the sub as from the conscious."

Never So Few

· A M E R I C A N   M I S C E L L A N Y ·

Henry Ford (1863-1947)

[*The following appeared in the Hearst papers for April 27, and 28, 1938, being a copyrighted account of an interview with Henry Ford:*]

When I was a young man I, like so many others, was bewildered. I found myself asking the question . . . "What are we here for?" I found no answer. Without some answer to that question life is empty, useless. Then one day a friend handed me a book. . . . That little book gave me the answer I was seeking. It changed my whole life. From emptiness and uselessness, it changed my outlook upon life to purpose and meaning. I believe that we are here now and will come back again. . . . Of this I am sure . . . that we *are* here for a purpose. And that we go on. Mind and memory—they are the eternals.

[*Another interview with Ford is reported thus by the well-known journalist George Sylvester Viereck (San Francisco Examiner, August 26, 1928):*]

I adopted the theory of Reincarnation when I was twenty-six. . . . Religion offered nothing to the point. . . . Even work could not give me complete satisfaction. Work is futile if we cannot utilize the experience we collect in one life in the next. When I discovered Reincarnation it was as if I had found a universal plan. I realized that there was a chance to work out my ideas. Time was no longer limited. I was no longer a slave to the hands of the clock. . . .

The discovery of Reincarnation put my mind at ease. . . . If you preserve a record of this conversation, write it so that it puts men's minds at ease. I would like to communicate to others the calmness that the long view of life gives to us.

Genius is experience. Some seem to think that it is a gift or talent, but it is the fruit of long experience in many lives. Some are older souls than others, and so they know more.

William Randolph Hearst (1863-1951)

[In one of his daily columns "In the News" (Los Angeles Examiner, March 27, 1941) Hearst wrote of the town, San Miguel de Allende, near Monterrey, Mexico:]

The architecture in this town is particularly striking. Singularly enough, most of it was designed and constructed by Severino Gutierrez, an Indian who had no trained and technical knowledge and who drew all his plans with a stick in the sand. Reincarnation may be a fantastic theory, but this Indian genius could not have inherited an amazing talent which none of his ancestors possessed. How then, could he have acquired it except by personal experience in some previous existence?

Harry Houdini (1874-1926)
PSEUDONYM OF EHRICH WEISS

[An interview recorded in The Free Press reports the famous Houdini as having said:]

I firmly believe, and this belief is based on investigation, observation, and, in a measure, personal experience—that somehow, somewhere, and sometime, we return in another human form, to carry on, as it were, through another lifetime, perhaps through many succeeding lifetimes, until some strange destiny is worked out to its ultimate solution. . . .

I, myself, have entered some Old World city for the first time in my life, so far as I was aware, and found the streets familiar, known just where to go to locate a certain house, for instance. Things have come to me that it seemed could only have been results of some former experience. I seemed from earliest childhood to have a grasp upon certain faculties and a knowledge not according to my years—as if the understanding were from past education and that I had entered the world with certain fixed principles and ideas that could not have been at that time the result of any present education.

Homer Lea (1876-1912)

Few today recall General Homer Lea, the American cripple who overthrew the Manchu Dynasty of China, setting in motion the wheels of a new Asiatic era before ever setting foot on Asian soil. *

As a small boy he had a dream which left an unforgettable impression. In it appeared strange men and strange sounds. At ten, the dream reappeared. This time he knew the men to be Chinese soldiers. The dream came for the third time at sixteen; and this time he knew the sounds for Chinese war trumpets. It returned a fourth time, years later, just before his departure for China.

After leaving college he turned his entire attention to military strategy. In some way he gained ascendency over the Chinese youth of San Francisco and Los Angeles, organized them, cut off their queues—the mark of servitude to the Manchu Dynasty—and began shipping them to China. Shortly afterward he followed. Then began the first successful rebellion. Lea came back with a price on his head, in all Oriental usage a disgraced man, yet Kang Yu Wei, ex-Premier of China, and Liang Ki Chew, an Imperial Prince, attached themselves to him like servitors. His military record caused him at various times to be consulted by Lord Roberts, Commander-in-chief of the British Army, and Kaiser Wilhelm. The latter had a special carriage built to enable Lea to see army maneuvers.

Lea came to know Dr. Sun Yat Sen; and together they plotted and carried out the uprising which made a Republic—in name—of China. He died soon after, having played jackstraws with the destinies of more human beings than Napoleon probably ever realized were in the world. Like Napoleon, he considered himself a "man of destiny"; and like Napoleon, speculated upon his own peculiarities as derived from other lives of the past. A Buddhist

---

* An account of General Lea's life was published in the Los Angeles *Times,* November 15, 1931, by Harry Carr, a personal acquaintance.

monk, "reading" his palm, grew pale and pronounced the hand that of a king—or so they say.

Edgar Cayce (1877-1945)

During the past few decades considerable interest in reincarnation has been aroused through the reputed healings of Edgar Cayce, who it is claimed had the power of reading the past lives of people and detecting karmic causes leading to present troubles. Two books on Cayce's life work are: Many Mansions, by Dr. Gina Cerminara (Wm. Sloane) and There is a River, by Thomas Sugrue (Henry Holt).

Dr. Pearl Cleveland Wilson (1882-   )

EMERITUS PROFESSOR OF CLASSICS, HUNTER COLLEGE

To one with a conviction that the individual is far more than a physical body and that what is often called "chance" is the result of laws still unrecognized, reincarnation explains much that has long puzzled the observing eye and the reflecting mind. Other explanations offered by various religions seem vague when compared with it. Why do men living good lives suffer? Reincarnation gives the answer to this and similar questions with clarifying logic. Moreover, the concept of living which it provides makes even performance of necessary routine no longer dull by offering assurance that no good thought and no helpful act is ever wasted.

Frances P. Bolton (1885-   )

REPRESENTATIVE FROM OHIO, U. S. CONGRESS

[Extracts from Representative Bolton's address over Edward R. Murrow's radio program "This I Believe," and published in Vol. 2 of Murrow's book of that title:]

When I was but twelve, death entered my life. The dear old rector of a near-by mission chapel took me on his knee and told me very gently that I must not be unhappy, for God had put my mother to sleep until the Resurrection Day. My revolt was immediate and violent. I . . . ran out the door to the sea beach where I had taken all my child agonies. . . . A flame of indignation consumed me, as I shook my fists at the sky, calling out with all the passion within me, "That isn't true, God! and I must know what is. Do anything you want to me, but let me find truth."

My search has led me to the place from which I can say with entire simplicity that I believe that you and I are part and parcel of the stream of Universal Life—as water drops are part of the Great Sea. I believe that what we call a life span is but one of an endless number of lifetimes during which, bit by bit, we shall experience all things. . . .

I believe with the ancient Aryans [Hindus] that, and I quote:

> Never the Spirit was born, the
> Spirit shall Cease to be never;
> Never was time it was not;
> End and Beginning are dreams!
> [The Bhagavad-Gita]

. . . This I do humbly believe.

Charles A. Lindbergh (1902-   )

Charles Lindbergh's The Spirit of St. Louis (Scribner, 1953), is far more than a tale of courage and adventure concerning his historic flight across the Atlantic. It reveals the strange dissociation of states of consciousness that went on within himself as the thirty-four hour flight proceeded and he waged a superhuman battle to keep awake. (He had not slept during the night and day preceding.) First, a separation was observed to take place between mind and body—aspects of himself hitherto regarded as indivisible. Overwhelmed with drowsiness the senses and organs sought sleep though obviously it meant their certain death, but the mind entity standing "apart" holds firm. In turn the mind becomes unable to preserve wakefulness, only to give way to a transcendent power that Lindbergh hardly suspected was part of his makeup. Finally, in mid-ocean, the conscious mind falls fast asleep, and this third element, this new "extraordinary mind" which at first he feared to trust, now directs the flight. Here, in brief, is what he says occurred:

The fuselage behind became crowded with ghostly human presences, transparent, riding weightless with him in the plane. No surprise is experienced at their arrival, and without turning his head he sees them all, for his skull has become "one great eye, seeing everywhere at once." They seem able to disappear or show themselves at will, to pass through the walls of the plane as though no walls existed. Sometimes voices from afar off resound in the plane, familiar voices, advising him on his flight, encouraging him, conveying messages unattainable in normal life.

What connection exists between these "spirits" and himself? It is more like a reunion of friends after years of separation, "as though I've known all of them before in some past incarnation." Perhaps they are the products of the experience of ages, dwellers of a realm closed to the men of our world. He feels himself in a transitional state between earthly life and a vaster region beyond, as though caught in the magnetic field between two planets and propelled by forces he cannot control "representing powers incomparably stronger than I've ever known." Only when his conscious direction of the plane's course seems imperative does he find himself momentarily wakened, to be soon followed by these long, strange interludes of "sleep" with eyes wide open.

Values are changing within his consciousness. For twenty-five years it has been imprisoned in walls of bone, and he had not recognized the endlessness of life, the immortal existence that lies outside. Is he already "dead" and about to join these "phantoms"? Death ceases to be the final end he thought it was. Simultaneously, he lives in the past, the present, and the future. Around him are "old associations, bygone friendships, voices from ancestrally distant times." Yes, he is flying in a plane over the Atlantic, but he is also living in ages long past.

PART THREE

Scientists and Psychologists on Reincarnation

Scientific truth is characterized by its exactness and the certainty of its predictions. But these admirable qualities are contrived by science at the cost of remaining on a plane of secondary problems, leaving intact the ultimate and decisive questions. . . . If the physicist detains, at the point where his method ends, the hand with which he delineates the facts, the human being behind each physicist prolongs the line thus begun and carries it on to its termination, as an eye beholding an arch in ruins will of itself complete the missing airy curve. . . .

The past century, resorting to all but force, tried to restrict the human mind within the limits set to exactness. Its violent effort to turn its back on last problems is called agnosticism. . . . How can we live turning a deaf ear to the last dramatic questions? Where does the world come from and whither is it going? Which is the supreme power of the cosmos, what the essential meaning of life? We cannot breathe confined to a realm of secondary and intermediate themes. We need a comprehensive perspective, foreground and background, not a maimed scenery, a horizon stripped of infinite distances. . . . We are given no escape from last questions. In one fashion or another they are in us, whether we like it or not.

Toward a Philosophy of History
José Ortega y Gasset

❀

ESSAY FROM ❀
"THE YALE REVIEW"

❀

[Before presenting the quotations from scientists and psychologists, the following essay, reprinted in part from the Spring, 1945 Yale Review, may be found an excellent approach to a scientific consideration of reincarnation and immortality:]

Belief in a Future Life

BY J. PAUL WILLIAMS, PROFESSOR, MT. HOLYOKE COLLEGE

Skepticism towards a belief in a future life is undoubtedly widespread. In fact, it is common to hear people disclaim any interest in the subject. "My grandfather believed in a hereafter," writes a famous editor, "and felt that life would be unbearable without the belief. My father doubted, but hoped for it. For myself, I must confess that the prospect arouses dread more than anything else, and my children, so far as I can see, care nothing about it one way or the other." . . .

Yet when one gets beneath the superficial patter of everyday talk, one finds that this attitude of disinterest is often a veneer and does not reflect the true feelings of many men and women. Most of us, even though we may feel that we can never have any genuine knowledge of the hereafter, are deeply interested in the problem of our own personal destiny. . . .

I contend—on what I believe to be purely rational grounds—that it is more reasonable to believe in a future life than to disbelieve in it. Further, I contend that one can believe in it without the fear that one is yielding to the urge to do wishful thinking or to indulge an ancient conception which has been outmoded by the discoveries of modern science.

There is no better approach to a defense of this position than a consideration of some of the causes which have led to skepticism concerning the future life. With many people, one of these causes has been a violent reaction against the naïve conceptions of heaven and hell which they were taught in their youth. Some of the metaphors of the Bible have been taken with such great literalness* that many pious folk believed that some of their neighbors would spend eternity in a lake of fire burning with sulphur, and that the righteous would go to a place which had gates of pearl and streets of gold. . . .

The study of comparative religions has also been a cause of the reaction against the traditional teachings; for it shows how ideas of the hereafter vary with the demands of the cultures which give them birth. The Moslem lives on the desert; thus his Paradise is a verdant oasis. . . . The Eskimo hell is a very cold place; the American Indian expected to arrive finally at the happy hunting ground. The early Teuton dreamed of Valhalla, where heroic warriors battled during the day and then, miraculously healed of their wounds, banqueted lustily at night. . . . Many moderns, largely because of their reaction against crude ideas of a future life, have given up all hope of a hereafter and have, in fact, accepted a positive disbelief in it. But to my mind they have thrown out the baby with the bath. They are like people who stop eating meat simply because one serving of meat made them ill.

Another cause for the current skepticism concerning the future life is that many people have given up a belief in the soul. Probably there is no question in philosophy which has more in it of meaning for practical living than the question, "What is the nature of human nature?" or, in the terms of theology, "What is the nature of man?" Is a man just a body, as some of our contemporaries believe? Or is he just a soul, as some others hold? Or is he a body that has a soul? Or (and this is a different proposition) is he a soul that has a body?

The thinker whose philosophy has been etched by the "acids of modernity" tends to reject any idea of a soul and to assert that a human being is just a physical mechanism: iron, sulphur, sodium, carbon, water, and other elements, all combined in very complex ways. This belief, of course, makes impossible a belief in a future life. Frequently men accept this materialistic

* [Dr. Paul Tillich, of Harvard University Divinity School, in his article "The Lost Dimension of Religion" (*Saturday Evening Post*, June 14, 1958), pointed out: "The first step toward the non-religion of the Western world was made by religion itself. When it defended great symbols, not as symbols, but as literal stories, it had already lost the battle. In doing so the theologians (and today many religious laymen) helped to transfer the powerful expressions of the dimension of depth into objects or happenings on the horizontal plane. There the symbols lose their power and become an easy prey to physical, biological and historical attack." Eds.]

view of man because here again they are reacting to a naïve idea. Many primitive peoples identify the soul with the breath—which disappears at death—and many who supposedly are more civilized have thought of the soul as a misty sort of matter, ectoplasm perhaps, which departs from the body when life departs. Our very competent biologists, having dug around in the human anatomy, and having found no such substance, have come to the conclusion that the soul, in the old-fashioned sense at least, is nonexistent. This tendency to reject the idea of the soul is so pronounced in our modern world that many people who state emphatically their belief that human beings are more than just physical mechanisms prefer not to use the word *soul* with its traditional connotations. They prefer the terms *self* or *personality*.

Before coming to the arguments which support a belief in a future life I should like to make four observations.

[1] . . . the term *immortality* is being deliberately avoided here. The customary meaning of this word is that after death we shall come to life and then shall live forever, through all eternity. Now, it is easier for me to believe simply that human beings will live again than that they will live forever. To my mind, the mystery which surrounds the problem of what is at either end of the eternity of time in the midst of which we live is so deep that human speculation has no chance of penetrating it. . . . Thus only one of the arguments to be mentioned supports immortality.

[2] . . . All we can hope to do is to arrive at a faith that belief in the future life is more rational than disbelief, or that disbelief is more rational than belief. For, the discussion lies in an area in which there are no scientific data on which to build arguments—unless we accept as such the data presented by psychic research. . . .

[3] One's emotional orientation to the problem of the future life is materially advanced when one realizes that the two great religions of the East —Hinduism and Buddhism—assume that the future life is a fact. They teach that man is reborn into the world over and over again, and they view the prospect with much anxiety. Thus one major function of these religions is to teach men how to avoid being reborn. It is not "wishful thinking" from the Hindu or Buddhist point of view to expect to live again; rather it is stark realism. But it would be "wishful thinking" from their point of view really to believe that religion has found a way to get man off of the "wheel of life."

[4] Finally, this discussion is to deal with personal survival; not "the immortality of good influence," or future life for the species, or the kind of survival in which our personalities are absorbed and lost in the Being of God, as a drop of water falls back into the ocean and loses its identity. Our concern here is with the continuance of our individuality, of our awareness of ourselves and of our environment.

The argument for the future life which logically precedes all others is the simple one that if man is a soul it is not unreasonable to suppose that he survives death. If man is simply a body, a physio-chemical reaction, and nothing more, it is obvious that he does not live again as such a body. If, however, man is—or perhaps has—a soul, the door is left open to the possibility that the soul persists after death. Thus the case for the future life is no stronger than is the case for the existence of the soul.

Are human beings souls? . . .

I am among those who feel that they must believe in souls simply because they experience them. It may be that my family, the students I meet on the campus, the friends I play cards with are just bodies, machines, not essentially different from the images I see on a movie screen, images that move and talk. But I find that a very hard position to accept. It is much easier to account for one's experience of people and for one's knowledge of himself on the assumption that the essential human being is more than just a physio-chemical reaction. Is man a living soul? For answer observe people: watch a group of boys playing football; read Shakespeare; look into the eyes of one beloved.

The idea that human beings are just bodies is one phase of the notion that nothing exists but matter, that spirit is nonexistent, that mind is but matter in motion. This position is one that some scientists have expounded dogmatically. Because of the prestige of these men, many people have jumped to the conclusion that anyone who is thoroughly abreast of modern thought will discard faith in anything that is non-material and will, of course, discard faith in a soul. Yet there are other scientists, men of equal prestige, who do not accept the faith that the universe is composed exclusively of matter and assert their belief that faith in a future life is rational. But as a matter of fact scientists are in no better position than are the rest of us to decide whether matter and mind are both real. That is a question for philosophy. And we must all, consciously or unconsciously, be philosophers.

The belief that there are in the universe other realities than matter is a basic assumption, a point at which thinking starts. Traditionally most men have believed that they experience the many manifestations of mind. In this modern day it is still rational to hold that just as real as our experience of food, of bomb-sights . . . is our experience . . . of courage that conquers every fear, of hope that a better world can be established.

Accept if you can the belief that we are souls; that still does not mean that a future life is proved. Do these souls survive death? Our only experience of life is in connection with the body. Some people would contend that we must deduce from this simple fact the conclusion that where there is no body there is no life. But this is not a necessary conclusion. William James pointed out that we can take two positions concerning the relation between the body and life: one is that the body *produces* life; the other that the body *reflects* life. Light is produced by a candle; if the candle is put out its light disappears. Light is reflected by a mirror; if the mirror is taken away the light still continues. Now is it not at least as easy to suppose that the body reflects the soul as it is to suppose that it produces the soul? It may be that this human carcass, full of aches and diseases, heir to boils and rheumatism, produces things like "Hamlet," the theory of evolution, psychoanalysis, and the fortieth chapter of Isaiah, but it is a great deal easier for me to believe that these things are the work of living souls who used bodies as instruments.

If we assume that the soul is reflected rather than is produced by the body, then it is rational to believe that the soul can exist apart from the body. The fact that we have no direct experience of souls which do exist apart from matter is a serious weakness in the argument, but it need not force us to the conclusion that they cannot so exist. The typical reaction of the materialists to this kind of reasoning is an appeal to stick to the known facts. But the materialistic scientist certainly does not limit himself to immediately experienced data. The limits of our experience are so narrow that if we did not permit our thinking to go beyond them, human thought would be puny indeed. Who ever experienced an atom or an electron? . . . The whole conception of the atomic structure is an inference; it is believed because it is consistent with the way in which the elements combine, because it explains why under certain conditions peculiar markings appear on photographic plates. . . . Yet we do not accuse the physicist of irrationality when he says that the solid matter of a rock is really composed of tiny solar systems in which electrons revolve at incredible speed around protons. . . . Who can demonstrate that when a scrap of paper falls into a wastebasket it pushes the earth downward and that this motion of the earth will, in turn, affect every object in the universe? Yet this conclusion follows from Newton's laws of motion. Let no one think that he has reached perfection in his habits of thought if he accepts inferential logic in physics but rejects it in theology.

Another argument in favor of a future life is the simple fact that we are alive now. Here we are, set in the midst of an infinity of time. It is impossible for us to imagine a limit to time. . . . If that is true, then the chances are infinitely against us that we should be alive at any specific time. But here we are. The only way to get rid of the infinity of chances which are against us is to assume that we are like time; that is, that we too are infinite.

This argument turns out to be a defense of immortality. Usually thinking about personal immortality takes this form—a human being is created somewhere near the time of his birth, finally he dies, and then he becomes immortal. The conception I am suggesting, however, is that in addition to living after this life is ended we have lived before it began. This is a logically necessary assumption, if one accepts the force of the argument in any measure. For since infinity is infinitely greater than any part of infinity, the chances of living during any part of eternity, say forever after birth, are infinitely against one. Thus the possibility that we have lived before this life is as good as the possibility that we will live after this life. But, it may be said, we have no memory of any former existence. True, and therefore, if one accepts the argument, one is forced into the conclusion that some means has operated to prevent memory of previous existences.

Perhaps this kind of thinking is going too far with speculation. This may be so, but I gain comfort by pondering the fact that we live now.

The consideration which weighs most heavily with me in my acceptance of a belief in a future life is that a universe in which personality—the most precious thing we know—is preserved is a more rational universe than one in which personality is destroyed. One of the fundamental assumptions of modern thought is that the universe is consistent, that it conforms to certain laws and resists caprice. One of the important conclusions of science is that the sum total of matter and energy in the universe is a constant. Would not a consistent universe preserve its highest manifestation, personality, even as it preserves its lowest manifestation, matter? . . . George Herbert Palmer wrote of the death of his wife, "Though no regrets are proper for the manner of her death, who can contemplate the fact of it, and not call the world irrational if, out of deference to a few particles of disordered matter, it excludes so fair a spirit?" . . .

SCIENTISTS AND PSYCHOLOGISTS ON REINCARNATION

❀

It would be curious if we should find science and philosophy taking up again the old theory of metempsychosis, remodeling it to suit our present modes of religious and scientific thought, and launching it again on the wide ocean of human belief. But stranger things have happened in the history of human opinion.

James Freeman Clarke

Ancient and Medieval Physicians

Dr. Henry More, in his catalog of great thinkers who viewed with favor the idea of the pre-existence and rebirth of the soul, mentions Girolamo Cardan (1501-1576), the noted Italian physician, mathematician, and philosopher, as well as Johannes Fernelius (Jean Fernel 1497-1558), the French doctor and writer surnamed "the modern Galen." Dr. More further states that Fernelius had discovered that "those two grand-masters of medicine, Hippocrates and Galen" were also of the same persuasion.

Paracelsus (1493-1541)

Life is something spiritual. Life is not only in that which moves, such as men and animals, but in all things; for what would be a corporeal form without a spirit? The form may be destroyed; but the spirit remains and is living, for it is the subjective life. . . .

The body which we receive from our parents . . . has no spiritual powers, for wisdom and virtue, faith, hope and charity, do not grow from the earth. These powers are not the products of man's physical organization, but the attributes of another invisible and glorified body, whose germs are laid within man. The physical body changes and dies, the glorified body is eternal. This eternal man is the real man, and is not generated by his earthly parents. He does not draw nutriment from the earth, but from the eternal invisible source from which he originated. . . .

The temporal body is the house of the eternal, and we should therefore take care of it, because he who destroys the temporal body destroys the house of the eternal, and although the eternal man is invisible, he exists neverthe-less, and will become visible in time. . . . Some children are born from heaven, and others are born from hell, because each human being has his inherent tendencies, and these tendencies belong to his spirit, and indicate the state in which he existed before he was born. Witches and sorcerers are not made at once; they are born with powers for evil. The body is only an instrument; if you seek for man in his dead body, you are seeking for him in vain. . . . There is a continual process of death and regeneration going on in man. As a tree grows out of its seed, so the new life grows out of the old one.

> *Quoted in Paracelsus and the Substance of*
> *His Teachings by Franz Hartmann*

Georg Christoph Lichtenberg (1742-1799)

GERMAN PHYSICIST

I cannot get rid of the thought that I died before I was born. I feel so many things that, were I to write them down, the world would regard me as a madman. Consequently, I prefer to hold my peace.

> *Selbstcharacteristik*

Johann Ehlert Bode (1747-1826)

ASTRONOMER; BODE'S LAW NAMED AFTER HIM

Like his contemporary, Immanuel Kant, this celebrated German astron-omer speculated upon the soul's progress among the various heavenly bodies. Louis Figuier, the French science writer, stated in his book The Tomorrow of Death that Bode believed we start our evolutionary journey on the coldest planet of the solar system, advancing from planet to planet, ever closer to the sun, where the most perfect beings, he thought, will live.

Charles Bonnet and Johann Lavater (eighteenth century)
SWISS SCIENTISTS

[Writes Bertholet in The Transmigration of Souls:]

As Lessing tells us, his theory of metempsychosis was based upon the ideas of Charles Bonnet, a physicist of Geneva, who wrote a treatise in French in 1769 upon philosophical palingenesis, giving many so-called proofs to show how from the original matter of the brain all created beings were transformed from corporeal to ethereal natures. Bonnet's ideas seem to have fallen upon fruitful soil elsewhere. In 1770 Lavater translated his treatise into German with annotations, and his social environment also shows how the belief in soul-transmigration haunted the minds of that age. . . . The diary of a woman of Zurich, who may be quoted as an eye-witness of that interesting period, . . . says: "The friends of Lavater at Copenhagen believe in a transmigration of the soul. They believe that several of Jesus' apostles live again on earth, without any recollection of their former lives as apostles."

Sir Humphrey Davy (1778-1829)
ENGLISH CHEMIST

The external world is to us nothing but a cluster of sensations, and in looking back to the memory of our being we find one principle which may be called the monad or self, constantly present, intimately associated with a particular class of sensations, which we call our body, or organs. These organs are connected with other sensations, and move, as it were, with them in circles of existence, quitting for a time some trains of sensation to return to others, but the monad is always present. We can fix no beginning to its operations, we can place no limit to them.

We sometimes in sleep lose the beginning and end of a dream, and recollect the middle of it, and one dream has no connection with another, and yet we are conscious of an infinite variety of dreams, and there is a strong analogy for believing in an infinity of past existences which must have been connected. . . . Human life may be regarded as a type of infinite and immortal life, and its succession of sleep and dreams as a type of the changes of death and birth to which from its nature it is liable. . . .

The whole intellect is a history of change, according to a certain law, and we retain the memory only of those changes which may be useful to us. The child forgets what happened to it in the womb. The recollections of the infant likewise, before two years, are soon lost; yet many of the habits acquired in that age are retained for life. . . . In old age the mind, as it were, falls asleep, to awake in a new existence.

With its present organization the intellect of man is naturally limited and imperfect, but this depends upon its material machinery, and in a higher organized form it may be imagined to possess infinitely higher powers. It does not, however, appear improbable to me that some of the more refined machinery of thought may adhere, even in another state, to the sentient principle, for though the organs of gross sensation, the nerves and brain, are destroyed by death, yet something of the more ethereal value may be less destructible, and I sometimes imagine that many of those powers which have been called instinctive belong to the more refined clothing of the spirit. Conscience, indeed, seems to have some undefined source, and may bear relations to a former state of being.

Consolations in Travel, Dialogue IV

Sir David Brewster (1781-1868)

SCOTTISH PHYSICIST

[*This celebrated scientist, noted especially for discoveries in the polarization of light, wrote in 1854 a book entitled* More Worlds Than One, the Creed of the Philosopher and the Hope of the Christian, *in answer to an attack by a churchman on the theory that the other planets and stars are inhabited. Brewster believed that man will incarnate on other planets and worlds, and stated:*]

In what regions of space these mansions are built—on what sphere the mouldering dust is to be gathered and revived, and by what process the immortal being is to reach its destination, Reason does not enable us to determine; but it is impossible for intellectual man . . . to doubt a moment that on the celestial spheres his future is to be spent—spent doubtless, in lofty inquiries—in social intercourse—in the renewal of domestic ties. . . . With such a vista before us, so wide in its expanse, and so remote in its termination, what scenes of beauty—what forms of the sublime— what enjoyments, physical and intellectual, may we not anticipate,—wisdom to the sage, rest to the pilgrim—and gladness to the broken in heart!

Thomas H. Huxley (1825-1895)
BRITISH BIOLOGIST AND DARWINIST

In the doctrine of transmigration, whatever its origin, Brahminical and Buddhist speculation found, ready to hand, the means of constructing a plausible vindication of the ways of the Cosmos to man. . . . This plea of justification is not less plausible than others; and none but very hasty thinkers will reject it on the ground of inherent absurdity. Like the doctrine of evolution itself, that of transmigration has its roots in the world of reality; and it may claim such support as the great argument from analogy is capable of supplying.

Evolution and Ethics

Sir Edward B. Tylor (1832-1917)
CALLED THE FATHER OF ANTHROPOLOGY

[*In Tylor's well-known work* Primitive Culture (*Vol. 2, Chapter 12*) *he makes the following comment after comparing the various concepts of reincarnation among primitive tribes and ancient peoples:*]

So it may seem that the original idea of transmigration was the straightforward and reasonable one of human souls being reborn in new human bodies. . . .

Camille Flammarion (1842-1925)
FRENCH ASTRONOMER AND WRITER

If the human soul survives the physical organism, it existed before this physical organism; there is the same eternity behind us as before us. . . . Each of us . . . enters this world with special aptitudes, the origin of which cannot be found in heredity. . . .

From the philosophic and religious point of view, let us be Pythagoreans who have reappeared in the twentieth century, with its astronomical knowledge. . . . Are we returning, therefore, in our twentieth century, to doctrines enunciated seven thousand years ago? Yes, and no. Yes, in the sense that the ancients knew more about these things than is generally supposed. No, in the sense that present scientific methods have brought practical confirmation and the beginning of an explanation.

Death and Its Mystery (Vol. 3)

Thomas Edison (1847-1931)

[Edison was one of the early members of the first reincarnationist association in the West, the Theosophical Society. During his last illness reporters inquired if he believed in survival after death. He answered: "The only survival I can conceive is to start a new earth cycle again" (St. Louis Star-Times). On his eightieth birthday he was asked: "Do you believe man has a soul?" His reply was:]

No one understands that man is not a unit of life. He is as dead as granite. The unit of life is composed of swarms of billions of highly charged entities which live in the cells. I believe that when a man dies, this swarm deserts the body and goes out into space, but keeps on and enters another cycle of life and is immortal.

[In The Diary and Sundry Observations of Thomas Alva Edison, Edison expanded on these ideas, stating, in part:]

I cannot believe for a moment that life in the first instance originated on this insignificant little ball which we call the earth. . . . The particles which combined to evolve living creatures on this planet of ours probably came from some other body elsewhere in the universe.

I don't believe for a moment that one life makes another life. Take our own bodies. I believe they are composed of myriads and myriads of infinitesimally small individuals, each in itself a unit of life, and that these units work in squads—or swarms, as I prefer to call them—and that these infinitesimally small units live forever. When we "die" these swarms of units, like a swarm of bees, so to speak, betake themselves elsewhere, and go on functioning in some other form or environment. . . . The more we learn the more we realize that there is life in things which we used to regard as inanimate, as lifeless.

Sir Oliver Lodge (1851-1940)

PHYSICIST AND AUTHOR

The experience and memory of the past survive in our very organization; we are the product of evolution through the ages. Conscious memory may fail—does fail—but the effect of experience lasts. . . . The doctrine is old; Plato taught it before the time of Christ, Wordsworth taught it early in the last century—the doctrine that when we enter into flesh we leave behind all memory of previous existences; all, except for occasional dim and shadowy recollections which, though they may be stronger in infancy, occasionally surprise the grown man also. . . . Crowds of unsuspected things are awaiting our discovery. . . . The doctrine of evolution—evolution of capacity for knowledge—is profoundly true with respect to the spirit of man.

Reason and Belief

Louis Figuier (1819-1894)
FRENCH NATURALIST AND SCIENCE WRITER

Descartes and Leibnitz have demonstrated that the human understanding possesses ideas called *innate*, that is to say, ideas which we bring with us to our birth. This fact is certain. In our times, the Scotch philosopher Dugald Stewart, has put Descartes' theory into a more precise form, by proving that the only really *innate* idea, that which has universal existence in the human mind after birth, is the idea or the *principle of causality*, a principle that makes us say and think that there is no effect without cause, which is the beginning of reason. . . .

Innate ideas and the principle of causality are explained very simply by the doctrine of the plurality of existences; they are, indeed, merely deductions from that doctrine. A man's soul, having already existed . . . has preserved the trace of the impressions received during that existence. It has lost, it is true, the recollection of actions performed during its former incarnation, but the abstract facts . . . must remain in the soul in its second incarnation. . . . Natural aptitudes, special faculties, vocations, are the traces of impressions formerly received, of knowledge already acquired, and, being revealed from the cradle, cannot be explained otherwise than by a life gone by. . . . The soul of the man remains always the same, in spite of its numerous peregrinations.

The Tomorrow of Death

Gustaf Strömberg (1882-   )
ASTRONOMER

[*Dr. Albert Einstein wrote concerning Strömberg's book,* The Soul of the Universe, *"What impressed me particularly was the successful attempt to pick out of the bewildering variety of researches that which is of essential value, and to present it in such a way that the concept of the Oneness of all knowledge can for the first time be stated with definite intent." The fol-*

lowing is taken from the review of the book contained in Time for April 29, 1940:]

Memory is independent of matter. If it can survive replacement of (cerebral) matter during life, why should it not survive the dissolution of the brain cells after death? "The memory of an individual . . . is written in indelible script in space and time—it has become an eternal part of a Cosmos in development."

Dr. Strömberg defines the soul as "the ego of a human being . . . something which gives unity to the mental complex of a man." Though immaterial, he considers it a real structure, like a field of force. Therefore it cannot be annihilated without violating a law analogous to the purely physical law of conservation of mass and energy. Exactly what experiences the human soul may have after death, the author does not presume to say. He thinks the transmigration of souls entirely possible.

Dr. Hermann Weyl (1885-1955)

MATHEMATICIAN

[From Dr. Weyl's book The Open World, being originally three lectures on metaphysical implications of science, (Yale University Press):]

Physics has never given support to that truly consistent determinism which maintains the unconditioned necessity of everything which happens. . . . Kant's solution of the dilemma [regarding free will and determinism] can only be carried through honestly if one believes in the existence of the individual from eternity to eternity, in the form of a Leibniz monad, say, or by metempsychosis as the Indians and Schopenhauer believe. Nevertheless, it is of sufficient importance that physics has always admitted a loophole in the necessity of Nature.

Julian Huxley (1887-   )

BIOLOGIST

Egg and sperms carry the destiny of the generations. The egg realizes one chance combination out of an infinity of possibilities: and it is confronted with millions of pairs of sperms, each one actually different in the combination of cards which it holds. Then comes the final moment in the drama—the marriage of egg and sperm to produce the beginning of a large individual. . . . Here too, it seems to be entirely a matter of chance which particular union of all the millions of possible unions shall be consummated. One might have produced a genius, another a moron . . . and so on. . . . With a realization of all that this implies, we can banish from human thought a host of fears and superstitions. No basis now remains for any doctrine of metempsychosis.

What Dare I Think (1931)

[NOTE: *See page 169 concerning a reported conversation between Julian Huxley and George Russell on heredity and reincarnation.*]

W. C. Alverez (1884-   )

EMERITUS MEMBER OF THE MAYO CLINIC

A wise man will often turn his tense nerves into useful servants. With their help he may achieve success in life and may find much beauty in living. Many a man has taken his stormy emotions, his great sensitiveness, his vivid imagination and his great reactiveness—all of which often cause him pain and distress—and, combining them perhaps with a gift for music or writing or artistry, has become a great success as a composer, novelist or artist. . . . Many times I have cursed the sensitive and complaining nerves which my mother bequeathed me. But then I have said, "No. If I am to have another incarnation, I'll take those nerves again, rather than my father's placid, less bothersome ones."

Los Angeles Times, March 24, 1952

Raynor C. Johnson (1901-   )

PHYSICIST

[Dr. Johnson, an eminent British physicist, holds doctorates in both science and philosophy. At present he is Master of Queen's College, University of Melbourne. In his book The Imprisoned Splendour (Harpers), Chapter 18 entitled "Pre-existence, Re-incarnation and Karma" is thus introduced:]

It is probably true to say that a number of my readers have already reacted to the title of this chapter with some measure of emotional interest or aversion. Some people seem curiously and almost instinctively interested in these topics, others, frequently religious-minded people, feel antagonistic, as though some strange pagan faith was subtly menacing their cherished beliefs. The average thoughtful Western man has in general given little consideration to these matters, although his reticence does not always match his knowledge. In any attempt to formulate a philosophy of life and endeavour to see meaning in our pilgrimage, these ancient beliefs cannot be lightly set aside. It is our duty to weigh them carefully, and without prejudice, in order to see if they illuminate for us tracts of experience which would otherwise remain dark and mysterious. . . .

The idea of re-incarnation presents no logical difficulties, whatever be the emotional reaction to it. What the soul has done once by the process of incarnation in a physical body, it can presumably do again. (By the term "soul" we mean that individualised aspect of the Self, including . . . the Intuitive self—and Higher Mind, all of which are regarded as immortal.) We should of course bear in mind that what is meant by the phrase "have lived before" is not that the physical form Raynor Johnson has lived on earth previously, but rather that Raynor Johnson is only a particular and temporary expression of an underlying immortal soul which has adopted previous and quite possibly different appearances.

Matthew Luckiesh (1889-   )

[*This well-known research-engineer and scientist once wrote:*]

Reincarnation of the soul has been dreamed of and desired by many peoples. . . . After all these years we are still uncertain of the destiny of that intangible part of us—the soul or mind-entity. Can we suppress a smile when we admit that knowledge has proved reincarnation and practically eternal life for dead matter, but has revealed as yet no such proof for our so-called souls?

We lie down at night and our minds rest in unconsciousness. The atoms in the textiles which cover us are as vibrant with life as those in our bodies. . . . These movements of these small elemental bodies go on whether we waken or die, and they go on doing this forever. . . . We can imagine many interesting migrations of matter during the course of which many reincarnations take place. [A vivid picture of the adventures of an atom is then provided.] This is the merest glimpse of its eternal life—unchanged although reincarnated countless times. . . . The irony of it! Knowledge has first proved the eternal life of matter.*

[*Of course Dr. Luckiesh can hardly rule out the possibility that the universal law which causes the ceaseless re-embodiment of matter does not*

* *The Esoteric Tradition*, by Dr. Gottfried de Purucker, Vol. II p. 641.

equally apply to the realm of soul (*if it does exist*), for in his book Foundations of the Universe he states, after having described the imperfections of
the senses as recording instruments:]

Perhaps this emphasizes the extreme limitations of our human senses
in appraising all that may exist in the universe around us. With our mere
human senses we may be living in a world within a world. Anything is possible beyond our experience. Our imagination could conjure up another
world coincident with our 'human' world, but unseen, unfelt and unknown to us. Although we know a great deal of the physical world in
which we live, beyond the veil unpenetrated by our senses may be other
worlds coincident.*

Rebirth of the Universe?

New scientific findings indicate the universe may be pulsing like a gigan-
tic heart, expanding and contracting in periods of many billions of years.
The findings also indicate that the present rate of expansion may be slowing down and that eventually a period of contraction will follow. . . . If
later information confirms that the universe is, indeed, oscillating, the inference will be that it has gone through many births and deaths. Since its
latest re-birth five or six billion years ago, the universe has been steadily
evolving. But if its expansion rate is slowing, at some future time the universe will begin to contract again.

New York Herald Tribune, December 15, 1956

William James (1842-1910)
PSYCHOLOGIST AND PHILOSOPHER

[Professor James's essay on Human Immortality, an Ingersoll lecture
first delivered at Harvard in 1893, shows how the assumption that physiological psychology has taken away the basis for belief in immortality is
totally without scientific justification. It rests on the view that the brain
functions only in a productive capacity in relation to thought. The brain,
however, could as easily transmit ideas that have an origin elsewhere. As he
puts it:]

---

* From Matthew Luckiesh, *Foundations of the Universe*. Copyright 1924, D. Van
Nostrand Co., Inc., Princeton, New Jersey.

According to the state in which the brain finds itself, the barrier of its obstructiveness may also be supposed to rise or fall. It sinks so low, when the brain is in full activity, that a comparative flood of spiritual energy pours over. At other times, only such occasional waves of thought as heavy sleep permits gets by. And when finally a brain stops acting altogether, or decays, that special stream of consciousness which it subserved will vanish entirely from this natural world. But the sphere of being that supplied the consciousness would still be intact; and in that more real world with which, even whilst here, it was continuous, the consciousness might, in ways unknown to us, continue still.

[*In his preface to the second edition of the above essay, Wm. James enlarges upon his views and touches upon reincarnation:*]

So many critics have made one and the same objection to the doorway to immortality which my lecture claims to be left open by the "transmission-theory" of cerebral action, that I feel tempted, as the book is again going to press, to add a word of explanation. If our finite personality here below, the objectors say, be due to the transmission through the brain of portions of a pre-existing larger consciousness, all that can remain after the brain expires is the larger consciousness itself as such. . . . But this, the critics continue, is the pantheistic idea of immortality, survival, namely, in the soul of the world; not the Christian idea of immortality, which means survival in strictly personal form. . . .

The plain truth is that *one may conceive the mental world behind the veil in as individualistic a form as one pleases, without any detriment to the general scheme by which the brain is represented as a transmissive organ.* If the extreme individualistic view were taken, one's finite mundane consciousness would be an extract from one's larger, truer personality, the latter having even now some sort of reality behind the scenes. And in transmitting it . . . one's brain would also leave effects upon the part remaining behind the veil; for when a thing is torn, both fragments feel the operation.

And just as (to use a very coarse figure) the stubs remain in a check-book whenever a check is used, to register the transaction, so these impressions on the transcendent self might constitute so many vouchers of the finite experiences of which the brain had been the mediator; and ultimately they might form that collection within the larger self of memories of our earthly passage. . . .

It is true that all this would seem to have affinities rather with pre-existence and with possible re-incarnations than with the Christian notion of immortality. But my concern in the lecture was not to discuss immortality in general. It was confined to showing it to be *not incompatible* with the brain-function theory of our present mundane consciousness. I hold that it is so compatible, and compatible moreover in fully individualized form. The reader would be in accord with everything that the text of my lecture intended to say, were he to assert that every memory and affection of his present life is to be preserved, and that he shall never *in sæcula sæculorum* cease to be able to say to himself: "I am the same personal being who in old times upon the earth had those experiences."

James Ward (1843-1925)

PHILOSOPHER AND PSYCHOLOGIST

[*James Ward was Professor of Mental Philosophy at Cambridge from 1897 to 1925. He received doctorates in science from both Cambridge and Oxford, and was a Fellow of the British Academy and the New York Academy of Sciences.*]

We can hardly frame more than the vaguest conjectures how . . . the [disembodied] soul or spirit proceeds, if needs be, to clothe itself anew; albeit we have no reason to regard it, let me remark again, as reduced in the interim to the level of a naked monad. . . .

The objection to transmigration or metempsychosis has been met by assuming that the personal discontinuity is only temporary, and that the successive lives of a given subject may be eventually connected through continuous but latent memories that are revived after death or when all the soul's *Wanderjahre* are over.* But even so, if this series is to have any real continuity or meaning, if it is to be not merely a series but a progression, then at every return to life, either Providence must determine, or the naturient soul must itself select, its appropriate reincarnation. Otherwise, if disembodied souls are to be blown about by the winds of circumstance like other seeds, we should only have a repetition of that outrageous fortune which the doctrine of transmigration was supposed to redress. . . .

This difficulty in turn has been met by the further and bolder assumption, that disembodied souls do in fact steer their own way back to a suitable rebirth. An atom liberated from its molecular bonds is described as manifesting an unwonted activity, technically known as "the nascent state"; but still it does not recombine indifferently with the first free atom that it encounters, but only with one for which it has an "affinity." And [quoting

---

* So, for example, Professor Campbell Fraser thinks. Cf. his *Theism*, Vol. II, p. 249. And still more definitely Renouvier, *Le Personnalisme*, 1903, p. 220. A similar view was held by Max Drossbach, J. Reynaud and many others. (James Ward.)

McTaggart] "there seems to be nothing more strange or paradoxical in the suggestion that each person enters into connexion with the body that it is most fitted to be connected with him." . . . A liberated spirit ought to be credited with vastly more *savoir vivre* than a liberated atom. Further it must be allowed that this suggestion is quite in keeping with the conservation of values, which men like Lotze and Höffding regard as axiomatic —at any rate experience often verifies, and never certainly belies it. Finally it minimises the objection to personal continuity that is often based on the facts of heredity. . . .

We say All men are mortal, but not one of us has experienced death; not one of us knows anything therefore of what for the subject immediately concerned it really is. If we knew that the individual's existence began with that of the body, we might argue that it would also probably end with it: but here again the empirical basis for such an argument fails us. . . . Altogether—so far as the mere persistence of the individual subject now actually existing goes—we may fairly maintain that the burden of proof after all rests with those who would dogmatically deny it. . . .

I make bold to deny, that the theory of pre-existence "creates new difficulties." It involves "a ramifying network" of assumptions unquestionably; but if it "is certainly not capable of positive disproof," the objector is bound to show that the result of the whole is worthless. Till then, summarily to reject it involves the still more extravagant assumption that we have exhausted all possibilities and that what may be only our lack of knowledge of its empirical conditions is tantamount to a proof of its impossibility.

The Realm of Ends
Gifford Lectures 1907-10

Carl G. Jung (1875-1961)

SWISS PSYCHIATRIST AND PSYCHOLOGIST

[Vol. 9 of Jung's Collected Works, Part I, entitled Archetypes and the Collective Unconscious, reprints his lecture delivered at the Eranos Meeting of 1939 "Concerning Rebirth" (revised 1950). After carefully defining five main types of rebirth, namely, metempsychosis, reincarnation, resurrection, rebirth within one life, and transformation, he concerns himself not with reincarnation as a philosophical and metaphysical truth, but with the psychology behind all these concepts of rebirth. Quoting from the lecture:]

Rebirth is not a process that we can in any way observe. We can neither measure nor weigh nor photograph it. It is entirely beyond sense perception. We have to do here with a purely *psychic* reality, which is transmitted to us only indirectly through personal statements. One speaks of rebirth; one professes rebirth; one is filled with rebirth. This we accept as sufficiently real. . . . I am of the opinion that the psyche is the most tremendous fact of human life. . . . The mere fact that people talk about re-birth, and that there is such a concept at all, means that a store of psychic experiences designated by that term must actually exist.

Rebirth is an affirmation that must be counted among the primordial affirmations of mankind. These primordial affirmations are based on what I call archetypes. . . . There must be psychic events underlying these affirmations which it is the business of psychology to discuss—without entering into all the metaphysical and philosophical assumptions regarding their significance.

[*A few of Jung's statements in this lecture on an immortal entity within the mortal man seem pertinent:*]

When a summit of life is reached, when the bud unfolds and from the lesser the greater emerges, then, as Nietzsche says, "One becomes Two," and the greater figure, which one always was but which remained invisible, appears to the lesser personality with the force of a revelation. He who is truly and hopelessly little will always drag the revelation of the greater down to the level of his littleness, and will never understand that the day of judgment for his littleness has dawned. But the man who is inwardly great will know that the long expected friend of his soul, the immortal one, has now really come, "to lead captivity captive"; that is, to seize hold of him by whom this immortal had always been confined and held prisoner, and to make his life flow into that greater life. . . . Christ himself is the perfect symbol of the hidden immortal within the mortal man. . . .

In addition to the technical processes of transformation there are also natural transformations. All ideas of rebirth are founded on this fact. Nature herself demands a death and a rebirth. . . . We are that pair of Dioscuri, one of whom is mortal and the other immortal, and who, though always together, can never be made completely one. The transformation processes strive to approximate them to one another, but our consciousness is aware of resistances, because the other person seems strange and uncanny, and because we cannot get accustomed to the idea that we are not absolute master in our own house. . . . It is my own transformation—not a personal transformation, but the transformation of what is mortal in me into what is immortal. It shakes off the mortal husk that I am and awakens to a life of its own.

Dr. J. B. Rhine (1895-   )

DIRECTOR OF PARAPSYCHOLOGY LABORATORY, DUKE UNIVERSITY

[*The extracts that follow are taken from an article that appeared in The American Weekly for April 8, 1956 entitled "Did You Live Before?" in which Dr. Rhine, at the request of the editors of the Weekly, discusses the famous case of Bridey Murphey.**]

In brief, *Bridey Murphy* is the story of Ruth Simmons [Virginia Tighe], a young housewife living in Pueblo, Colorado. . . . One evening in 1952 she agreed to be the subject of a hypnotism experiment. The hypnotist was a young businessman, Morey Bernstein. At first he led her back through what we commonly call age-regression. . . . Eventually she remembered the toys she loved when she was only one year old. There was nothing unusual about this, but in a second session the hypnotist suggested, "Your mind will be going back . . . back until you find yourself in some other scene, in some other place, in some other time. You will be able to talk to me about it and answer my questions."

The gist of her response was that she was a little Irish girl named Bridey Murphy, who lived in Cork with her mother Kathleen, her barrister father Duncan, and one brother. . . . The year was 1806. She told how, at fifteen, she attended Mrs. Strayne's school in Cork "studying to be a lady," and how she later married Brian MacCarthy and went to live in Belfast. As the sessions continued, all recorded on tape, the life story carried on through the years, up to Bridey's death at the age of sixty-six. She claimed that, after bodily death, Bridey existed in the spirit world for forty years, then was reborn in Iowa, in 1923, to take up her life as Ruth— the present Ruth Simmons.

Checking later with the Irish Consulate, the British Information Service, the New York Public Library and other sources, Mr. Bernstein learned that a number of Bridey's statements were consistent with historical fact. If Ruth, who never had visited Ireland, had no normal way of knowing these things, didn't this raise the question: Does reincarnation really occur? . . .

In the first place nobody knows, and there is no way of finding out, that

---

* [Over a million copies were sold of *The Search for Bridey Murphy* by Morey Bernstein (Doubleday, Jan. 1956; Pocket Books, June 1956), the book having been printed in more than 30 countries. For an up-to-date survey of the facts in this much discussed case see chapter "How the Case of The Search for Bridey Murphy Stands Today" in Prof. C. J. Ducasse's book *A Critical Examination of the Belief in a Life After Death* (C. C. Thomas, Springfield, Ill., 1961). Eds.]

the hypnotized girl did not already have all the verified facts somewhere in her memory. We are told that Ruth came of part Irish ancestry. What stories did she hear, far back in her girlhood, as she listened to someone talking of the old country? What had she read or otherwise absorbed that could have been woven into the tale of Bridey? . . .

It also is possible that this young woman could have gained her knowledge through telepathy or clairvoyance, two forms of which we call extrasensory perception (ESP). Science has shown by careful experiment that ESP, or the acquisition of knowledge beyond the reach of the senses, is a normal capacity of human beings. . . . [Also] for a careful study of so important a matter as reincarnation, it would be necessary to know what went on in the conversations that took place with the girl awake, between sessions, as well as when hypnotized. . . .

If we are to consider the question seriously, and try to find some proof of reincarnation, leading a person back through hypnotic regression—as was done in this case—is the wrong road to take. Science should first attempt to discover whether there is a spirit personality which can exist apart from its body. . . . Let's look at some of these efforts. Since they concern spirit survival, they also have a bearing on the possibility of reincarnation. They began long ago with the study of remarkable persons who claimed that, while in a trance, they could receive messages from spirits trying to reach living people. Some of the messages seemed most convincing but—just as in the Bridey Murphy case—no one ever has been able to prove that the medium does not learn the facts on which she bases messages through telepathy or clairvoyance, instead of getting them from a spirit in the great beyond.

Here at Duke University, we have turned from examining the beliefs of groups and cults to a collection of individual experiences for some clue to an answer to the question—"Do spirits survive?" We have collected thousands of incidents, several hundred of which seem to indicate that the teller of the tale has had contact with a loved one who has died. [Three such incidents are given.]

For the careful thinker I need not warn against the tendency to take these experiences in themselves as final and adequate evidence of anything. . . . But just as one must not take them as proof, so one cannot and should not dismiss them all as worthless superstition or mere coincidence. It is enough at this stage to know that in these experiences something of the unrecognized nature of man probably is being revealed.

Let us make our explorations as carefully as possible and go as cautiously into interpretations and applications as the gravity of the issues deserves. Let us get to the facts about men as we do about atoms. As we anxiously scan the skies for the new menace science has brought out of the hidden resources of nature, it is timely, is it not, for the scientist to peer over the edge of his physical foundations and ask: What, if anything, may follow the final obliterating blast?

Ian Stevenson (1918-   )

PSYCHIATRIST, CHAIRMAN DEPARTMENT OF PSYCHIATRY,
UNIVERSITY OF VIRGINIA SCHOOL OF MEDICINE

[*In July 1959, Harper's magazine published an article by Dr. Stevenson entitled "The Uncomfortable Facts About Extrasensory Perception." In 1960 his 44-page essay "The Evidence for Survival from Claimed Memories of Former Incarnations" was the prize-winning essay of the American Society for Psychical Research contest in honor of William James, one of its early presidents. Parts I and II appeared respectively in the April and July issues of the Journal of the Society. Dr. Stevenson studied hundreds of instances where children or adults seemed to remember a past life, and presents a select few "in the evaluation of which reincarnation becomes a very serious contender as the most plausible explanation of the empirical facts." With one exception, the claimed memories upon which Dr. Stevenson bases the following conclusions arose naturally and spontaneously in normal states of consciousness:*]

The writer of a review of this kind has the privilege and perhaps the obligation of saying how he personally interprets the data. I will say, therefore, that I think reincarnation the most plausible hypothesis for understanding the cases of this series. This is not to say that I think they prove reincarnation either singly or together. Indeed, I am quite sure they do not. But for each of the alternative hypothesis I find objections or shortcomings which make them for me unsuitable explanations of all the cases, although they may apply to some. . . .

A large number of cases in which the recall of true memories is a plausible hypothesis should make that hypothesis worthy of attention. I think the number of cases in the present collection confers that respectablity on the hypothesis, even though many of these cases may have particular aspects which make some other hypothesis more plausible in such cases. Expectations can harmfully influence perceptions. If we proceed in an investigation with the expectation of confirming a particular hypothesis, we may think we discover more evidence for it than we do. But the reverse type of misperception can also occur with equal harm. If we reject offhand, as most Westerners are inclined to do, the hypothesis of reincarnation, we may exclude from our investigations those conditions which could permit further relevant data to emerge. . . .

The evidence I have assembled and reviewed here does not warrant any firm conclusion about reincarnation. But it does justify, I believe, a much more extensive and more sympathetic study of this hypothesis than it has hitherto received in the West. Further investigation of apparent memories of former incarnations may well establish reincarnation as the most probable explanation of these experiences. Along this line we may in the end obtain more convincing evidence of human survival of physical death than from other kinds of evidence. In mediumistic communications we have the problem of proving that someone clearly dead still lives. In evaluating apparent memories of former incarnations, the problem consists in judging whether someone clearly living once died. This may prove the easier task and, if pursued with sufficient zeal and success, may contribute decisively to the question of survival.

Buddhist Psychology

[*From* Buddhist Psychology *by Mrs. C. A. F. Rhys Davids, second edition, 1924·*]

The psychology of to-day tries to build up the mind of the individual from the racial mind of the past. It has to deal in masses, for it has not the Buddhist secret of rebirth. The psychology of to-morrow will investigate the past of the individual—the last bit of that past; and it will find itself up against the Buddhist doctrine of rebirth. The next step will be to inquire into the psychology of our future—into what *we* rise up as, when *we* discard this body, the whence of that new body and the nature of it. It is no idle quest, but of tremendous practical importance. . . . We all die, and very soon. Are we always going to be so childish as to be content, not only with creeds, but with sciences that leave us in ignorance of death, and so in the fear of death?

[*From* Zen Buddhism and Psychoanalysis (Harpers, 1960) *by Suzuki Fromm, and De Martino, are taken the extracts below by Dr. Erich Fromm the internationally renowned Psychoanalyst. A statement from Dr. Suzuki on Zen views concerning reincarnation may be found in the Anthology at page 17. To what degree the Western enthusiasm for Zen Buddhism has included and will include a serious consideration of this doctrine remains to be seen.*]

There is an unmistakable and increasing interest in Zen Buddhism among psychoanalysts. . . . Cf. Jung's introduction to D. T. Suzuki's *Zen Buddhism* (London, Rider, 1949); the French psychiatrist Benoit's work on Zen Buddhism, *The Supreme Doctrine* (New York, Pantheon Books, 1955). The late Karen Horney was intensely interested in Zen Buddhism during the last years of her life. The conference held in Cuernavaca, Mexico, at which the papers published in this book were presented, is another symptom of the interest of psychoanalysts in Zen. . . . Any psychologist, even twenty years ago, would have been greatly surprised—or shocked—to find his colleagues interested in a "mystical" religious system such as Zen Buddhism. He would have been even more surprised to find that most of the people present were not just "interested" but deeply concerned, and that they discovered that the week spent with Dr. Suzuki and his ideas had a most stimulating and refreshing influence on them, to say the least. . . .

The study of Zen Buddhism has been of vital significance to me and, as I believe—is significant for all students of psychoanalysis. . . . [It] helps man to find an answer to the question of his existence, an answer which is essentially the same as that given in the Judaeo-Christian tradition, and yet which does not contradict the rationality, realism, and independence which are modern man's precious achievements. Paradoxically, Eastern religious thought turns out to be more congenial to Western rational thought than does Western religious thought itself.

PART FOUR

Scientists and Psychologists on Immortality and Soul

AND RELATED CONCEPTS

❀ O N   I M M O R T A L I T Y ❀
A N D   S O U L

❀

The quotations that follow have a proper place in an anthology on reincarnation, it would appear, even though rebirth itself is not directly mentioned. Once admit that a permanent ego may exist, sooner or later some
theory of rebirth must be formulated. After death the ego must live somewhere, and in view of the known order of nature must have some vehicle
through which to manifest its powers and communicate with others. "The
soul's immortality demands embodiment here or elsewhere, and to be embodied means reincarnation."

Charles Darwin (1809-1882)

With respect to immortality, nothing shows me [so clearly] how strong
and almost instinctive a belief it is, as the consideration of the view now
held by most physicists, namely, that the sun with all the planets will in
time grow too cold for life, unless indeed some great body dashes into
the sun, and thus gives it fresh life. Believing as I do that man in the distant future will be a far more perfect creature than he now it, it is an in-
tolerable thought that he and all other sentient beings are doomed to

complete annihilation after such long-continued slow progress. To those who fully admit the immortality of the human soul, the destruction of our world will not appear so dreadful.

Letters

Albert Einstein (1879-1955)

It is enough for me to contemplate the mystery of conscious life, perpetuating itself through all eternity—to reflect upon the marvelous structure of the universe, which we can dimly perceive—and to try humbly to comprehend even an infinitesimal part of the *intelligence* manifested in nature. . . .*

❀

The most beautiful and most profound emotion we can experience is the sensation of the mystical. It is the sower of all true science. He to whom this emotion is a stranger, who can no longer wonder and stand rapt in awe, is as good as dead. To know that what is impenetrable to us really exists, manifesting itself as the highest wisdom and the most radiant beauty which our dull faculties can comprehend only in their primitive forms—this knowledge, this feeling is at the center of true religiousness.†

❀

I maintain that cosmic religious feeling is the strongest and noblest incitement to scientific research. A contemporary has said, not unjustly, that in this age of ours the serious scientific workers are the only profoundly religious people.

The World As I See It

Alexis Carrel (1873-1944)

The soul is the aspect of ourselves that is specific of our nature and distinguishes man from all other animals. We are not capable of defining this familiar and profoundly mysterious entity. What is thought, that strange being, which lives in the depths of ourselves without consuming a measurable quantity of chemical energy? Is it related to the known forms of

* Quoted in *The Autobiography of Robert A. Millikan*, Prentice Hall, p. 287.
† Quoted in *The Universe and Dr. Einstein* by Lincoln Barnett (Mentor Book).

energy? Could it be a constituent of our universe, ignored by the physicists, but infinitely more important than light?

The mind is hidden within the living matter, completely neglected by physiologists and economists, almost unnoticed by physicians. And yet it is the most colossal power of this world. . . . Should it be considered as an immaterial being, located outside space and time, outside the dimensions of the cosmic universe, and inserting itself by an unknown procedure into our brain, which would be the indispensable condition of its manifestations and the determining agent of its characterstics? . . .

Our mind has a natural tendency to reject the things that do not fit into the frame of the scientific or philosophical beliefs of our time. After all, scientists are only men. They are saturated with the prejudices of their environment and their epoch. They willingly believe that facts that cannot be explained by current theories do not exist. . . . At the present time, scientists . . . still look upon telepathy and other metaphysical phenomena as illusions. Evident facts having an unorthodox appearance are suppressed. . . . The inventory of the things which could lead us to a better understanding of the human being has been left incomplete. We must, then, go back to a naïve observation of ourselves in all our aspects, reject nothing and describe simply what we see.

Man, the Unknown

Heber D. Curtis (1872-1942)

ASTROPHYSICIST

I personally find it impossible to regard Handel's "Largo," Keats's "Ode to a Grecian Urn," and the higher ethics as mere by-products of the chemical interaction of a collection of hydrocarbon molecules. With energy, matter, space and time continuous, with nothing lost or wasted, are we ourselves the only manifestation that comes to an end, ceases, is annihilated at three score years and ten?

What we crudely call the spirit of man makes new compounds, plays with the laws of chemical action, guides the forces of the atom, changes the face of the earth, gives life to new forms and takes it away from millions of animals and plants. Here is a flame that controls its own flaming, a creative spirit which cannot reasonably be less than the continuity it controls. This thing, soul, mind or spirit, cannot well be an exception. In some way, as yet impossible to define, it too, must possess continuity.

Los Angeles Times, Dec. 31, 1926

Thomas H. Huxley (1825-1895)

BIOLOGIST

Looking at the matter from the most rigidly scientific point of view, the assumption that, amidst the myriads of worlds scattered through endless space, there can be no intelligence, as much greater than man's as his is greater than a blackbeetle's; no being endowed with powers of influencing the course of nature as much greater than his, as his is greater than a snail's, seems to me not merely baseless, but impertinent. Without stepping beyond the analogy of that which is known, it is easy to people the cosmos with entities, in ascending scale. . . .

I understand the main tenet of Materialism to be that there is nothing in the universe but matter and force. . . . *Kraft und Stoff*—force and matter—are paraded as the Alpha and Omega of existence. . . . Whosoever does not hold it is condemned by the more zealous of the persuasion to the Inferno appointed for fools or hypocrites. But all this I heartily disbelieve. . . . There is a third thing in the universe, to wit, consciousness, which . . . I can not see to be matter or force, or any conceivable modification of either. . . .

The student of nature, who starts from the axiom of the universality of the law of causation, can not refuse to admit an eternal existence; if he admits the conservation of energy, he can not deny the possibility of an eternal energy; if he admits the existence of immaterial phenomena in the form of consciousness, he must admit the possibility, at any rate, *of an eternal series of such phenomena.* (Italics ours.)

Essays Upon Some Controverted Questions

Max Planck (1858-1947)

PHYSICIST

There is a point, one single point in the immeasurable world of mind and matter, where science and therefore every causal method of research is inapplicable, not only on practical grounds but also on logical grounds, and will always remain inapplicable. This point is the individual ego. It is a small point in the universal realm of being; but in itself it is a whole world, embracing our emotional life, our will and our thought. This realm of the ego is at once the source of our deepest suffering and at the same time of our highest happiness. Over this realm no outer power of fate can ever have sway. . . .

There can never be any real opposition between religion and science;

for the one is the complement of the other. Every serious and reflective person realizes, I think, that the religious element in his nature must be recognized and cultivated if all the powers of the human soul are to act together in perfect balance and harmony. And indeed it was not by any accident that the greatest thinkers of all ages were also deeply religious souls, even though they made no public show of their religious feeling. . . . Every advance in knowledge brings us face to face with the mystery of our own being.

Where is Science Going?

Erwin Schrödinger (1887-1961)

PHYSICIST, NOBEL PRIZE 1933

(1) My body functions as a pure mechanism according to the Laws of Nature.

(2) Yet I know, by incontrovertible direct experience, that I am directing its motions, of which I foresee the effects, that may be fateful and all-important, in which case I feel and take full responsibility for them.

The only possible inference from these two facts is, I think, that I—I in the widest meaning of the word, that is to say, every conscious mind that has ever said or felt "I"—am the person, if any, who controls the "motion of the atoms" according to the Laws of Nature. . . . In itself, the insight is not new. . . . From the early great Upanishads the recognition ATMAN = BRAHMAN (the personal self equals the omnipresent, all-comprehending eternal self) was in Indian thought considered, far from being blasphemous, to represent the quintessence of deepest insight into the happenings of the world. The striving of all the scholars of Vedanta was . . . really to assimilate in their minds this grandest of all thoughts.

Consciousness is never experienced in the plural, only in the singular. . . . Consciousness is a singular of which the plural is unknown. . . .

If you analyze [this "I"] closely you will, I think, find that it is just a little bit more than a collection of single data (experiences and memories), namely the canvas [or ground-stuff] *upon which* they are collected. . . . You may come to a distant country, lose sight of all your friends . . . acquire new [ones]. . . . Less and less important will become the fact that, while living your new life, you still recollect the old one. . . . Yet there has been no intermediate break, no death. And even if a skilled hypnotist succeeded in blotting out entirely all your earlier reminiscences, you would not find that he had killed *you*. In no case is there a loss of personal existence to deplore. Nor will there ever be.

What is Life? *

* Cambridge University Press.

W. F. G. Swann (1884-)

PHYSICIST, FORMER DIRECTOR OF THE BARTOL RESEARCH FOUNDATION

[See Preface for the first portion of the following quotation:]

We must not be too astonished at the invocation of an entity which does not call for expression in terms of space and time. After all, I may speak of such things as good and evil without accompanying them with coordinates x, y, z, t, to express where they are and when they were there.

I shall not be surprised to find the new entity playing a part in the survival of pattern, so dominant in living things. I hesitate to limit its potentialities by giving it a name already appropriated and endowed with properties of vagueness too foggy to be permitted in scientific discussion, and so I will not call it by the name "soul." If it is to be of service, it must not shrink away from its duties and take refuge as part of high-sounding sentences. Its functions and modes of operation must be well-defined and it is only natural that in conventional science it will have to go through the process of skeptic criticism which has fallen to the lot of all of its predecessors in the materialistic realm.

I should expect to find it play a role in those phenomena which for long have lain in the borderland between what is accepted by all and what is accepted only by few, even though representatives of the few may be found in all periods of man's history. I refer to such things as extrasensory perception, the significance of the immortality of man, clairvoyance, and allied phenomena, and the significance of the fact that our universe exhibits what we may call a planned design, whether or not we are willing to admit the hazy notion of a planner, or say what we mean by that postulate.

"The Living and the Dead," Saturday Review, June 4, 1960

[The New York Times for March 24, 1957, reports on another lecture of Dr. Swann:]

In the course of time, some ten to twelve billion years from now, the hydrogen fuel in the sun will be exhausted and the sun will start to cool, and . . . may thus end as a cold, dead star, exploding into a mass of very dense, lifeless fragments. The fate that awaits the sun, it appears from scientific evidence now available, also awaits the universe as a whole. Yet scientists on occasion leave room for doubt that such, indeed, is the ignoble destiny awaiting the cosmos, as was shown recently in an address before the Franklin Institute by Prof. W. F. G. Swann, director of the institute's Bartol Research Foundation and one of the country's leading physicists.

As we peer about in the universe, Professor Swann said, we see certain stars which have attained this degree of old age. It seems that in about ten or twelve billion years' time "we may expect to find nothing but the dead remnants of a glorious past, with the universe no more than a huge cemetery with no further life or potentiality of activity."

"The spectacle," he continued, "is a depressing one and one may well wonder whether any real intent of a purpose would have been achieved by it. Was the purpose really to create a fifteen billion year spectacle? . . . Are we merely confronted with an end which is naught but a confession of failure? Or has this titanic episode constituted simply a part of something else, something else which has not yet revealed itself, at any rate in its entirety, to those creatures, man and his kind, who have formed part of the material picture?

"Has this material universe constituted merely the chrysalis from which a very much more beautiful structure has been born, or is to be born, a structure in which the things to be spoken of are such things as souls, things, which have left behind the battles of their birth, and form a spiritual world where . . . death is no longer the inevitable end of the strife?

"If, indeed, such is the case, we may join the bard of Avon in likening all that we see around us as but a vision doomed to melt into thin air, in which the great globe itself and everything on it shall dissolve. But here, instead of joining in the dramatists's thought that not a rack will remain behind, we shall see something remaining, something that is indeed very real, something that was hidden from us in large measure during our mortal lives, but which will remain as the only final reality after the material universe, which gave it birth, has died."

Sir Charles S. Sherrington (1861-1952)

FATHER OF NEUROPHYSIOLOGY; NOBEL PRIZE 1932

Mind, for anything that perception can compass, goes . . . in our spatial world more ghostly than a ghost. Invisible, intangible . . . it remains without sensual confirmation and remains without it for ever. Stripped to nakedness there remains to it but itself. What then does that amount to? All that counts in life. Desire, zest, truth, love, knowledge. . . .

Man on His Nature
Gifford Lectures 1937-38

W. Grey Walter (1910-   )

Dr. Walter, a foremost authority on "brain waves," in a book entitled The Living Brain, now asserts that man's mind does not live by brain alone. Dr. Walter, successor to the fame of Sir Charles Sherrington in the field of cerebral research, is sure that no amount of further experimentation will explain all the mysterious powers of mind in terms of familiar physical laws. The author notes that with the construction of instruments for measurement of brain waves, it was thought by some enthusiastic physiologists that we could soon do away with words such as "mind" and "soul." But ESP phenomena cannot be explained, by any stretch of the imagination, in terms of brain waves. Thus, the more we know about the brain, the less we are apt to think that the brain is the whole of man. Dr. Walter writes:

Very early in the human story the brain must have acquired the mechanism of what we recognise in action as imagination, calculation, prediction. . . . The operation of these mental controls . . . can be recorded as electrical eddies swirling in subtle patterns through the brain. But our most sensitive instruments, amplifying the electrical charges ten million times or more, detect only isolated and intermittent elements of these higher functions in the brains of other animals.

Thus the mechanisms of the brain reveal a deep physiological division between man and ape, deeper than the superficial physical differences of most distant origin. If the title of soul be given to the higher functions in question, it must be admitted that the other animals have only a glimmer of the light that so shines before men.

The Living Brain

Sir Francis Walshe

NEUROLOGIST

From sheer psychological and philosophical necessity, traditional common-sense philosophy from the earliest Greeks to Aquinas accepted the existence in man of an essential immaterial element . . . setting him above the merely animal. This element they called psyche, entelechy, anima or soul.

It has also to be recognized that for the soul's functioning as an essential element in the hylomorphic human person, it needs sense data, of which the brain is the collecting, integrating and distributing mechanism. Yet it would be quite childish to identify the instrument with its user, even though the user be dependent upon the instrument for operating. . . . We shall have to accept the ancient concept of the soul again: as an immaterial, noncorporeal part of the human person, and yet an integral part of his nature, not just some concomitant aspect of man, but something without which he is not a human person. . . .

There is a sense in which the present is an age of which a characteristic is its failure to understand the status of its own abstractions, and this, perhaps, is the inevitable fruit of the divorce of natural science from metaphysics, to have achieved which was the empty triumph of the nineteenth century. . . . For me, the chill physico-mathematical concept of the human mind is a muddy vesture of decay in which I am not willing to be enfolded. It is unworthy of the dignity of Man. And if any say that this is not a scientific attitude I am unmoved by the irrelevance, for, outside its proper field of discourse, the word "science" does not intimidate me. Man was not made for science, but science by man, who remains more and greater than his creations.

"Thoughts upon the Equation of Mind with Brain"
Brain—A Journal of Neurology, March 1953

Erich Fromm (1900-   )

PSYCHOANALYST

Academic psychology, trying to imitate the natural sciences and laboratory methods of weighing and counting, dealt with everything except the soul. It tried to understand those aspects of man which can be examined in the laboratory and claimed that conscience, value judgments, the knowledge of good and evil are metaphysical concepts, outside the problems of psychology; it was more often concerned with insignificant problems which fitted an alleged scientific method than with devising new methods to study the significant problems of man. Psychology thus became a science lacking its main subject matter, the soul. . . . [In] Egypt the priests were the "physicians of the soul," in . . . Greece this function was at least partly assumed by philosophers. . . . Because the word *soul* has associations which include these higher human powers [of love, reason, conscience, values] I use it here and throughout these chapters rather than the words "psyche" or "mind."

Psychoanalysis and Religion

Life in its biological aspects is a miracle and a secret, and man in his human aspects is an unfathomable secret. . . . The further we reach into the depth of our being, or someone else's being, the more the goal of full knowledge eludes us. Yet we cannot help desiring to penetrate into the secret of man's soul, into the nucleus of "he." . . . Psychology can show us what man is *not*. It cannot tell us what man, each one of us, *is*. The soul of man, the unique core of each individual, can never be grasped and described adequately.

"Man is Not a Thing"
Saturday Review, Mar. 16, 1957

Carl G. Jung (1875-1961)

PSYCHIATRIST

In the same way that our misconception of the solar system had to be freed from prejudice by Copernicus, the most strenuous efforts of a well-nigh revolutionary nature were needed to free psychology . . . from the prejudice that the psyche is, on the one hand, a mere epiphenomenon of a biochemical process in the brain or, on the other hand, a wholly unapproachable and recondite matter. The connection with the brain does not in itself prove that the psyche is an epiphenomenon, a secondary function causally dependent on biochemical processes. . . .

The phenomena of parapsychology . . . warns us to be careful for they point to a relativization of space and time through psychic factors which casts doubt on our naïve and overhasty explanation of the parallels between the psychic and the physical. For the sake of this explanation people deny the findings of parapsychology outright, either for philosophical reasons or from intellectual laziness. This can hardly be considered a scientifically responsible attitude, even though it is a popular way out of a quite extraordinary intellectual difficulty. To assess the psychic phenomenon, we have to take account of all the other phenomena that come with it, and accordingly we can no longer practice any psychology that ignores the existence of the unconscious or of parapsychology.

The structure and physiology of the brain furnish no explanation of the psychic process. The psyche has a peculiar nature which cannot be reduced to anything else.

The Undiscovered Self

J. B. Rhine (1895-   )

DIRECTOR OF PARAPSYCHOLOGY LABORATORY, DUKE UNIVERSITY

The scientific tests that were initiated by prophetic dreams have already led to the discovery of a new fact about the human mind, a discovery so radical as to call for an eventual revolution in basic human thought. Perhaps the most significant finding that has emerged is this: there is now known to be present in human personality an aspect that is unbounded by the space and time of matter—hence a nonphysical or spiritual aspect. Its boundaries and its capacity for growth may well be beyond the limits of our present powers to conceive.

"Do Dreams Come True?"
Readers Digest, March 1955

By far the largest common ground thus far recognized by religion and parapsychology is that of the problem of spirit survival—the question whether there exists in human personality anything that can effectively endure beyond the death of the bodily organism. . . . The very basic fact of the establishment of psi occurrence furnishes an applicable principle of great significance to this problem of spirit survival. If there were no evidence of anything transcending physical law, if there were no defiance of the limits of mechanistic interpretation of man and the living world, there would be no point at all in thinking further about the survival problem.

"What Next in Parapsychology?" *

A type of lawfulness peculiar to mind and contrary to physics is increasingly evident in the extra-sensory perception and psychokinetic researches. Without these researches and with only the facts of the biological sciences to go on, it is hard to see how any kind of immortality would be possible. The brain-dominating, or cerebro-centric view of personality, would not allow it. In that view the brain is primarily and completely the center of man. But if the psyche is a force and a factor in its own right, with laws and ways peculiarly non-physical, the survival hypothesis has at least a logical chance.

If the mind is different from the physical brain system, it could have a different destiny, could perhaps be independent, separable, unique. This degree of simple possibility must not, of course, be mistaken for probability; but the mere logical possibility is itself very important. . . . Is it not then provocative, to say the least, to discover certain capacities of mind that appear to operate beyond the boundaries of space and time within which our sensorial, bodily system has to live and move? Here, surely, if ever, "hope sees a star" and the urge toward an inquiry into the question of survival receives valuable impetus and encouragement.

N. Y. Herald-Tribune, Feb. 27, 1944
From Journal of Parapsychology

* *Beyond the Five Senses,* ed. Eileen Garrett, J. B. Lippincott, 1957.

William James (1842-1910)
PSYCHOLOGIST AND PHILOSOPHER

[Writing of mysticism, and using as a frame of reference several quoted passages from H. P. Blavatsky's translation of The Voice of the Silence, William James remarked in Varieties of Religious Experience:]

There is a verge of the mind which these things haunt; and whispers therefrom mingle with the operations of our understanding, even as the waters of the infinite ocean send their waves to break among the pebbles that lie upon our shores. That doctrine, for example, that eternity is time-less, that our "immortality," if we live in the eternal, is not so much future as already now and here, which we find so often expressed to-day in certain philosophic circles, finds its support in a "hear, hear!" or an "amen," which floats up from that mysteriously deeper level. We recognize the passwords to the mystical region as we hear them, but we cannot use them ourselves; it alone has the keeping of "the password primeval."

Appendix

[See page 39 for historical facts surrounding the issuance of these Anathemas.]

• THE ANATHEMAS AGAINST ORIGEN* •
The Fifth Ecumenical Council
The Second Council of Constantinople
A.D. 553

I If anyone assert the fabulous pre-existence of souls, and shall assert the monstrous restoration which follows from it: let him be anathema.

II If anyone shall say that the creation of all reasonable things includes only intelligences without bodies and altogether immaterial, having neither number or name, so that there is unity between them all by identity of substance, force and energy, and by their union with and knowledge of God, the Word; but that no longer desiring the sight of God, they gave themselves over to worse things, each one following his own inclinations, and that they have taken bodies more or less subtile, and have received names, for among the heavenly Powers there is a difference of names as there is also a difference of bodies; and thence some became and are called Cherubims, other Seraphims, and Principalities, and Powers, and Domina-

---

* Taken from *A Select Library of Nicene and Post-Nicene Fathers of the Christian Church*, Vol. 14, Series 2, entitled "The Seven Ecumenical Councils of the Undivided Church," edited by Henry R. Percival, M.A., D.D. (New York: Charles Scribner's Sons, 1900), pp. 318-20. The words in brackets are Percival's own editing. Where he used Greek letters, however, the English equivalents have been inserted.

tions, and Thrones, and Angels, and as many other heavenly orders as there may be: let him be anathema.

III If anyone shall say that the sun, the moon, and the stars are also reasonable things, and that they have only become what they are because they turned towards evil: let him be anathema.

IV If anyone shall say that the reasonable creatures in whom the divine love had grown cold have been hidden in gross bodies such as ours, and have been called men, while those who have attained the lowest degree of wickedness have shared cold and obscure bodies and are become and called demons and evil spirits: let him be anathema.

V If anyone shall say that a psychic condition has come from an angelic or archangelic state, and moreover that a demoniac and a human condition has come from a psychic condition, and that from a human state they may become again angels and demons, and that each order of heavenly virtues is either all from those below or from those above and below: let him be anathema.

VI If anyone shall say that there is a twofold race of demons, of which the one includes the souls of men and the other the superior spirits who fell to this, and that of all the number of reasonable beings there is but one which has remained unshaken in the love and contemplation of God, and that that spirit is become Christ and the king of all reasonable beings, and that he has created all the bodies which exist in heaven, on earth, and between heaven and earth; and that the world which has in itself elements more ancient than itself, and which exist by themselves, viz: dryness, damp, heat and cold, and the image to which it was formed, was so formed, and that the most holy and consubstantial Trinity did not create the world, but that it was created by the working intelligence which is more ancient than the world, and which communicates to it its being: let him be anathema.

VII If anyone shall say that Christ, of whom it is said that he appeared in the form of God, and that he was united before all time with God the Word, and humbled himself in those last days even to humanity, had (according to their expression) pity upon the divers falls which had appeared in the spirits united in the same unity (of which he himself is part) and that to restore them he passed through divers classes, had different bodies and different names, became all to all, an Angel among Angels, a Power among Powers, had clothed himself in the different classes of reasonable beings with a form corresponding to that class, and finally has taken flesh and blood like ours and is become man for man; [if anyone says all this] and does not profess that God the Word humbled himself and became man: let him be anathema.

VIII   If anyone shall not acknowledge that God the Word, of the same substance with the Father and the Holy Ghost, and who was made flesh and became man, one of the Trinity, is Christ in every sense of the word, but [shall affirm] that he is so only in an inaccurate manner, and because of the abasement, as they call it, of the intelligence; if anyone shall affirm that this intelligence united to God the Word, is the Christ in the true sense of the word, while the Logos is only called Christ because of this union with the intelligence, and *e converso* that the intelligence is only called God because of the Logos: let him be anathema.

IX   If anyone shall say that it was not the Divine Logos made man by taking an animated body with a rational spirit (anima rationalis) and VOEPA, that he descended into hell and ascended into heaven, but shall pretend that it is the NOUS which has done this, that NOUS of which they say (in an impious fashion) he is Christ, properly called, and that he is become so by knowledge of the Monad: let him be anathema.

X   If anyone shall say that after the resurrection the body of the Lord was ethereal, having the form of a sphere, and that such shall be the bodies of all after the resurrection; and that after the Lord himself shall have rejected his true body and after the others who rise shall have rejected theirs, the nature of their bodies shall be annihilated: let him be anathema.

XI   If anyone shall say that the future judgment signifies the destruction of the body and that the end of the story will be an immaterial [false appearance?] and that thereafter there will no longer be any matter, but only spirit: let him be anathema.

XII   If anyone shall say that the heavenly Powers and all men and the Devil and evil spirits are united with the Word of God in all respects, as the NOUS which is by them called Christ and which is in the form of God, and which humbled itself as they say; and [if anyone shall say] that the kingdom of Christ shall have an end: let him be anathema.

XIII   If anyone shall say that Christ [i.e., the NOUS] is in no wise different from other reasonable beings, neither substantially nor by wisdom nor by his power and might over all things but that all will be placed at the right hand of God, as well as he that is called by them Christ [the NOUS], as also they were in the feigned pre-existence of all things: let him be anathema.

XIV   If anyone shall say that all reasonable beings will one day be united in one, when the hypostases as well as the numbers and the bodies shall have disappeared, and that the knowledge of the world to come will carry with it the ruin of worlds, and the rejection of bodies as also the abolition of [all] names, and that there shall be finally an identity . . . of the hypostasis; moreover, that in this pretended apocatastasis, spirits only will continue to exist, as it was in the feigned pre-existence; let him be anathema.

XV   If anyone shall say that the life of the spirits shall be like to the life which was in the beginning while as yet the spirits had not come down or fallen, so that the end and the beginning shall be alike, and that the end shall be the true measure of the beginning; let him be anathema.

If anyone does not anathematize Arius, Eunomius, Macedonius, Apollinaris, Nestorius, Eutyches and Origen, as well as their impious writings, as also all other heretics already condemned and anathematized by the Holy Catholic and Apostolic Church, and by the aforesaid four Holy Synods and (if anyone does not equally anathematize) all those who have held and hold or who in their impiety persist in holding to the end the same opinion as those heretics just mentioned: let him be anathema.

· THE ANATHEMATISMS OF THE EMPEROR JUSTINIAN AGAINST ORIGEN ·

Constantinople, A.D. 553

I   Whoever says or thinks that human souls pre-existed, *i.e.*, that they had previously been spirits and holy powers, but that, satiated with the vision of God, they had turned to evil, and in this way the divine love in them had died out and they had therefore become souls and had been condemned to punishment in bodies, shall be anathema.

II   If anyone says or thinks that the soul of the Lord pre-existed and was united with God the Word before the Incarnation and Conception of the Virgin, let him be anathema.

III   If anyone says or thinks that the body of our Lord Jesus Christ was first formed in the womb of the holy Virgin and that afterwards there was united with it God the Word and the pre-existing soul, let him be anathema.

IV   If anyone says or thinks that the word of God has become like to all heavenly orders, so that for the cherubim he was a cherub, for the seraphim a seraph: in short, like all the superior powers, let him be anathema.

V   If anyone says or thinks that at the resurrection, human bodies will rise spherical in form and unlike our present form, let him be anathema.

VI   If anyone says that the heavens, the sun, the moon, the stars, and the waters that are above heavens, have souls, and are reasonable beings, let him be anathema.

VII   If anyone says or thinks that Christ the Lord in a future time will be crucified for demons, as he was for man, let him be anathema.

VIII   If anyone says or thinks that the power of God is limited, and that he created as much as he was able to compass, let him be anathema.

IX   If anyone says or thinks that the punishment of demons and of impious men is only temporary, and will one day have an end, and that a restoration will take place of demons and of impious men, let him be anathema.

Anathema to Origen and to that Adamantius, who set forth these opinions together with their nefarious and execrable and wicked doctrine, and to whomsoever there is who thinks thus, or defends these opinions, or in any way hereafter at any time presume to protect them.

❀

❀ **ACKNOWLEDGMENTS** ❀

❀

Very grateful thanks are due to the following publishers, authors, or copyright holders, for granting permission to quote from the works indicated below:

Allen & Unwin, Ltd., London. *Towards Democracy* and *The Art of Creation* by Edward Carpenter; *Thus Spake Zarathustra* by Friedrich Nietzsche, translated by Thomas Common; *Education and the Good Life* by Bertrand Russell (distributed by Liveright Publishing Corp. in U.S.); *Where is Science Going?* by Max Planck; *Lines of Life* by H. W. Nevinson; *Pre-existence and Reincarnation* by W. Lutoslawski; *Rumi, Poet and Mystic*, translated by R. A. Nicholson; *The Hibbert Journal*, "Varieties of Belief in Reincarnation" by Dr. E. G. Parrinder; *The Halt in the Garden* by Robert Hillyer (confirmed by Robert Hillyer and Alfred A. Knopf, New York); *The Secret* by Laurence Binyon.

The American-Scandinavian Foundation, New York. For excerpt from Bjornstjerne Bjornson's poem "Psalms," Vol. 3, *Scandinavian Classics*.

Anthroposophic Press, Inc., New York. For excerpt on Cardinal Mercier from *Reincarnation as a Phenomenon of Metamorphosis*, by Dr. Guenther Wachsmuth, translated by Olin D. Wannamaker.

Appleton-Century-Crofts, Inc., New York. *The Glimpse* by Arnold Bennett; *Death and Its Mystery* by Camille Flammarion.

Edward Arnold (Publishers) Ltd. *The Human Situation* by W. Macneile Dixon; *Some Dogmas of Religion* by J. E. McTaggart; *From Religion to Philosophy* by F. M. Cornford; *Verses from Pushkin and Others*, translated by Oliver Elton (poem of Alexander Blok).

The Aryan Path, Bombay, India. For excerpts from five articles.

Mrs. George Bambridge, Doubleday & Company, Inc., New York, and Macmillan Company of Canada Ltd. For excerpt from "The Sack of the Gods" from *Naulahka* by Rudyard Kipling.

A. S. Barnes & Company, Inc., New York, and The Bodley Head Ltd., London. *Reincarnation and Karma* by L. Stanley Jast.

Mr. Clifford Bax. For excerpt from his poem "The School of Plato," *Poems Dramatic and Lyrical*.

Beacon Press Inc., Boston. *Indian Thought and Its Development* by Albert Schweitzer.

Algernon Blackwood. Permission from the owner of the copyright of *Julius Le Vallon* by Algernon Blackwood.

The Bodley Head Ltd., London. *The Creed of Buddha* by Edmond Holmes; *The Collected Poems of Margaret L. Woods; Modern Russian Poetry, and Anthology,* for poems of Konstantin Balmont and Valery Brusov.

Bollingen Foundation, New York. *The Archetypes and the Collective Unconscious* by C. G. Jung. Bollingen Series XX, Bollingen Foundation, New York.

Representative Frances P. Bolton. For excerpt from Edward R. Murrow's *This I Believe* (Vol. 2), Simon & Schuster, New York.

Albert & Charles Boni, Inc., New York. *Prophets of the New India* by Romain Rolland.

Ellen Bosanquet. *Value and Destiny of the Individual* by Bernard Bosanquet.

Buddhist Society, London. *The Essence of Buddhism* by D. T. Suzuki.

Cambridge University Press, London & New York. *Examination of McTaggart's Philosophy* by C. D. Broad; *The Neoplatonists* by Thos. Whittaker; *Studies in Hegelian Cosmology* by J. E. McTaggart; *What is Life?* by Erwin Schrödinger; *Man on His Nature* by Sir Charles Sherrington; *Realm of Ends* by James Ward.

Chatto and Windus Ltd., London. *Letters of Feodor Dostoevsky,* translated by Ethel C. Mayne.

The Clarendon Press, Oxford University. *Proclus—The Elements of Theology* by E. R. Dodds.

Constable and Company Limited, London. *Six Theosophic Points* by Jacob Boehme, translated by John Rolleston Earle.

Coward-McCann, Inc., New York. "Interpretive Essays" by Henri Borel, contained in *Laotzu's Tao and Wu-Wei,* copyright 1919, used by permission of Coward-McCann, Inc.; "The Uniter of Souls" by Feodor Sologub, translated by John Cournos, contained in *A Treasury of Russian Life and Humor,* edited by John Cournos, copyright, 1943, by Coward-McCann, Inc.

The Cresset Press, London. Poem "Pre-existence" by Frances Cornford.

Cunningham Press, Alhambra, Calif. Essay "Some Modern Perspectives on Buddha's Thought" contained in The Dhammapada.

Walter de la Mare, Literary Trustees of, and The Society of Authors, London. *The Return* by Walter de la Mare.

J. M. Dent & Sons Ltd., London. *Greek Religious Thought* by F. M. Cornford.

Dial Press, Inc., New York. For excerpt reprinted from *That Day Alone* by Pierre Van Paassen. Copyright, 1941, by Pierre Van Paassen and used with the permission of the publishers, The Dial Press.

Dodd, Mead & Company, New York. *Our Eternity* and *Treasure of the Humble* by Maurice Maeterlinck.

Doubleday & Company, Inc., New York. For excerpt from "Heir and Serf" in *Poems and Portraits* by Don Marquis. Copyright, 1922, by Don Marquis. Reprinted by permission Doubleday and Company, Inc.; excerpt from *The Summing Up* by W. Somerset Maugham. Copyright, 1938, by W. Somerset Maugham. Reprinted by permission of Doubleday and Company, Inc.; *Collected Verse of Rudyard Kipling.*

E. P. Dutton & Co., Inc., New York. *The Story of San Michele* by Axel Munthe; *Seven Years in Tibet* by Heinrich Harrer; Everyman Library editions, *The Life of Mazzini* by Bolton King, and *Leibniz' Philosophical Writings* translated by Mary Morris.

Encyclopædia Britannica, Chicago. Articles "Priscillian" (11th edition); "Neoplatonism" (1959 edition).

Farrar, Straus & Cudahy, Inc., New York, and W. H. Allen & Co., Ltd., London. Excerpt from *Four Great Oaks* by Mildred McNaughton. Copyright, 1946, by Mildred McNaughton. Used by permission of Farrar, Straus & Cudahy, Inc., and W. H. Allen & Co. Ltd.

Funk & Wagnalls Company, New York. *Victor Hugo's Intellectual Autobiography,* translated by Lorenzo O'Rourke.

Golden Eagle Books Limited, Dublin. *A Servant to the Queen* by Maud Gonne MacBride.

Victor Gollancz, Ltd., London. *Puzzled People;* Lord Riddell's *Intimate Diary of the Peace Conference and After,* confirmed by Harcourt, Brace & World, New York.

Sir Rider Haggard, Executors of estate of. *She,* and *The Days of My Life* by Sir Rider Haggard.

Harcourt, Brace & World, New York. Excerpt from *Challenge* by Louis Untermeyer, copyright, 1914, by Harcourt, Brace & World, Inc.; renewed, 1942, by Louis Untermeyer. Reprinted by permission of the publishers; *The Travel Diary of a Philosopher* by Count Keyserling.

Harper & Brothers, New York. *Transmigration of Souls* by D. Alfred Bertholet; *Undine* by Olive Schreiner; "My Platonic Sweetheart" from *The Mysterious Stranger and Other Stories* by Mark Twain; *Sweet Rocket* by Mary Johnston; *The Naked Truth* by Clare Sheridan; *What Dare I Think* by Julian Huxley; *Man the Unknown* by Alexis Carrel; *The Perennial Philosophy* by Aldous Huxley; *Pleasant Valley* by Louis Bromfield; *The Imprisoned Splendour* by Raynor C. Johnson; *The Magicians* by J. B. Priestley; *Far Memory* by Joan Grant; *The Religions of Man* by Prof. Huston Smith; *Zen Buddhism and Psychoanalysis* by Suzuki, Fromm, and De Martino.

Harvard University Press, Cambridge, Mass. *Metempsychosis* by G. F. Moore; *The Dawn of Philosophy* by Georg Misch; The Loeb Classical Library edition, *The Odes of Pindar*, translated by Sir John Sandys.

Holt, Rinehart and Winston, New York. Excerpt from *Complete Poems of Robert Frost*; copyright 1930, 1949, Holt, Rinehart and Winston, Inc. Reprinted by permission of the publisher, Holt, Rinehart and Winston, Inc., *The Two Sources of Morality and Religion* by Henri Bergson; *Anthony Adverse* and *Bedford Village* by Hervey Allen.

Houghton Mifflin Company, Boston. *Selected Poems of William Vaughn Moody; The Soul of the Indian* by Chas. Eastman; *Religion and Immortality* by G. Lowes Dickinson; *John of the Mountains* by John Muir.

The Hutchinson Publishing Group, London. *Om* by Talbot Mundy; *Collected Poems of Arthur Edward Waite; Pythagoras and the Delphic Mysteries* by Edouard Schuré.

The Johns Hopkins Press, Baltimore. Article "The Phædrus and Reincarnation" by Dr. R. S. Bluck, from *American Journal of Philology*.

Alfred A. Knopf, Inc., New York. *Merely Players* by Claude Bragdon.

Little, Brown & Company, Boston. *The Undiscovered Self* by C. G. Jung.

Liveright Publishing Corporation, New York. For excerpt from: *Napoleon* by Emil Ludwig, by permission of Liveright, Publishers, N. Y. Copyright © 1954, Liveright Publishing Corp. For excerpt from The Dybbuk, by S. Ansky. By permission of Liveright, Publishers, N. Y. Copyright © 1954, by Henry G. Alsberg & Winifred Katzin, translators.

Longmans, Green & Co. Limited, London. *The Philosophy of Plotinus* by Wm. R. Inge.

Luzac & Company Ltd., London. *Buddhist Psychology* by Mrs. C. A. F. Rhys Davids.

Macmillan & Co. Ltd., London. *Northern Tribes of Central Australia* by Spencer & Gillen; *The Candle of Vision* by George W. Russell (confirmed by Diarmuid Russell); *The Soul of a People* and *The Inward Light* by H. Fielding Hall; *Head in Green Bronze* by Sir Hugh Walpole (confirmed by the latter's Literary Executors).

The Macmillan Company, New York. *The Assurance of Immortality* by Dr. Harry Emerson Fosdick; *The Philosophy of Ibn 'Arabī* by Rom Landau; *Complete Works of Friedrich Nietzsche* (Vol. 16, essay "Eternal Recurrence"); The Sacred Writings of the Sikhs, translated by Khushwant Singh; Poem "A Creed" from *Collected Poems* by John Masefield. Copyright, 1912, by The Macmillan Company, renewed 1940 by John Masefield. Used by permission of The Macmillan Company. Poem "Bright Sun" by Andrey Biely, from *A Treasury of Russian Verse* edited by Avram Yarmolinsky. Copyright, 1949, by The Macmillan Company and used with their permission. Poem "The Chinese Nightingale" from *Collected Poems* by Vachel Lindsay. Copyright, 1917, by The Macmillan Company, renewed 1945 by Elizabeth C. Lindsay. Used by permission of The Macmillan Company. Poem "A Prelude and a Song" from *Collected Poems* by James Stephens. Copyright, 1912, by The Macmillan Company, renewed 1940 by James Stephens. Used by permission of The Macmillan Company.

Dr. W. H. Magee (John Eglinton). *A Memoir of Æ* by John Eglinton.

Manas Publishing Company, Los Angeles. Article "Heredity, Environment and the 'Soul.'"

Edwin Markham's poem "The Crowning Hour" reprinted by permission of Virgil Markham.

Mary Yost Associates, New York. *A History of Spiritualism* by Sir Arthur Conan Doyle. Reprinted by permission of the Estate of Sir Arthur Conan Doyle.

Methuen & Co. Ltd., London. *Reason and Belief* by Sir Oliver Lodge; *Lohengrin and Parsifal* by A. L. Cleather & Basil Crump.

William Morrow & Company, Inc., New York. *The Desert Year* by Joseph Wood Krutch. Copyright, 1951 and 1952, by Joseph Wood Krutch; *In the Wet* by Nevil Shute. Copyright, 1953, by William Morrow & Company, Inc.

D. L. Murray, and Hodder & Stoughton Limited, London. *Come Like Shadows* by D. L. Murray.

John Murray, London. For excerpts from the following books in the Wisdom of the East Series: *Musings of a Chinese Mystic* edited by Lionel Giles; *Karma and Rebirth* by Christmas Humphreys; *Buddhist Psalms*, translated by S. Yamabe and L. Adams Beck.

The New Age Magazine, Washington, D.C. "Freemasonry and Reincarnation" by C. I. McReynolds.

The New American Library of World Literature, Inc., New York. *Teachings of the Compassionate Buddha*, edited by Edwin A. Burtt.

New York Herald Tribune, article in *Today's Living*, "Dali Greets the World" by Ben Martin.

The New York Times Magazine, article on Jean Sibelius by Howard Taubman; article "Tragic Decline of the Humane Ideal" by André Maurois.

W. W. Norton & Company, Inc., New York, by permission of. For excerpts reprinted from *Toward a Philosophy of History* by José Ortega y Gasset; *The Living Brain* by W. Grey Walter. Copyrights respectively 1941 and 1953, by W. W. Norton & Company, Inc.

The Open Court Publishing Company, La Salle, Illinois. *Nature, Mind and Death* by C. J. Ducasse; *The Fragments of Empedocles*, translated by Wm. E. Leonard.

Pantheon Books Inc., New York. *Doctor Zhivago* by Boris Pasternak.

M. C. Peto, Tadworth, Surrey, England. "The Case for Reincarnation" by Rev. Leslie D. Weatherhead.

Philosophical Library, New York. *The World as I See It* by Albert Einstein; *The Diary and Sundry Observations of Thomas Alva Edison*.

G. P. Putnam's Sons, New York. *Life of Apollonius of Tyana* by Philostratus, translated by F. C. Conybeare; *Zones of the Spirit*, by August Strindberg; copyright, 1913, by G. P. Putnam's Sons. *Goethe* by Emil Ludwig; copyright, 1928, by G. P. Putnam's Sons. *The Nazarene* by Sholem Asch, copyright 1939, by Sholem Asch.

Random House Inc., New York. *War and Peace* by Leo Tolstoy; *The Brothers Karamazov* by Feodor Dostoevsky; *Best Plays by Chekhov*.

Dr. J. B. Rhine. "Do Dreams Come True" from *The Reader's Digest;* "Did You Live Before?" from *The American Weekly;* excerpt from *Journal of Parapsychology;* "What Next in Parapsychology" from *Beyond the Five Senses*, edited by Eileen Garrett: latter permission confirmed by Parapsychology Foundation, Inc., New York.

Routledge & Kegan Paul Ltd., London. *Giordano Bruno, His Life, Thought and Martyrdom* by Wm. Boulting; *Paracelsus and the Substance of His Teachings* by Franz Hartmann; *The World As Will and Idea* by Arthur Schopenhauer, translated by R. B. Haldane and J. Kemp.

Saturday Review, New York. "Man is Not a Thing" by Dr. Erich Fromm; "Walt Whitman's Buried Masterpiece" by Malcolm Cowley; William Faulkner's acceptance speech on receipt of Nobel prize; "The Living and the Dead" by Dr. W. F. G. Swann (the latter permission confirmed by the original source, *Journal of the Franklin Institute*, Philadelphia).

Charles Scribner's Sons, New York. Excerpts from the following books are used by permission of Charles Scribner's Sons: *Never So Few* (pp. 199-200) by Tom T. Chamales, © copyright 1957 Tom T. Chamales. "The Emperor Julian" from *The Collected Works of Henrik Ibsen*, Volume V (p. 393) translated by William Archer; copyright 1907, Charles Scribner's Sons; renewal copyright, 1935, Frank Archer. *From Here to Eternity* (pp. 647, 648, 723) by James Jones, copyright, 1951, James Jones.

Julia M. Seton. *The Gospel of the Red Man* by Ernest Thompson Seton and Julia M. Seton.

G. Bernard Shaw, The Public Trustee of, and The Society of Authors, London. *Saint Joan* and *Back to Methuselah* by Bernard Shaw.

Irving Shepard, Jack London Ranch, Glen Ellen, Calif. *The Star Rover* by Jack London.

Sidgwick & Jackson Ltd., London. *Collected Poems of John Drinkwater; Two Blind Countries* by Rose Macaulay.

Dr. Ian Stevenson and American Society for Psychical Research, Inc. "The Evidence for Survival from Claimed Memories of Former Incarnations" from the Journal of that Society.

Sunrise Magazine, Pasadena, Calif. "The Transcendentalists on Reincarnation."

The Theosophical Publishing House, London, Ltd. *Reincarnation, a Study of Human Evolution* by Dr. Theophile Pascal.

The Theosophical Publishing House, Adyar, Madras, India. *Reincarnation*, and *The Ancient Wisdom* by Annie Besant; *Theosophy and Modern Thought* by C. Jinarajadasa.

The Theosophy Company, Los Angeles, Calif. *The Friendly Philosopher* by Robert Crosbie.

Dr. Paul Tillich. "The Lost Dimension of Religion" (*Saturday Evening Post*); "Symbols of Eternal Life."

Tweedsmuir estate, and Hodder & Stoughton Limited, London. *Memory Hold-the-Door* by John Buchan.

University of California Press, Berkeley. Poem "An Epitaph" by Andrey Biely, from *The Frenzied Poets* by Oleg A. Maslenikov.

Mrs. Lydia Vachell. *The Other Side* by H. A. Vachell.

Vedanta Society of Southern California. As publisher and copyright holder of The Bhagavad-Gita, translated by Swami Prabhavananda and Christopher Isherwood.

The Viking Press, Inc., New York. A *Prison, a Paradise* by Loren Hurnscot.

Sir Francis Walshe, and editor of magazine *Brain*, Sir W. Russell Brain. Article "Thoughts Upon the Equation of Mind with Brain."

John M. Watkins, publishers, London. *The Masonic Initiation* by W. L. Wilmshurst.

H. G. Wells, Executors of estate of. *The Dream* by H. G. Wells.

The Yale Review, New Haven, Conn. "Belief in a Future Life" by J. Paul Williams.

Deep appreciation is expressed to those who assisted in translating from German, Russian, Danish, and Hungarian authors excerpts from works which have not hitherto appeared in English.

Index

What a handful of dust is man to think such thoughts! Or is he, perchance, a prince in misfortune, whose speech at times betrays his birth? I like to think that, if men are machines, they are machines of a celestial pattern, which can rise above themselves, and, to the amazement of the watching gods, acquit themselves as men. I like to think that this singular race of indomitable, philosophising, poetical beings, resolute to carry the banner of Becoming to unimaginable heights, may be as interesting to the gods as they to us, and that they will stoop to admit these creatures of promise into their divine society.

W. Macneile Dixon

THE THEOSOPHICAL PUBLISHING HOUSE

Wheaton, Ill., U.S.A.

Madras, India

London, England

Publishers of a wide range of titles on many
subjects including:

Mysticism

Yoga

Meditation

Extrasensory Perception

Religions of the World

Asian Classics

Reincarnation

The Human Situation

Theosophy

Distributors for the Adyar Library Series
of Sanskrit Texts, Translations and Studies

The Theosophical Publishing House, Wheaton,
Illinois, is also the publisher of

QUEST BOOKS

Many titles from our regular clothbound list in
attractive paperbound editions

For a complete list of all Quest Books write to:

QUEST BOOKS
P.O. Box 270, Wheaton, Ill. 60187